EXECUTIVE COMPUTING

Beware of all enterprises that require new clothes, and not rather a new wearer of clothes. If there is not a new man, how can the new clothes be made to fit?

Henry David Thoreau

EXECUTIVE COMPUTING

HOW TO GET IT DONE ON YOUR OWN

JOHN M. NEVISON

John M. Nevison Associates
Concord, Massachusetts

Addison-Wesley Publishing Company
Reading, Massachusetts • Menlo Park, California
London • Amsterdam • Don Mills, Ontario • Sydney

**This book is in the
Addison-Wesley Microcomputer Books
Executive Series**

Seventh Printing, December 1983

The language BASIC was developed at Dartmouth College by John G. Kemeny and Thomas E. Kurtz.

VisiCalc™ is a trademark of Personal Software, Inc., and is a copyrighted computer program of Software Arts, Inc. Used with permission.

All of the computer programs in this book are © copyright 1980 by John M. Nevison Associates and may be stored and retrieved electronically solely for personal educational use, but not for transmission to any other individual or agency without the prior written permission of John M. Nevison Associates. Used with permission of John M. Nevison Associates.

Excerpts from *Walden, The Writings of Henry D. Thoreau*, edited by J. Lyndon Shanley (copyright © 1971 by Princeton University Press), CEAA edn. pp. 10–323. Reprinted by permission of Princeton University Press.

Library of Congress Cataloging in Publication Data

Nevison, John M
   Executive Computing—how to get it done on your own.

   (Joy of computing)
   Includes bibliographical references and index.
   1. Business—Data processing—Case studies. 2. Computer programs—Problems, exercises, etc. I. Title.
II. Series.
HF5548.2.N415   658'.054   80-28977
ISBN 0-201-05248-2

ISBN 0-201-05248-2
   GHIJKL–AL–8987654

To Nancy and Laura

Foreword

Executive computing is an idea about getting work done. It is the kind of idea that strikes you with its simplicity—once it has been demonstrated. Jack Nevison demonstrates it here, with sparkling clarity.

Executive computing begins with the conviction that executives can learn about programming more easily than programmers can learn about business. While it can be frustratingly difficult to explain your methods to someone else, it can be remarkably easy to weave them into your own computer program.

This book challenges you to become computer-literate. Being literate about computing is like being literate about reading and writing: it means you can actually perform on your own. You may not be so proficient in writing a computer program that you will put the data-processing department out of business, but you will know enough to get some work out of the computer by yourself. By doing some jobs on your own, you will find you have dramatically improved your ability to communicate with your data-processing department.

As Jack demonstrates in every chapter, writing a program is a way of analyzing a problem. He follows the rules of his earlier book, *The Little Book of BASIC Style*, and shows us here that a styled BASIC program can be an unexpectedly clear statement of a problem-solving procedure. In fact, you may find that as you become computer-literate you will discover new ways of thinking about your business.

Whether this is your introduction to computing or a step toward more advanced work, I think you will find *Executive Computing* an invaluable experience.

Bruce Herzberg

December 1980

Preface

*To be a philosopher is not merely to have subtle thoughts . . .
It is to solve some of the problems of life, not only theoretically, but practically.*

Henry David Thoreau

This book is for the business person who wants to get work done
with the help of a computer—from the busy executive who owns a
microcomputer to the business student who needs a practical way to
apply a quantitative method. In order to use this book comfortably, the
reader should already have written and run a few BASIC programs (see
Appendix A if BASIC is new to you).

TO HELP YOU HELP YOURSELF

The heart of this book is the idea that a business method can be
expressed conveniently as a computer program. Each of the 25 cases
tries to illustrate a fundamental business method and suggest some ways
to apply it. The method is pulled together in the computer program at
the end. Because a case must be the simple version of the story, its
program is not really an end; it is a beginning—a place where you can
start to journey toward the program you need to solve your own particular problem. So if you find a particular case especially interesting, start
programming after you stop reading.

As you become familiar with the individual programs used to solve
the various cases, you may elect to combine several to solve your own
particular problem. Through modification and combination, you should
be able to compose an approach to a wide variety of problems in a
relatively short time.

For those who wish to test the waters before they jump in, exercises are included with each case. They are not difficult, but they do require more time than traditional exercises.

If you are interested in pursuing a subject beyond the depth of this book, the references at the end of each chapter should help you on your way.

The appendixes at the end of the book offer several kinds of additional help. The first provides a brief introduction to BASIC and a set of structural guidelines for writing and combining programs. The second includes a set of 16 utility programs to be used on their own or in larger programs. The third presents tips to help you buy a personal computer. The fourth describes another tool for manipulating tabular data.

BASIC

This book uses the computer language BASIC because it is:

- available on almost every computer
- quick to learn
- simple to read
- easy to understand
- powerful to use

The language BASIC is convenient, but not necessary. The ideas in the book are important; the computer language in which they are expressed is not. Whatever language you have available to you will work. BASIC is widely used and you should have no trouble finding a book that will explain the elements of the language (see Appendix A and its references). From there, the conversion to another language should be a straightforward task. If you attend to the principles of Appendix A, you should be able to transfer the ideas quickly and easily.

All of the programs in this book have been run on a Radio Shack TRS-80 computer with 16,000 characters of memory (16K) and Level II BASIC. This computer's successor, the Model III, presently sells for less than $1000. See Appendix C for additional details on equipment.

VISICALC

VisiCalc is a new computer product that turns a computer into an electronic blackboard on which you can write a table of numbers and modify it in many ways. It is an extremely handy way to deal with tabular information. Any program in this book that can be constructed using VisiCalc is marked with an asterisk (*) in the Program Index. See Appendix D for further details.

ACKNOWLEDGMENTS

It is a real pleasure to thank all those who have been involved in this book's evolution.

Teledata, Inc., of Hanover, New Hampshire, generously contributed computer resources that sped the writing and rewriting of the text and the programs. Business ideas and criticisms came from Michael Chu of City Investing, Lou Fernandez, Robert Montgomery of Corning, and Chris Nevison of Colgate University. Sharp comments on English came from Bruce Herzberg. Additional helpful remarks came from Bill Dickson, Tom Dwyer, and Steve Stadler. My colleagues at Nevison Associates, Tim Stein and Sandy Sorkin, improved both ideas and computer programs. Elisabeth Micheli painstakingly styled these programs for the TRS-80. Addison-Wesley's Bill Gruener and Gail Goodell provided unflagging support and encouragement. Barbara Pendergast meticulously edited the manuscript. The guest-cook problem was inspired by Toni McJennett. The largest debt of gratitude is again to Nancy Ross McJennett whose three performances as understanding wife, attentive mother, and concerned book designer made this book possible.

Quotes from Henry David Thoreau's *Walden* introduce each chapter with a remark that is intended to relieve the text's narrow focus.

J.M.N.

Concord, Massachusetts
December 1980

Contents

PART I   THE EXECUTIVE OFFICE

1   Introduction: Looking at Numbers   3
Compound Growth   3
Pricing in Inflation   4
The Program INFLATE   6
Graphing Sales   7
The Office   13
The Program SALES   13

2   The Long-Range Plan   15
Beginning Assumptions   16
Growth Rates   18
The Program PLAN   19
Cash Flow   22
The Program CASHPLAN   26
Budget Help   29
The Program TABLE   31

3   The Strategic Review   35
A Look at Cost   35
Analysis   37
The Program X-RAY   39
The Value of Experience   43
The Program SHARE   47
Competitive Growth   49
The Program GROWTH   56
Final Results   65

4   Present Value and Future Risk   67
Four Methods   68
The New Policy   72
The Program PRESENT   73
Risk   75
The Program RISKY   82

5   The Corporation's Data   85
Structure   86
The Corporate Data Base   88
Data-Base Users   89
The Program QUERY   93

PART II   LINE MANAGEMENT

6   Project Planning, Scheduling, and Control   99
Help with Dinner   99
The Program GANTT   103
From Jobs to Networks of Jobs   104
The Gantt Chart Revisited   106
The Predecessor Table   107
The Program CPM-I   109
Scheduling with a Scarce Resource   114
The Program CPM-II   117
Controlling the Project   125
The Program CPM-III   128
Timely Estimates   139
Guessing the Task   140
The Tasks Together   145
The Program TIMELY   146

7   The Model Inventory   149
Model of Material   150
The Program INVENTRY   154
Carrying Inventory Versus Replenishing Inventory   156
The Program INV   161
Replenishment Delay   161
Demand   161
The Program INVENT   167
Cost of Incurring Shortages   170
Balancing Costs   170
Quantity Discounts and Changes in Supply   170

8   The Diet Problem: Linear Programming   173

The Program DIET   176
Reflection   178
The Tucker Tableau   179
The Eight-Step Simplex Method   181
The Answers   185
A Related Problem   185
Dial a Benefit   186
Applications   189
Equalities   189
The Program SIMPLEX   193
Transportation Problems   202

9   The Raincoat Problem: Decision Analysis   207

A Computer Program   209
The Program DECIDE   212
A Marketing Decision   216
The End Game   218

**10   Looking Ahead: Next Month's Sales,
Next Week's Meetings   221**

The Program LINEFIT   222
Next Month's Forecast   226
The Program NEXTMNTH   229
Next Week's Meetings   233
The Program FINDTIME   239

APPENDIXES

A   Introduction to BASIC and Program Structure   249

BASIC in Action   249
Style and Structure   259
Program Paragraphs   265
The Larger Program   268

B   Utility Programs   273

READ   274
PERCENT   275
MAX   276
SORT   277
SORTII   278

PLOT   280
HIST   282
PIE   284
AMORT   288
DEPA   289
DEPB   291
DEPC   292
SMOOTH   293
BETA   295
BAR   296
SEVEN   299

C   Current Equipment   305
Know Your Needs   305
Get Good Service   306
Buy a Brand Name   306

D   About VisiCalc   309

Program Index   313

Index   315

PART I

THE EXECUTIVE OFFICE

1

Introduction:
Looking at Numbers

The first ice is especially interesting and perfect, being hard, dark, and transparent, and affords the best opportunity that ever offers for examining the bottom where it is shallow.

Henry David Thoreau

Steven Cauldwell knew there were several advantages to writing his own computer programs, but he had no idea which one was the most important. He knew that writing a program forced him to express ideas in a different way and that just the effort of reexpression often taught him something new. For example, he had learned how to rework the simple idea of compound growth into a tool for dealing with pricing in inflationary periods.

COMPOUND GROWTH

Compound growth was a simple idea by itself. Growth at 15 percent was the same as multiplying by a factor of 1.15. In other words, the new sum would be 1.15 times the old sum. In BASIC that was:

```
LET S = 1.15 * S
```

The line read backwards. The initial S was on the right-hand side of the equal sign. The new S on the left-hand side was the result. When he made a four-line program and numbered each statement, the computer would do the statements in order:

3

```
10      LET S = 100
20      LET S = 1.15 * S
30      PRINT S
40      END
```

and the answer would appear as

```
115
```

The initial idea had a simple consequence. To compound interest for five years, the same operation could be repeated five times. By using the NEXT statement to send the computer back to the FOR statement, he made the computer loop back and reuse the same statements:

```
10      LET S = 100
20    '
30      FOR Y = 1 TO 5
40          LET S = 1.15 * S
50          PRINT Y, S
60      NEXT Y
70    '
80      END
```

(Lines 20 and 70 are blank lines with an apostrophe mark. They do nothing but make the program easier to read.) The computer used the old statements with new values each time it went around the loop. The results were:

```
1       115.
2       132.25
3       152.088
4       174.901
5       201.136
```

PRICING IN INFLATION

Pricing in an inflationary period was an elaboration of the idea behind compound growth. But different costs each had different inflation rates. Labor costs went up at a 1.15 rate each year, while raw materials went up at a 1.03 rate. If the dollar price contained 56 cents of raw material and 21 cents of labor, what happened to the profit margin when the price went up at a rate of 1.12 a year?

The program to answer the question was:

```
270      LET P = 100
280      LET R = 56
290      LET L = 21
300      PRINT 0; R, L, R+L, P, (P−(R+L))/P * 100
310      FOR Y = 1 TO 5
315          LET P = 1.12 * P
320          LET R = 1.03 * R
330          LET L = 1.15 * L
340          PRINT Y; R, L, R+L, P, (P−(R+L))/P * 100
350      NEXT Y
999      END
```

The result was:

YR	MAT	LABOR	TOTL CST	PRICE	MARGIN
0	56.00	21.00	77.00	100.00	23%
1	57.68	24.15	81.83	112.00	27%
2	59.41	27.77	87.18	125.44	30%
3	61.19	31.94	93.13	140.49	34%
4	63.03	36.73	99.76	157.35	37%
5	64.92	42.24	107.16	176.23	39%

The price growth rate of 1.12 was clearly high, so Cauldwell retyped the price growth using 1.10 and reran the program. The margin was still too high. He quickly tried 1.08, 1.06, and finally 1.07 to find the value that preserved his margin.

In going from the compound growth to the pricing model, Cauldwell learned that an idea expressed as a computer program was almost always capable of refinement. He could, if he chose, go still further and make a model with five or six cost components. So the first big advantage of computing was the freedom to reexpress and refine an idea.

The computer program illustrated a second benefit: ease of calculation. It was easier and faster for Caudwell to write and revise the computer program than to find the answer any other way. With algebra he always worried about making an error; with his calculator he would not have seen the whole picture.

There was a third benefit: ease of reuse. The most obvious reuse was when the rates changed—and they were always changing. Now that the program was written, it could be saved and reused quickly when circumstances demanded a revised plan.

A fourth benefit was related to the ease of reuse: the ability to ask "what if?" questions. A computer program could be viewed as a set of assumptions, and what the computer did was draw the necessary conclusions in a fraction of a second. So if he wanted to use INFLATE to find out what a different future inflation rate would mean to his margin, he could. In fact, by trying out a few cases, he could develop his intuition about what the future might hold, both its threat and its promise. That was certainly a big advantage of computing.

THE PROGRAM INFLATE

```
100 REM    INFLATE    1 JANUARY 1980   STEVE CAULDWELL
110 '
112 REM    © COPYRIGHT 1980 JOHN M. NEVISON ASSOCIATES
114 '
120 REM    REVEALS PROFIT MARGIN IN AN INFLATIONARY
130 REM    WORLD WHERE RAW MATERIAL COSTS, LABOR COSTS,
140 REM    AND PRICES EACH GROW AT A DIFFERENT RATE.
145 '
150 REM    VARIABLES:
154 REM        L . . . . . . . . . . . . LABOR COST
155 REM        P . . . . . . . . . . . PRICE
156 REM        R . . . . . . . . . . . RAW MATERIAL COST
158 '
200        PRINT "YR   RAW MAT.", "LABOR", "TOTAL COST",
210        PRINT "PRICE", "MARGIN (%)"
211        PRINT
220 '
270        LET P = 100
280        LET R = 56
290        LET L = 21
300        PRINT  0; R, L, R+L, P, (P-(R+L))/P * 100
310        FOR Y = 1 TO 5
315            LET P = 1.12 * P
320            LET R = 1.03 * R
330            LET L = 1.15 * L
340            PRINT  Y; R, L, R+L, P, (P-(R+L))/P * 100
350        NEXT Y
999        END
```

If you have never seen a BASIC computer program before, you should pause here and read Appendix A. If you have read programs before, then this one should hold no surprises for you.

The program uses three variables, R for raw materials, L for labor, and P for price. First the program prints out the headings for the results. The calculations then begin, and after printing the beginning values at time zero, the program prints out each year's values for five successive years.

To try a different price increase, you only have to retype the line LET P = 1.12 * P with a new rate.

_____ *Exercises* _____

1. Verify that a price increase of 1.07 holds the margin constant. Is it exactly the right answer?
2. Suppose raw materials costs were 40 cents, energy costs were 16 cents, and labor costs were 21 cents. If the costs grow as before and energy costs grow at a rate of 1.35, what happens to the margin if the price increases at 1.15? Revise INFLATE to include the energy costs.

GRAPHING SALES

Steven Cauldwell was the Chief Executive Officer of Chordata, and his days were filled to overflowing. Just before he left the office one night, he learned that a meeting that was supposed to be held at the end of the week had been moved up to eight thirty the next morning. The meeting was with Frank Bradshaw, the director of the Bear Division. Bear Division made household appliances. It was the company's biggest division and its sales had not been doing well. It was nine o'clock at night. Cauldwell's problem was that he had only the rest of the evening to go over the figures and find out what had been happening.

The figures he had in front of him were the monthly sales for the last five years. He also had similar sales figures for each of Chordata's other three divisions. Cauldwell recalled a graph he had seen in a recent article that he felt would give him a quick yet comprehensive means of looking at the sales figures. The graph had two parts: a bar-chart summary of the average sales for several past years, and a line graph of the last twelve months' sales. It looked like the one shown in Fig. 1.1.

Fig. 1-1   A Sales Summary

Such a graph would show at a glance what he needed to know.

Cauldwell settled down to work out a computer program to plot his graph. He worked into the program backwards, first writing the section that would print out the monthly line graph.

```
800 REM    MONTHLY LINE GRAPH
810 '
820     DIM S(12)
830     FOR M = 1 TO 12
840         READ S(M)
850         DATA 14, 20, 22, 24, 26, 15, 16, 20, 26, 23, 19, 17
860         PRINT TAB(S(M));"*"
870     NEXT M
999     END
```

The program would print a month's sales on each line so that the year would run down the page. To make the graph, he turned the paper on its side and connected the asterisks with a pencil. The results looked like this:

The next part he wrote was the routine to print out the bar charts of the past years' average monthly sales. The program read the yearly average, Y, and printed a bar of asterisks out to Y.

He estimated some rough data for a test run.

```
500 REM    YEARLY BAR CHARTS
510 '
520        FOR I = 1 TO 4
530            READ Y
540            DATA 15, 18, 19, 21
545            FOR J = 1 TO Y
550                PRINT "*";
560            NEXT J
570            PRINT
580        NEXT I
590 '
800 REM    MONTHLY LINE GRAPH
810 '
820        DIM S(12)
830        FOR M = 1 TO 12
840            READ S(M)
850            DATA 14, 20, 22, 24, 26, 15, 16, 20, 26, 23, 19, 17
860            PRINT TAB(S(M));"*"
870        NEXT M
999        END
```

When he ran the whole program it looked like this:

Ten minutes after starting to work, Cauldwell had completed the essential computer program. He wanted a graph that was easy to read, so he continued to revise and improve his initial effort. After making the printing look good, he turned his attention to the data. It arrived monthly, so his final program would have to tally the past years' sales to get the yearly totals and averages. He wanted the program to print the most recent twelve months' figures so that his secretary could reuse the program next month by adding the new month's data and advancing the current month number by one.

He continued his backwards course from results to initial conditions. As he added the sections that read the new data, he discarded his initial test data. He included the names of the months so they could be printed on the graph. Finally, he added comments at every step so the final version would be easy to read. (A commentary on this program appears at the end of the chapter.)

```
100 REM    SALES   17 AUGUST 1980   STEVEN CAULDWELL
110 '
120 REM    © COPYRIGHT 1980 JOHN M. NEVISON ASSOCIATES
130 '
140 REM    THIS PROGRAM PRINTS A GRAPH (*) OF MONTHLY SALES
150 REM    FIGURES FOR THE COMPANY. PREVIOUS FOUR CALENDAR
160 REM    YEARS ARE BAR CHARTS.
180 '
190 REM    VARIABLES:
200 REM       I,J . . . . . . . . . . . INDEX VARIABLES
210 REM       L$(). . . . . . . . . . LABELS FOR MONTHS
220 REM       M. . . . . . . . . . . INDEX OF MONTHS
230 REM       S(). . . . . . . . . . SALES PER MONTH
240 REM       Y() . . . . . . . . . AVERAGE YEARLY SALES
250 '
260 REM    DIMENSIONS:
270        DIM L$(60), S(60)
280 '
290 REM    CONSTANTS:
300 '
310        FOR M = 37 TO 60
320           READ L$(M)   'LABEL FOR MONTHS
330        NEXT M
340        DATA JAN,FEB,MAR,APR,MAY,JUN,JUL,AUG,SEP,OCT,NOV,DEC
350        DATA JAN,FEB,MAR,APR,MAY,JUN,JUL,AUG,SEP,OCT,NOV,DEC
360 '
370        FOR M = 1 TO 48
380           READ S(M)    'SALES PER MONTH (PAST 4 YEARS)
390        NEXT M
400        DATA 10, 14, 16, 18, 20, 16, 15, 13, 11, 13, 14, 15
410        DATA 10, 15, 19, 20, 21, 20, 19, 15, 17, 20, 22, 21
420        DATA 12, 17, 19, 23, 22, 19, 18, 15, 18, 20, 23, 23
430        DATA 15, 17, 21, 27, 25, 20, 19, 14, 20, 22, 24, 26
440 '
450        LET C = 7        'NUMBER OF CURRENT MONTH (JUL)
460        FOR M = 48 + 1 TO 48 + C
470           READ S(M)   'SALES PER MONTH (CURRENT YEAR)
480        NEXT M
490        DATA 15, 16, 20, 26, 23, 19, 17
500 '
510 '
```

```
520 REM    MAIN PROGRAM
530 '
540 REM    CALCULATE AVERAGE YEARLY SALES
550 '
560        LET Y(1) = S(1)+S(2)+S(3)+S(4)+S(5)+S(6)+S(7)
570        LET Y(1) = Y(1) + S(8)+S(9)+S(10)+S(11)+S(12)
580        LET Y(1) = Y(1)/12
590 '
600        LET Y(2) = S(13)+S(14)+S(15)+S(16)+S(17)+S(18)+S(19)
610        LET Y(2) = Y(2) + S(20)+S(21)+S(22)+S(23)+S(24)
620        LET Y(2) = Y(2)/12
630 '
640        LET Y(3) = S(25)+S(26)+S(27)+S(28)+S(29)+S(30)+S(31)
650        LET Y(3) = Y(3) + S(32)+S(33)+S(34)+S(35)+S(36)
660        LET Y(3) = Y(3)/12
670 '
680        LET Y(4) = S(37)+S(38)+S(39)+S(40)+S(41)+S(42)+S(43)
690        LET Y(4) = Y(4) + S(44)+S(45)+S(46)+S(47)+S(48)
700        LET Y(4) = Y(4)/12
710 '
720 REM    PRINT OUT GRAPH
730 '
740 REM    TOP SCALE
750 '
760        PRINT "          0              10            20";
765        PRINT "              30            40"
770        PRINT "      +----------+----------+";
775        PRINT "----------+----------+"
780     '
790 REM    YEARLY BAR CHARTS
800 '
810        FOR I = 1 TO 4
815           PRINT "      I"
820           PRINT" "; I+75; " I";
830           FOR J = 1 TO INT(Y(I) + .5)
840               PRINT "*";
850           NEXT J
860           PRINT
870        NEXT I
880 '
890 REM    MONTHLY POINTS OF MOST RECENT 12 MONTHS
900 '
910        FOR M = 48 + C - 11 TO 48 + C
915           PRINT "     I"
920           PRINT " "; L$(M); " I";
930           PRINT TAB(S(M) + 6); "*"
940        NEXT M
950 '
960        END
```

When he ran the final program it looked like this:

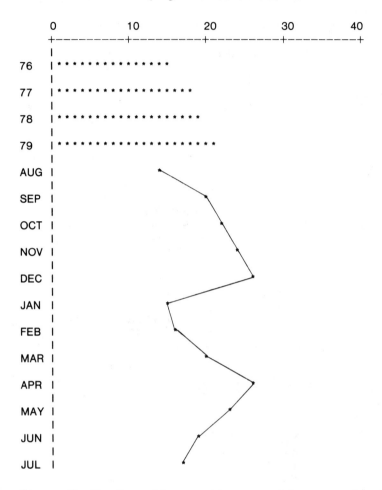

Steven Cauldwell working on his own at home produced an up-to-date report in about an hour. More exactly, he produced a device that would manufacture an up-to-date report. The device, the computer program, would produce a report each month from now on. His secretary could perform the job. So Cauldwell received the benefits of the immediate report and established a way to create new reports in the future.

He also found a way to become intimately acquainted with the sales figures of his ailing division. After completing his program, he modified it to show the graphs of the same twelve months in each of the preceding years. He was thoroughly prepared for his meeting the next day.

THE OFFICE

After his promotion a year ago, Cauldwell had made sure that the entire staff was trained to write simple computer programs. They attended a two-day course which refreshed what some had learned in business school and gave the novices enough background to proceed on their own.

His second innovation was the purchase—with the help of his Director of Data Processing—of several small computers for the executive office. He kept one of these computers in his study at home. The small computers could do two things: they could run programs and they could serve as terminals to interrogate the company's big computer for data from the central files.

At work the next day, Cauldwell used his new graphs to go over Bear Division's problems with its general manager, Frank Bradshaw. The two of them ironed out several issues that had led to the summer decline. Bear Division won a long-sought-after increase in its capital-equipment budget for the next year.

After the meeting Cauldwell stepped into the office of Peter Bates, his director of long-range planning. He dropped a copy of the computer program and its output on his desk. "I think from now on I want to look at these figures in graph form," he began. "Could you build files for our other divisions' data and show my secretary how to update everything when next month's figures come in?

"Behind each graph should be a table with supporting figures. And it would be a big help if we consolidated the four divisions into one overall corporate picture."

Peter Bates leaned forward and examined the program. He knew that what he needed to do would take only a few hours of work.

"When do you need it?" he asked.

"Day after tomorrow."

"Okay," Bates said, "I'll get right to it."

THE PROGRAM SALES

(Program appears earlier in text.)

The program illustrates several features of BASIC.

REM or an apostrophe mark (') indicates a remark, often called a comment. All the REM statements and apostrophes set off instructions intended for the author of the program.

Normal variables to which numbers can be assigned are single letters of the alphabet such as I, J, or M. A variable that can take a string of characters is a letter followed by a dollar sign ($) such as L$. L$ can be assigned "J" or "JAN" or "FEB" or any other string of characters and is called a string variable. A variable can also be a letter followed by a numeral (see S9 in the program CASHPLAN in Chapter 2).

Sometimes one letter is used to create many variables by subscripting the letter, for example S(34) or Y(3). In this program, we use L$() subscripted in any one of 60 ways, S() in 60 ways, and Y() in 4 ways. If you subscript a variable larger than 10, the DIM (for dimension) statement tells BASIC to reserve sufficient space for the variable.

The program reads values for variables L$(37) through L$(60) (the first 36 are left blank—why?). Then it reads monthly sales for S(1) through S(48) and reads S(49) to the current month.

Next, the program computes four yearly averages, Y(1), Y(2), Y(3), and Y(4).

Finally, the program uses the PRINT conventions to make the desired graph. If you don't understand these tricks, try out a few lines on your own computer and see how they work. If you don't have a computer handy, take the tricks on faith. Their details are not important.

_____ *Exercises* _____

1. Alter the program to print out a graph of 1978's sales.
2. Help Peter Bates by extending the program SALES to print a table of data to support the graph.
3. Alter the program so it would read two more divisions' data and print out a graph and a table for each.
4. Alter the program so it would do a corporate graph and table after it does the individual divisions.
5. Pick a problem of your own and imitate Steven Cauldwell's method of writing the program:
   a) Draw an example of the results.
   b) Write the last part of the program with PRINT statements to give the picture when you have the numbers.
   c) Write the first part of the program that reads the raw data.
   d) Write the middle part that computes the needed results.
   e) Style the whole program so that it can be easily read.

References

1. Dwyer, Thomas A., and Critchfield, Margot, *BASIC and the Personal Computer*, Reading, MA: Addison-Wesley, 1978.
2. Kemeny, John G., and Kurtz, Thomas E., *BASIC Programming*, Third Edition, New York: Wiley, 1980.
3. Nevison, John M., *The Little Book of BASIC Style*, Reading, MA: Addison-Wesley, 1978.

2

The Long-Range Plan

In the long run men hit only what they aim at. Therefore,
though they should fail immediately, they had better aim at
something high.

Henry David Thoreau

Rose Thompson thought she was doing okay. Wolf Division manufactured industrial tools, and for the last two years she had been investing in new equipment to make it possible to use integrated circuits in the tools. The next few years looked very good. Thompson foresaw no more major capital expenditures and sales going up at 15 percent a year. Her sales for the next year would probably be $107 million, and her debt right now was $28 million and holding steady.

Thompson's trouble was she wanted more than just a good feeling; she wanted to know. Her reputation and her bonus rode on the division's performance. Besides that, during the budget review, Corporate might well ask what would happen if her assumptions about sales were either high or low. She called in George Lee, a marketing analyst who had recently completed his MBA training before joining the division.

"George, these figures are where I think we will be next year. Take the numbers and work up an income statement for the next five years. You should try and make it possible to alter the growth rates from year to year.

"I checked with Simon Wilson in Data Processing and he can give us a small computer like the ones they have in the corporate office. We're getting it on loan for a month.

"I would like you to see if the job is something we can do and if it is, whether we can do it in the next month. Wilson said that if we need a computer long term, he could oversee the purchase. That's another question. Should we think about having a computer around over the long term?"

After Lee left, Thompson felt much better. Now she could concentrate on her twelve-month operating budget for next year. She knew that the long-range plan was in good hands.

BEGINNING ASSUMPTIONS

Two days later George Lee had already answered most of Thompson's questions. He had tried out the computer and found that it understood BASIC, the computer language he had studied in school.

Thompson's request was clear: based on the growth of sales and next year's initial figures, extend the Division's income statement for four more years. Lee knew that he could write the program and that a program was the appropriate way to handle the problem. The program would allow them to examine the consequences of alternative scenarios.

He set out the equations from the memo, noting the BASIC statement beside each.

1. Current debt is $28 million and constant.
     LET D = 28000   (Numbers are in thousands.)
2. Sales are to be $107 million.
     LET S = 107000
3. Cost of goods sold is 48 percent of sales.
     LET C = .48 * S
4. Gross profit is sales minus cost of goods sold.
     LET G = S − C
5. Depreciation is constant at $3.5 million.
     LET B = 3500
6. Selling, general, and administrative costs (SG&A) are 32.7 percent of sales.
     LET A = .327 * S
7. Total fixed costs are depreciation plus SG&A.
     LET F = B + A
8. Interest on debt is 14.5 percent per year.
     LET I = .145 * D   (Current debt is $28 million)
9. Profit before taxes is gross profit minus fixed costs and interest.
     LET P = G − (F + I)
10. Tax is 42 percent of profit before taxes.
     LET X = .42 * P

11. Net income is profit before taxes minus taxes.

```
LET N = P - X
```

George pulled the three initial variables out of the list:

```
LET S = 107000
LET B = 3500
LET D = 28000
```

The growth assumption was that sales would increase at 15 percent.

```
LET S = 1.15 * S
```

Lee looked at his notes for a few minutes and he thought he saw how to write the program. Lay down the initial equations. Calculate the dependent variables in the income statement. Print out the results for the year. Apply the annual growth to the sales to get the beginning of the next year, go back to calculate the second year's income statement, and so on. Continue doing this loop until all five years were done.

The heart of his program looked like this (without the printing):

```
375 REM    FUNDAMENTAL VARIABLES
380        LET S(1) = 107000
385        LET B(1) = 3500
390        LET D(1) = 28000
395 '
400        FOR Y = 1 TO 5
405 REM    DEPENDENT VARIABLES
410            LET C(Y) = .48 * S(Y)
415            LET G(Y) = S(Y) - C(Y)
420            LET A(Y) = .327 * S(Y)
425            LET F(Y) = A(Y) + B(Y)
435            LET I(Y) = .145 * D(Y)
445            LET P(Y) = G(Y) - F(Y) - I(Y)
450            LET X(Y) = .42 * P(Y)
455            LET N(Y) = P(Y) - X(Y)
520 '
525 REM    NEXT YEAR'S FUNDAMENTALS
530            LET S(Y+1) = 1.15 * S(Y)
535            LET B(Y+1) = B(Y)
540            LET D(Y+1) = D(Y)
545        NEXT Y
550 '
```

The results were:

			(IN $1,000'S)		
	1980	1981	1982	1983	1984
SALES	107,000	123,050	141,508	162,734	187,144
COST OF GOODS	51,360	59,064	67,924	78,112	89,829
GROSS PROFIT	55,640	63,986	73,584	84,621	97,315
DEPRECIATION	3,500	3,500	3,500	3,500	3,500
SELLNG GENL & ADMN	34,989	40,237	46,273	53,214	61,196
FIXED COSTS	38,489	43,737	49,773	56,714	64,696
INTEREST	4,060	4,060	4,060	4,060	4,060
PROFIT BEFORE TAX	13,091	16,189	19,751	23,848	28,559
TAX	5,498	6,799	8,295	10,016	11,995
NET PROFIT	7,593	9,389	11,456	13,832	16,564
DEBT	28,000	28,000	28,000	28,000	28,000

The results answered Thompson's basic request. Lee now turned his attention to the second part of Thompson's request. He had to make a plan that could be tailored to the division's expected growth rates.

GROWTH RATES

In the initial model sales grew at a rate of 1.15 in the second and subsequent years. The initial program could be changed to accommodate a change in this rate by simply retyping the growth equation. The standard change was no problem. If, however, one wanted to vary the growth rates from year to year, the program needed more flexibility.

One way to give it this flexibility, George thought, would be to store all the growth rates in a table.

Growth-Rate Table			
		Year	
	2	3	4	5
Sales growth	1.15	1.15	1.15	1.15

He read a set of growth rates, H( ), from a DATA statement in his BASIC program:

```
READ H(2), H(3), H(4), H(5)
DATA 1.15, 1.15, 1.15, 1.15
```

The growth rate $H(3)$ was the growth rate for the third year's sales. The value of $H(3)$ was 1.15. Lee changed the growth equation to use the growth rates from the table:

```
LET S(Y+1) = H(Y+1) * S(Y)
```

Because the table had exactly the same values the program had used in its first run, Lee expected the results would be the same. He ran the program to verify that they were. When the program worked, Lee knew he could vary the growth rate in any year by retyping only one line of data.

THE PROGRAM PLAN

```
100 REM    PLAN   7 OCTOBER 1980    GEORGE LEE
105 '
110 REM    © COPYRIGHT 1980 JOHN M. NEVISON ASSOCIATES
115 '
120 REM    CALCULATE INCOME STATEMENT.
130 '
135 REM    VARIABLES:
140 REM       A(Y) ......... SELLING GENERAL AND
142 REM                      ADMINISTRATIVE COSTS
145 REM       B(Y) ......... DEPRECIATION
150 REM       C(Y) ......... COST OF GOODS SOLD
160 REM       D(Y) ......... DEBT
170 REM       F(Y). ......... FIXED EXPENSES
180 REM       G(Y) ......... GROSS PROFIT
182 REM       H(Y) ......... GROWTH RATE OF SALES
185 REM       I(Y) ......... INTEREST ON DEBT
190 REM       N(Y) ......... NET PROFIT
200 REM       P(Y) ......... PROFIT
205 REM       P$ ........... PRINT TEMPLATE
210 REM       R ............ ROW INDEX
215 REM       R$(). ......... ROW LABEL
225 REM       S(Y) ......... SALES
235 REM       X(Y) ......... TAX
240 REM       Y ............ YEAR INDEX
245 '
```

```
250 REM   DIMENSIONS:
255       DIM R$(15)
260 '
265 REM   SALES GROWTH TABLE
270       READ H(2), H(3), H(4), H(5)
275       DATA 1.15, 1.15, 1.15, 1.15
280 '
285 REM   MAIN PROGRAM
290 '
295 REM   FOR FIVE YEARS, CALCULATE THE INCOME STATEMENT.
310 '
315 REM   ASSUMPTIONS. SALES START AT 107,000 AND GROW AT
320 REM   A RATE OF 1.15 A YEAR.  COGS AND SG&A ARE A
325 REM   PERCENTAGE OF SALES.  DEPRECIATION IS CONSTANT.
327 REM   LAST YEAR'S DEBT WAS 28,000.
330 '
375 REM   FUNDAMENTAL VARIABLES
380       LET S(1) = 107000
385       LET B(1) = 3500
390       LET D(1) = 28000
395 '
400       FOR Y = 1 TO 5
405 REM   DEPENDENT VARIABLES
410           LET C(Y) = .48 * S(Y)
415           LET G(Y) = S(Y) − C(Y)
420           LET A(Y) = .327 * S(Y)
425           LET F(Y) = A(Y) + B(Y)
435           LET I(Y) = .145 * D(Y)
445           LET P(Y) = G(Y) − F(Y) − I(Y)
450           LET X(Y) = .42 * P(Y)
455           LET N(Y) = P(Y) − X(Y)
520 '
525 REM   NEXT YEAR'S FUNDAMENTALS
530           LET S(Y+1) = H(Y+1) * S(Y)
535           LET B(Y+1) = B(Y)
540           LET D(Y+1) = D(Y)
545       NEXT Y
550 '
555 REM   PRINT OUT THE RESULTS
560       LET P$ = "%              %  ###,###   ###,###"
565       LET P$ = P$ + "  ###,###   ###,###   ###,###"
568       PRINT "                        (IN $1,000'S)"
570       PRINT "                 1980    1981";
575       PRINT "    1982    1983    1984"
580       PRINT
```

```
585        FOR R = 1 TO 11
590            READ R$(R)          'ROW LABEL
595        NEXT R
600        DATA SALES, COST OF GOODS, GROSS PROFIT, DEPRECIATION
605        DATA SELLNG GENL & ADMN, FIXED COSTS, INTEREST
610        DATA PROFIT BEFORE TAX, TAX, NET PROFIT
620        DATA DEBT
625  '
630        PRINT USING P$; R$(1), S(1), S(2), S(3), S(4), S(5)
635        PRINT USING P$; R$(2), C(1), C(2), C(3), C(4), C(5)
640        PRINT USING P$; R$(3), G(1), G(2), G(3), G(4), G(5)
645        PRINT
650        PRINT USING P$; R$(4), B(1), B(2), B(3), B(4), B(5)
655        PRINT USING P$; R$(5), A(1), A(2), A(3), A(4), A(5)
660        PRINT USING P$; R$(6), F(1), F(2), F(3), F(4), F(5)
665        PRINT
670        PRINT USING P$; R$(7), I(1), I(2), I(3), I(4), I(5)
675        PRINT
680        PRINT USING P$; R$(8), P(1), P(2), P(3), P(4), P(5)
685        PRINT USING P$; R$(9), X(1), X(2), X(3), X(4), X(5)
690        PRINT USING P$; R$(10), N(1), N(2), N(3), N(4), N(5)
695        PRINT
700        PRINT
735        PRINT
740        PRINT USING P$; R$(11), D(1), D(2), D(3), D(4), D(5)
745        END
```

The program features the use of subscripted variables to read and hold the values of the growth-rate table and the five-year statement.

After the program has read its growth rates and initial variables, it goes into a loop that repeats five times, once for each year. The first part of the loop computes the variables that depend on the initial values. At the end of this first part the values for a year's income statement have been completed. The second part of the loop prepares the initial conditions for the next year. When the loop starts its second round it can do the second year's dependent variables because the initials were set up at the bottom of the first round. When the loop does its fifth round it does the fifth year's dependent variables and then sets up a sixth year's initial variables, which are never used.

Upon completing the loop, the program moves on to printing the results accumulated in the subscripted variables. Should any of the tricks employed in the print statements not work on your computer, check your BASIC manual for the alternative commands. The program shown here will run on a Radio Shack TRS-80 computer.

_____ *Exercises* _____

1. Try a different initial sales figure until you find the one that yields $3.5 million net profit at the end of the fifth year.
2. Change the initial amounts to reflect your business and put in growth rates that you believe are realistic. Run the program and see how your next five years might look.
3. Examine the assumptions embedded in the dependent equations of the income statement. Modify the equations to reflect your own business's assumptions.
4. Rewrite the initial program to show an income statement where sales vary, first year net profits are $16,000, and profits grow at 20 percent a year.

CASH FLOW

Rose Thompson saw that her work was not really over. The assumption that debt remained constant bothered her. In fact, she really used her debt as a buffer for her cash needs. She borrowed when she needed cash and she retired debt when she had a cash surplus.

After building the income statement, she could take a cut at the cash flow and model that for five years as well. The operating cash flow could be defined as the net income with the depreciation added back in. Some of the cash would cover the increase in working capital. Her sales turned over her cash three times a year so her change in working capital would be a third of the increase in her sales. The change in capital expenses could be approximated by her depreciation adjusted for inflation. The cash left over could be used to reduce her debt.

Thompson described the problem to George Lee, who came up with a block diagram to explain the addition (Fig. 2.1).

"The new BASIC statements might look like this," Lee explained.

```
LET O = N + B
LET W = .33 * (S9−1)/S9 * S(Y)
LET E = 1.09^Y * B
LET R = O − (W+E)
```

"But the problem," said Thompson, "is that if we have cash, we can reduce the debt. If we reduce the debt, the interest in our income statement is less. We then must readjust the income statement, then readjust the cash flow, and so on. Can you make the computer do that?"

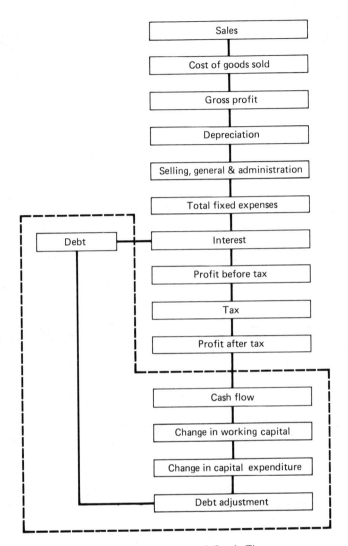

Fig. 2-1   Income Statement and Cash Flow

"Sure," said Lee, "give me a day or two."

Two days later, Lee answered Thompson's question with a revised set of results:

| | | | (IN $1,000'S) | | |
	1980	1981	1982	1983	1984
SALES	107,000	123,050	141,508	162,734	187,144
COST OF GOODS	51,360	59,064	67,924	78,112	89,829
GROSS PROFIT	55,640	63,986	73,584	84,621	97,315
DEPRECIATION	3,500	3,500	3,500	3,500	3,500
SELLNG GENL & ADMN	34,989	40,237	46,273	53,214	61,196
FIXED COSTS	38,489	43,737	49,773	56,714	64,696
INTEREST	3,637	3,054	2,276	1,260	−46
PROFIT BEFORE TAX	13,514	17,194	21,535	26,648	32,665
TAX	5,676	7,222	9,045	11,192	13,719
NET PROFIT	7,838	9,973	12,490	15,456	18,946
OPERATING CASH FLOW	11,338	13,473	15,990	18,956	22,446
CHANGE IN WRKNG CAP	4,606	5,297	6,091	7,005	8,055
CHANGE IN CAP EXPND	3,815	4,158	4,533	4,941	5,385
DEBT REDUCTION	2,917	4,018	5,367	7,011	9,005
DEBT	25,083	21,065	15,698	8,687	−318

"That's terrific," said Thompson. "These numbers are all consistent. Look, as we increase our profit and our margin, we are reducing our debt. That's encouraging. It would take forever to do this projection with my calculator. How did you get the computer to do it?"

"A simple idea, really," said Lee. "The program does it just the way we would do it by hand. Make a guess, see if the guess works, and if it doesn't, make another guess.

"Inside our guessing loop will be everything that changes as a result of our guess—the bottom of the income statement and the operating cash-flow figures. The loop variable is G for guess, D is the debt, and R is the reduction in the debt. D1 is the first guess at the new debt and D2 is the next guess at the new debt. The way it works is:"

```
425      LET D1 = D
430      FOR G = 1 TO 100
              (ALL THE FINANCIAL EQUATIONS ARE HERE)
485      LET D2 = D − R
490      IF ABS(D2 − D1) < .001 THEN 492 ELSE 496
492          LET D = D2
494          GOTO 520     'LOOP EXIT
496 '        IFEND
505          LET D1 = D2
510      NEXT G
520 '
```

"Let me see if I understand this," said Thompson. "This says that if the difference between the two guesses, (D2 − D1), is less than a small amount, then we are done. What does ABS mean?"

"It is BASIC for the absolute value. We don't know for sure which number is bigger in that subtraction so we take the absolute value to make sure the answer is positive. Then we check to see if it is small enough to quit."

"And we keep guessing until the two guesses are very close?"

"Yes," said Lee, "that's right. And we keep our initial debt, D, around so we can compute our new guess each time."

"This program is pretty tricky," said Thompson. "How did you figure it out?"

"I made a few tries before I got it right," confessed Lee. "But you don't need to worry about it any more. Now we have a method that we can always use."

"That's true," said Thompson. "I notice you set up the loop to go a hundred times. How many guesses did it really take to get close enough to quit?"

"Usually it quit after seven or eight guesses."

"Eight guesses per year," said Thompson. "That's five times eight, forty sets of calculations. I would never do that by hand. Very nice piece of work, Mr. Lee."

THE PROGRAM CASHPLAN

```
100 REM    CASHPLAN   15 OCTOBER 1980    GEORGE LEE
105 '
110 REM    © COPYRIGHT 1980 JOHN M. NEVISON ASSOCIATES
115 '
120 REM    A "WHAT-IF" FINANCIAL PLANNING MODEL THAT PRODUCES
125 REM    FIVE YEARS OF INCOME STATEMENTS AND CASH FLOWS.
130 '
135 REM    VARIABLES:
140 REM        A(Y) . . . . . . . . . SELLING GENERAL AND
142 REM                               ADMINISTRATIVE COSTS
145 REM        B(Y) . . . . . . . . DEPRECIATION
150 REM        C(Y) . . . . . . . . COST OF GOODS SOLD
155 REM        D1,D2 . . . . . . . ESTIMATES OF DEBT
160 REM        D(Y) . . . . . . . . DEBT
165 REM        E(Y) . . . . . . . . CHANGE IN CAPITAL EXPENSES
170 REM        F(Y). . . . . . . . . FIXED EXPENSES
175 REM        G . . . . . . . . . . . GUESS INDEX  (FOR DEBT)
180 REM        G(Y) . . . . . . . . GROSS PROFIT
185 REM        I(Y) . . . . . . . . . INTEREST ON DEBT
190 REM        N(Y) . . . . . . . . NET PROFIT
195 REM        O(Y) . . . . . . . . OPERATING CASH FLOW
200 REM        P(Y) . . . . . . . . PROFIT
205 REM        P$ . . . . . . . . . . PRINT TEMPLATE
210 REM        R . . . . . . . . . . . ROW INDEX
215 REM        R$() . . . . . . . . ROW LABEL
220 REM        R(Y) . . . . . . . . REDUCTION IN DEBT FROM CASH FLOW
225 REM        S(Y) . . . . . . . . SALES
230 REM        W(Y) . . . . . . . . CHANGE IN WORKING CAPITAL
235 REM        X(Y) . . . . . . . . TAX
240 REM        Y . . . . . . . . . . . YEAR INDEX
245 '
250 REM    DIMENSIONS:
255        DIM R$(15)
260 '
265 REM    CONSTANTS:
270        LET S9 = 1.15      'ANNUAL SALES GROWTH RATE
275 '
280 '
285 REM    MAIN PROGRAM
290 '
295 REM    FOR FIVE YEARS, CALCULATE THE INCOME STATEMENT AND
300 REM    CASH FLOWS.  ADJUST THE ANNUAL DEBT TO
305 REM    BOTH THE CASH FLOW AND THE INCOME STATEMENT.
310 '
```

```
315 REM    ASSUMPTIONS. SALES START AT 107,000 AND GROW AT
320 REM    A RATE OF 1.15 A YEAR. COGS AND SG&A ARE A
325 REM    PERCENTAGE OF SALES. DEPRECIATION IS CONSTANT.
327 REM    LAST YEAR'S DEBT WAS 28,000.
330 '
335 REM    CASH IS USED FOR WORKING CAPITAL, CAPITAL EXPENDI-
340 REM    TURES, AND REDUCTION OF DEBT. THE CHANGE IN
345 REM    WORKING CAPITAL IS ONE THIRD THE CHANGE IN SALES
350 REM    BECAUSE WORKING CAPITAL TURNS THREE TIMES A YEAR.
355 REM    THE CHANGE IN CAPITAL EXPENDITURE IS THE DEPRE-
360 REM    CIATION AT THE INFLATION RATE (1.09). EXTRA
365 REM    CASH IS USED TO REDUCE DEBT (OR MAKE LOANS).
370 '
375 REM    FUNDAMENTAL VARIABLES
380        LET S(1) = 107000
385        LET B(1) = 3500
390        LET D(1) = 28000
395 '
400        FOR Y = 1 TO 5
405 REM    DEPENDENT VARIABLES
410            LET C(Y) = .48 * S(Y)
415            LET G(Y) = S(Y) − C(Y)
420            LET A(Y) = .327 * S(Y)
422            LET F(Y) = A(Y) + B(Y)
425            LET D1 = D(Y)
430            FOR G = 1 TO 100
435                LET I(Y) = .145 * D1
445                LET P(Y) = G(Y) − F(Y) − I(Y)
450                LET X(Y) = .42 * P(Y)
455                LET N(Y) = P(Y) − X(Y)
460 '
465                LET O(Y) = N(Y) + B(Y)
470                LET W(Y) = .33 * (S9−1)/S9 * S(Y)
475                LET E(Y) = 1.09^Y * B(Y)
480                LET R(Y) = O(Y) − (W(Y) + E(Y))
485                LET D2 = D(Y) − R(Y)
490                IF ABS(D2−D1) < .001 THEN 492 ELSE 500
492                    LET D(Y) = D2
495                    GOTO 520             'LOOP EXIT
500 '                IFEND
505                    LET D1 = D2
510            NEXT G
515            STOP
520 '
525 REM    NEXT YEAR'S FUNDAMENTALS
530            LET S(Y+1) = S9 * S(Y)
535            LET B(Y+1) = B(Y)
540            LET D(Y+1) = D(Y)
545        NEXT Y
550 '
```

```
555 REM   PRINT OUT THE RESULTS
560       LET P$ = "%          %  ###,###   ###,###"
565       LET P$ = P$ + "   ###,###   ###,###   ###,###"
568       PRINT "                    (IN $1,000'S)"
570       PRINT "             1980    1981";
575       PRINT "   1982    1983    1984"
580       PRINT
585       FOR R = 1 TO 15
590           READ R$(R)     'ROW LABEL
595       NEXT R
600       DATA SALES, COST OF GOODS, GROSS PROFIT, DEPRECIATION
605       DATA SELLNG GENL & ADMN, FIXED COSTS, INTEREST
610       DATA PROFIT BEFORE TAX, TAX, NET PROFIT
615       DATA OPERATING CASH FLOW, CHANGE IN WRKNG CAP
620       DATA CHANGE IN CAP EXPND, DEBT REDUCTION, DEBT
625 '
630       PRINT USING P$; R$(1), S(1), S(2), S(3), S(4), S(5)
635       PRINT USING P$; R$(2), C(1), C(2), C(3), C(4), C(5)
640       PRINT USING P$; R$(3), G(1), G(2), G(3), G(4), G(5)
645       PRINT
650       PRINT USING P$; R$(4), B(1), B(2), B(3), B(4), B(5)
655       PRINT USING P$; R$(5), A(1), A(2), A(3), A(4), A(5)
660       PRINT USING P$; R$(6), F(1), F(2), F(3), F(4), F(5)
665       PRINT
670       PRINT USING P$; R$(7), I(1), I(2), I(3), I(4), I(5)
675       PRINT
680       PRINT USING P$; R$(8), P(1), P(2), P(3), P(4), P(5)
685       PRINT USING P$; R$(9), X(1), X(2), X(3), X(4), X(5)
690       PRINT USING P$; R$(10), N(1), N(2), N(3), N(4), N(5)
695       PRINT
700       PRINT
715       PRINT USING P$; R$(11), O(1), O(2), O(3), O(4), O(5)
720       PRINT USING P$; R$(12), W(1), W(2), W(3), W(4), W(5)
725       PRINT USING P$; R$(13), E(1), E(2), E(3), E(4), E(5)
730       PRINT USING P$; R$(14), R(1), R(2), R(3), R(4), R(5)
735       PRINT
740       PRINT USING P$; R$(15), D(1), D(2), D(3), D(4), D(5)
745       END
```

The program is a revision of the original program, PLAN. It is a good illustration of how an initial idea can be refined to provide additional results.

_____ *Exercises* _____

1. Alter the initial debt from $28,000 to $40,000. How does this change affect the profit after tax? What happens if the debt is only $18,000?
2. Find an annual report of a company you are interested in and try its data in CASHPLAN.

_____

BUDGET HELP

George Lee looked over his work. He was surprised to find that the computer program freed him from his bondage to number crunching. Previously, if he had time to make only three tries at a solution, he clung to his best set of numbers and defended them to the bitter end. But now, with a computer program, he could try 20 or 30 sets of numbers in the time it took to do the three by hand. The result was that he knew where the best range of values was. Then the world behind the numbers came back into focus and he found himself probing for further insights. Because the numbers were easily handled, they became less important. And because they were quickly handled, he had more time to explore. So his work improved both in quality of the numerical results and in quality of the insight into the world behind the numbers.

He saw one other big benefit: analytical insight. Any problem that could be quantified could be modeled in a small computer program. When he built the model, he understood the structure of the problem in a new way. He saw how the variables reacted with each other. On his way to practical answers, he developed analytical insight that would not have been possible without a computer.

"And some of this budgeting," thought Lee, "is manipulating a simple table."

He had an idea. It would be convenient to have a simple program that just added up the rows and columns of a table. The managers all did the same thing when they prepared next year's budgets for their groups. They laid out their projects over the four quarters to see where the dollars were bunched, and then tried to redistribute the costs so the four quarters were evenly balanced.

The advantage of a simple table program would be not in the initial run, but in the repeated runs. A user could modify any line by just retyping one line of the data and rerunning the program to see what the new table looked like. This ability to play with the figures quickly could save them some time preparing budgets.

He sketched out the idea of the program. It would have four columns, one for each quarter. The number of rows could be changed by the user. The program would give back the table with the row totals and the column totals and the grand total. The program's data looked like this:

```
400 '
410    DATA     0,  1234,  1234,  1234
420    DATA 40000, 60000,     0, 30000
430    DATA   333,   444,   333,   444
440    DATA  1200,  1824,  1560,  1960
450    DATA  8825,  9998,  4444,  7777
460    DATA 32111, 42222, 52333, 62444
470    DATA 44444, 33333, 22222, 11111
480 '
```

and made a table like this:

| | QUARTERS | | | | |
ROW	1	2	3	4	TOTAL
1	0	1,234	1,234	1,234	3,702
2	40,000	60,000	0	30,000	130,000
3	333	444	333	444	1,554
4	1,200	1,824	1,560	1,960	6,544
5	8,825	9,998	4,444	7,777	31,044
6	32,111	42,222	52,333	62,444	189,110
7	44,444	33,333	22,222	11,111	111,110
TOT	126,913	149,055	82,126	114,970	473,064

and could be altered and rerun like this:

| | QUARTERS | | | | |
ROW	1	2	3	4	TOTAL
1	0	1,234	1,234	1,234	3,702
2	40,000	30,000	30,000	30,000	130,000
3	333	444	333	444	1,554
4	1,200	1,824	1,560	1,960	6,544
5	8,825	9,998	4,444	7,777	31,044
6	32,111	42,222	52,333	62,444	189,110
7	44,444	33,333	22,222	11,111	111,110
TOT	126,913	119,055	112,126	114,970	473,064

Lee gave a short talk at the Wolf Division's monthly managers' meeting. He explained briefly how the program TABLE might be used and gave a live demonstration on a large television screen set up for the occasion. After the demonstration, Lee answered questions for a few minutes and sat down.

By the end of November, six people had set up copies of the program with their own figures. TABLE turned out to be a success. It was simple, easy to use, and practical. It did what Lee had hoped it would do. It gave managers the ability to juggle the figures in their budgets quickly and easily. Two of the six users made a point of telling him that the program had saved them a few hours of number crunching. One said she even tried a few novel combinations in order to arrive at her final budget for next year.

George was pleased that such a simple program could be so useful. He decided to purchase a computer for his office.

THE PROGRAM TABLE

```
100 REM    TABLE   25 OCTOBER 1980    GEORGE LEE
102 '
104 REM    © COPYRIGHT 1980 JOHN M. NEVISON ASSOCIATES
110 '
120 REM    A SIMPLE UTILITY TO READ A FOUR COLUMN
130 REM    TABLE, FOR EXAMPLE FOR FOUR QUARTERS.
140 REM    THE TABLE CAN BE UP TO 50 ROWS.  THE ACTUAL
150 REM    NUMBER OF ROWS IS N.
160 '
170 REM    TO USE THE TABLE, SET YOUR OWN NUMBER OF ROWS,
180 REM    TYPE IN YOUR TABLE WITH DATA STATEMENTS, AND
190 REM    WHEN YOU RUN THE PROGRAM IT WILL PRINT OUT
200 REM    ROW TOTALS, COLUMN TOTALS, AND THE GRAND TOTAL.
210 '
220 REM    TO TRY DIFFERENT IDEAS, JUST RETYPE THE LINE OF
230 REM    DATA THAT YOU WISH TO CHANGE
235 REM    AND RERUN THE PROGRAM.
240 '
250 REM    VARIABLES:
260 REM       C...........COLUMN COUNTER
265 REM       N...........NUMBER OF ROWS
270 REM       R...........ROW COUNTER
280 REM       S...........SUM BUILDER
290 REM       T().........TABLE OF VALUES
300 '
310 REM   DIMENSIONS:
320       DIM T(50,5)
330 '
```

```
340 REM    READ IN THE TABLE
345 '
350       LET N = 7
360       FOR R = 1 TO N
365          FOR C = 1 TO 4
370             READ T(R,C)
380          NEXT C
390       NEXT R
400 '
410       DATA       0,   1234,   1234,   1234
420       DATA 40000, 60000,      0, 30000
430       DATA    333,    444,    333,    444
440       DATA   1200,   1824,   1560,   1960
450       DATA   8825,   9998,   4444,   7777
460       DATA 32111, 42222, 52333, 62444
470       DATA 44444, 33333, 22222, 11111
480 '
490 REM   SUM EACH ROW AND PUT THE ANSWER
492 REM   AT THE END IN T(R,5).
495 '
500       FOR R = 1 TO N
510          LET T(R,5) = T(R,1) + T(R,2) + T(R,3) + T(R,4)
520       NEXT R
530 '
540 REM    SUM EACH COLUMN AND PUT THE ANSWER AT
550 REM    THE BOTTOM IN T(N+1,C).
555 '
560       FOR C = 1 TO 5
570          LET S = 0
580          FOR R = 1 TO N
590             LET S = S + T(R,C)
600          NEXT R
610          LET T(N+1,C) = S
620       NEXT C
630 '
640 REM    PRINT OUT THE TABLES WITH THE TOTALS
645 '
650       PRINT "            QUARTERS "
660       PRINT "ROW    1      2";
670       PRINT "     3      4     TOTAL"
680       PRINT
690       FOR R = 1 TO N
700          PRINT R;
710          FOR C = 1 TO 5
720             PRINT USING " ###,###", T(R,C);
730          NEXT C
740          PRINT
750       NEXT R
760 '
```

```
770         PRINT
780         PRINT "TOT";
790         FOR C = 1 TO 5
800            PRINT USING " ###,###", T(N+1,C);
810         NEXT C
820         PRINT
830  '
840         END
```

The program reads in a seven (or any number you wish) by four table, adds up the rows and the columns, and prints out the results.

The column sum is built by repeating the line,

LET S = S + T(R,C)

The calculation begins on the right-hand side of the equal sign (=) by taking the old value of S and adding to it the current value of T(R,C). The result of this addition (a single number) is then assigned to the variable on the left side of the equal sign—in this case, the new S. If the program is organized so that each time we cycle past this line we have a different T(R,C) then the program will repeatedly add the current T(R,C) to the running sum S. (If a line were inserted immediately beneath the above line that said PRINT S, we would see how S grew each time another T(R,C) was added to it.)

The section that prints the table does some tricks to make the numbers look good when they appear. Experiment with your BASIC to find the trick that will work for you.

_____ *Exercises* _____

1. Run the program with your own table of numbers. Modify it and rerun it.
2. Think of a table of numbers that you work with. Modify TABLE to read your table, do the correct arithmetic on the table, and print out the desired results. (Several of the later programs in this book are modifications of the program TABLE.)
3. Read Appendix D to see how you could use VisiCalc to work with a table of numbers.

_____

References

1. Dearden, John, *Cost Accounting and Financial Control Systems*, Reading, MA: Addison-Wesley, 1973.

2. Helfert, Erich A., *Techniques of Financial Analysis*, Homewood, IL: Richard D. Irwin, 1977.

3. Weston, J. Fred, and Brigham, Eugene F., *Managerial Finance*, Fourth Edition, New York: Holt, Rinehart, and Winston, 1972.

The Strategic Review

What recommends commerce to me is its enterprise and bravery.

Henry David Thoreau

Shortly after the start of the new year, Frank Bradshaw asked Steven Cauldwell to loan him Peter Bates. Bradshaw's Bear Division had finished the year poorly and he needed Bates to help him take a strategic look at his product mix. Cauldwell knew that the bulk of the planning for the coming year was completed, so he sent Bates out to help in late January.

A LOOK AT COST

When Bates arrived at Bear Division headquarters, he found an anxious Frank Bradshaw.

"We've got to get on top of our product mix," the general manager said. "We have some promising new products, some tired old lines, and some wishy-washy ones in the middle. Your job is to sort them out. We are the biggest division in Chordata and it's important that we get back on track quickly.

"Because we manufacture several products in our plants," Bradshaw continued, "fixed costs are hard to assign. Your first chore is to find out what to count that most closely corresponds to our real costs so we can apportion fixed costs to products. The answer may be manufactured units, or hours worked, or pieces of equipment set up, or even orders processed.

"Get back to me as soon as you have some answers. I'll be out of town until Friday afternoon."

"And what are the arrangements with your financial folks?" Bates asked.

"You have been given carte blanche. They should be able to fill you in on the direct costs, but go where you want to and talk to whomever you need to. I'll see you sometime next week?"

"Tight schedule, but okay," Bates nodded.

Nine days later Bates met with Bradshaw to show him his results. He found that the transaction that most closely reflected product costs was the number of purchase orders. Accompanying each order were administrative costs, set-up costs, and handling costs. Except for a few very large orders, the actual size of the order had little to do with the expense involved. A small order cost as much to process as a large order. The total number of orders for Bear Division was 213,000.

He showed Bradshaw his table of raw data that displayed the products' contributions and their total orders:

```
380 REM  PRODUCT LINE  CONTRIB(IN $1000)  ORDERS(IN 100)
385 '
390      DATA "TOASTER OVEN",      30520,       498
395      DATA "TOASTER       ",    15870,       660
400      DATA "FOOD PROCESR",      15870,       350
405      DATA "JUICER        ",     8280,       182
410      DATA "BLENDER        ",   10350,        64
415      DATA "CAN OPENER    ",     4140,       116
420      DATA "STEAM IRON    ",     3450,        78
425      DATA "HAIR CURLER   ",     2760,        73
430      DATA "PENCIL SHRPN ",      2760,       109
435 '
```

Working on a sheet of paper Bates explained how he had computed profits. "We start with the contribution, for example the Toaster Oven product line, which is 30,520,000. To get Toaster Oven's fixed cost, we take the fraction of orders processed, 49800/213000, times the total fixed cost, 39,000,000. That's 9,118,000. Profit is the difference between the two, 21,402,000."

"Sounds reasonable," said Bradshaw. "And the profit derived from this contribution reflects the managing efficiency of the product line?"

"To a point, yes," agreed Bates, "I included the profit-per-contribution dollar so the product lines could be compared. Here's what it all looks like."

TOTAL SALES: 275000
DIRECT COSTS: 181000
PRODUCT CONTRIBUTION -- 94000
PROFIT BEFORE TAX: 55000
FIXED COSTS -- 39000

	CONTRIB	%	FIXED CST	%	PROFIT	%	PROF/ CONTRIB-$
TOASTER OVEN	30,520	32	9,118	23	21,402	39	0.70
TOASTER	15,870	17	12,085	31	3,785	7	0.24
FOOD PROCESR	15,870	17	6,408	16	9,462	17	0.60
JUICER	8,280	9	3,332	9	4,948	9	0.60
BLENDER	10,350	11	1,172	3	9,178	17	0.89
CAN OPENER	4,140	4	2,124	5	2,016	4	0.49
STEAM IRON	3,450	4	1,428	4	2,022	4	0.59
HAIR CURLER	2,760	3	1,337	3	1,423	3	0.52
PENCIL SHRPN	2,760	3	1,996	5	764	1	0.28
TOTALS	94,000		39,000		55,000		0.59

"Wait a minute," said Bradshaw, "let me see if I understand this. You say that you removed direct costs from sales to get contribution and then you used the number of orders to apportion fixed costs to products. After the fixed costs have been subtracted we have a better picture of which products really made the profits last year."

"That's right," agreed Bates. "As you can see, Toaster and Pencil Sharpener are problems. And so are Can Opener and Hair Curler, probably. An interesting question to ask at this point is what happens if we sell more Toaster Ovens in place of Toasters? We can play some 'what if?' games with our product lines."

"Okay," said Bradshaw, "how do we ask 'what if?'"

ANALYSIS

Peter Bates lifted the small television screen and keyboard onto the table. "Glad you asked that. The program I wrote has a set of what I call 'change factors' built in at the top. For our initial table, all the factors were 1. If we want to double a product line, we can change its factor to 2. If we want to eliminate a product we can change its factor to 0."

"How hard is it to alter the factors?"

"Watch," said Bates. He turned on the small computer and loaded the program. He showed Bradshaw how the program looked. Then he typed on the screen:

DATA 1.5, 0, 1, 1, 1, 1, 2, 1, 0

"I just retyped one line in the program. The change cancelled Toaster and Pencil Sharpener and boosted Toaster Oven and Steam Iron." Bates typed RUN and the table appeared on the screen.

"Terrific," said Bradshaw, "Look at how our costs dropped and our profits rose." He leaned closer to study the screen. "What happens if we get rid of our other two weak product lines?"

"Why don't you find out?" said Bates, offering Bradshaw the seat in front of the screen.

Bradshaw hesitated, "I'm a lousy typist."

"Don't worry about it. If you make a mistake, you just back up and retype it."

Bradshaw sat down warily. He typed a data line with the new factors:

DATA 1.5, 0, 1, 1, 1.6, 0, 2, 0, 0

He typed RUN. The new table flashed on the screen:

TOTAL SALES: 275000
DIRECT COSTS: 181000
PRODUCT CONTRIBUTION -- 94000
PROFIT BEFORE TAX: 55000
FIXED COSTS -- 39000

	CONTRIB	%	FIXED CST	%	PROFIT	%	PROF/ CONTRIB-$
TOASTER OVEN	45,780	49	13,677	49	32,103	49	0.70
TOASTER	0	0	0	0	0	0	
FOOD PROCESR	15,870	17	6,408	23	9,462	15	0.60
JUICER	8,280	9	3,332	12	4,948	8	0.60
BLENDER	16,560	18	1,875	7	14,685	23	0.89
CAN OPENER	0	0	0	0	0	0	
STEAM IRON	6,900	7	2,856	10	4,044	6	0.59
HAIR CURLER	0	0	0	0	0	0	
PENCIL SHRPN	0	0	0	0	0	0	
TOTALS	93,390		28,150		65,240		0.70

"Theoretically we could increase our profits by 18 percent if we dropped Toaster, Can Opener, Hair Curler, and Pencil Sharpener and picked up the business with Toaster Oven, Blender, and Steam Iron. Not bad." Bradshaw appeared to have forgotten Bates. He studied the screen and continued to think out loud. "But Toaster Oven can't really sell that much more stuff. However, Food Processor sure could. Let's move Toaster Oven back down and raise Food Processor."

A few minutes later the new version of the table blinked on the screen. "Even doing it in a reasonable way gives us a 15 percent increase in profits. That's not just play; that's a real possibility.

"Why doesn't the top of the report agree with the bottom?" asked Bradshaw.

"The top five lines are the initial reality. It stays the same so you can always see how a change relates to the initial conditions."

Bradshaw nodded and turned back to study the screen.

Peter Bates leaned against the edge of a desk behind Bradshaw and said nothing. There were several more things to look at before any action could be taken. They had to look at market shares, distribution channels, potential market growth, cost controls, personnel, and finances. But things were off to a good start. Bradshaw was much more flexible than he expected.

Bradshaw got up from the terminal. "That was fun. Gave me some good ideas, too. Next on the agenda is some work with market share.

"By a week from Wednesday, I would like a breakdown of where our current products are. If that isn't finished, I'd like a once over lightly on the experience-curve principles and how they apply to our market-share work. By the way, why did you call the program X-RAY?"

"It's from a phrase of Peter Drucker's. He calls a related kind of analysis an 'x-ray' of a company. Some of the ideas behind this program are his, but most are mine. I used the name as a tribute to Drucker and because it is a memorable name."

THE PROGRAM X-RAY

```
100 REM   X-RAY    15 JANUARY 1981   PETER BATES
105 '
110 REM   © COPYRIGHT 1980 JOHN M. NEVISON ASSOCIATES
115 '
120 REM   THIS PROGRAM TAKES PRODUCT CONTRIBUTIONS AND
125 REM   PRODUCT TRANSACTIONS, BREAKS OUT PRODUCT FIXED
130 REM   COSTS FROM THE TOTAL FIXED COST, AND COMPUTES
132 REM   REAL PRODUCT PROFITS.
135 '
140 REM   THE PROGRAM ALSO COMPUTES PERCENTAGES OF
145 REM   COMPANY TOTALS AND A MEASURE OF PRODUCT
150 REM   PERFORMANCE, PROFIT PER CONTRIBUTION DOLLAR.
155 '
```

```
160 REM   TO ALTER THE PRODUCT MIX, CHANGE THE DATA FOR
165 REM   THE CHANGE FACTORS IN SUCH A WAY THAT THE
170 REM   TOTAL CONTRIBUTION REMAINS UNCHANGED.
175 '
180 REM   VARIABLES:
185 REM        C . . . . . . . . . . . FIXED COST ATTRIBUTABLE TO PRODUCTS
190 REM        C(I,1) . . . . . . . . PRODUCT FIXED COST
195 REM        C(I,2) . . . . . . . . PRODUCT FIXED COST (PERCENT OF TOTAL)
200 REM        D . . . . . . . . . . . DIRECT COSTS
205 REM        F(I) . . . . . . . . . CHANGE FACTORS
210 REM        I . . . . . . . . . . . . INDEX VARIABLE
215 REM        N$(I) . . . . . . . . NAME OF PRODUCT
220 REM        P . . . . . . . . . . . TOTAL PROFIT BEFORE TAX
225 REM        P(I,1) . . . . . . . . PRODUCT PROFIT
230 REM        P(I,2) . . . . . . . . PRODUCT PROFIT (PERCENT OF TOTAL)
235 REM        P$() . . . . . . . . PRINT TEMPLATES
240 REM        R(I,1) . . . . . . . PRODUCT CONTRIBUTION
245 REM        R(I,2) . . . . . . . PRODUCT CONTRIBUTION
247 REM                              (PERCENT OF TOTAL)
250 REM        S . . . . . . . . . . . TOTAL SALES
255 REM        T(I) . . . . . . . . . PRODUCT TRANSACTIONS
260 REM        T1,T2,T3,T4 . . . TALLY VARIABLES
265 '
270 REM   READ CHANGE FACTORS (ALL 1 INITIALLY)
275 '
280       FOR I = 1 TO 9
285           READ F(I)
290       NEXT I
295       DATA 1, 1, 1, 1, 1, 1, 1, 1, 1
300 '
305 REM   INITIAL CONDITIONS
310       READ S, D, P
315       DATA 275000, 181000, 55000
320       LET C = S − D − P
325 '
330 REM   READ THE PRODUCT'S NAME, CONTRIBUTION, AND
335 REM   TRANSACTIONS.  APPLY CHANGE FACTOR TO
337 REM   CONTRIBUTION.
340 REM   TALLY TRANSACTIONS.
345 '
```

```
350        FOR I = 1 TO 9
355            READ N$(I), R(I,1), T(I)
360            LET R(I,1) = F(I) * R(I,1)
365            LET T1 = T1 + T(I)
370        NEXT I
375  '
380 REM  PRODUCT LINE  CONTRIB(IN $1000)  ORDERS(IN 100)
385  '
390        DATA "TOASTER OVEN ",     30520,        498
395        DATA "TOASTER       ",    15870,        660
400        DATA "FOOD PROCESR",      15870,        350
405        DATA "JUICER        ",     8280,        182
410        DATA "BLENDER       ",    10350,         64
415        DATA "CAN OPENER   ",      4140,        116
420        DATA "STEAM IRON    ",     3450,         78
425        DATA "HAIR CURLER   ",     2760,         73
430        DATA "PENCIL SHRPN ",      2760,        109
435  '
440 REM   COMPUTE THE PRODUCT FIXED COST, C(). APPLY THE
445 REM   CHANGE FACTOR TO THE FIXED COST.  COMPUTE THE
450 REM   PROFIT, P(). TALLY CONTRIBUTIONS, FIXED COSTS,
452 REM   AND PROFITS.
455  '
460        FOR I = 1 TO 9
465            LET C(I,1) = T(I)/T1 * C
470            LET C(I,1) = F(I) * C(I,1)
475            LET P(I,1) = R(I,1) − C(I,1)
480            LET T2 = T2 + R(I,1)
485            LET T3 = T3 + C(I,1)
490            LET T4 = T4 + P(I,1)
495        NEXT I
500  '
505 REM   FIND THE PERCENTAGE CONTRIBUTION, FIXED COST,
510 REM   AND PROFIT.
515        FOR I = 1 TO 9
520            LET R(I,2) = R(I,1)/T2 * 100
525            LET C(I,2) = C(I,1)/T3 * 100
530            LET P(I,2) = P(I,1)/T4 * 100
535        NEXT I
540  '
```

```
545 REM    PRINT THE TABLE
550 REM    ***NOTE THAT THE PRINT USING STATEMENT MAY BE
555 REM    ***DIFFERENT ON YOUR COMPUTER.
560 '
565        LET P$(1) = " ###,###  ##"
570        LET P$(2) = " ###,###    "
575        PRINT "TOTAL SALES: "; S
580        PRINT "DIRECT COSTS: "; D
585        PRINT "PRODUCT CONTRIBUTION -- "; S – D
590        PRINT "PROFIT BEFORE TAX: "; P
595        PRINT "FIXED COSTS -- "; S – D – P
600        PRINT
605        PRINT "          CONTRIB   % FIXED CST  % PROFIT";
610        PRINT "   % PROF/CONTRIB-$"
615        PRINT
620        FOR I = 1 TO 9
625            PRINT N$(I);
630            PRINT USING P$(1); R(I,1), R(I,2);
635            PRINT USING P$(1); C(I,1), C(I,2);
640            PRINT USING P$(1); P(I,1), P(I,2);
645            IF R(I,1) < > 0 THEN 650 ELSE 660
650                PRINT USING " ##.##"; P(I,1)/R(I,1)
655                GOTO 670      'IFEND
660 '            ELSE
665                PRINT
670 '            IFEND
675        NEXT I
680        PRINT
685        PRINT "TOTALS     ";
690        PRINT USING P$(2); T2;
695        PRINT USING P$(2); T3;
700        PRINT USING P$(2); T4;
702        PRINT USING " ##.##"; T4/T2
705        END
```

The program begins with a solid set of comments on its use. The variable list explains how the variables will be used and serves as a dictionary for later quick reference.

The body of the code begins with the change factors, F(). Altering these factors will alter the levels of product activity: a two will double the activity; a zero will cancel the activity. Notice especially the line where the change factor is applied to contributions and the line where it is applied to costs. By swelling or shrinking these two items, the product's activity is altered.

The initial conditions are the basic data on the organization. From these conditions the fixed cost, C, is calculated. After the initial conditions, the product information is entered.

The program breaks out costs, calculates profits, tallies the columns, and finds the percentages.

After completing its calculations, the program prints out the results. The IF ... THEN ... ELSE construction avoids division by zero when a product's change factor is turned to zero. Additional details on this construction can be found in Appendix A.

_____ *Exercises* _____

1. Alter the change factors to try out what Frank Bradshaw suggested.
2. Try out a new set of your own change factors.
3. If you had to make the maximum profit, which product would you produce exclusively? Discuss why this is not a practical solution.
4. Apply the change factors, F( ), to transactions instead of costs. What's wrong with the results?
5. Try out X-RAY with a product mix of your own.

_____

THE VALUE OF EXPERIENCE

"Forgive me if this sounds like a lecture," said Peter Bates, "but this is what I did at the consulting firm before I joined up here. Please interrupt with questions."

"Don't worry, I will," said Frank Bradshaw.

"As the Second World War went on, a bomber became cheaper and cheaper to build. Each plane became cheaper because the plants making planes became more efficient — the industry as a whole learned how to make bombers better. This phenomenon can be graphed.

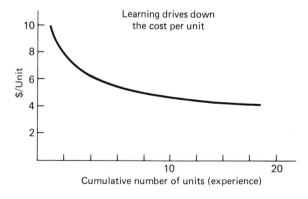

Fig. 3-1   A Learning Curve

"In the early 1960s the idea of this learning curve was broadened to be called an experience curve. Many industries exhibited the same phenomenon: their cost per unit (in constant dollars) dropped as the lifetime total number of units grew. This industry-wide drop covered more than the mere learning on the production line. It encompassed the whole business: finance, management, research and development, production, and marketing.

"An actual set of curves might look like the one in Fig. 3.2.

"The cost curve is for the individual firm in the market. The price curve is for the market as a whole. The horizontal axis is for cumulative volume of units made; the vertical axis is dollars per unit.

"One of the consequences of the cost curve is that if three firms have different cumulative volumes and different levels of experience, their costs will be different. For example, Firm A has the lowest cost and Firm C has the highest cost in the figure shown here."

"And they all charge the same price?" asked Bradshaw.

"In the simple model, yes. The industry price is determined from the sum of their individual volumes. In this example, it's the point X."

"The horizontal axis of X does not look like the sum of the horizontal axis values of A, B, and C," said Bradshaw. "Why not?"

"That's because both axes are telescoped by being on a logarithmic scale. The scales straighten out the experience curves and have the side effect of foreshortening the scales. It takes as far to get from 1

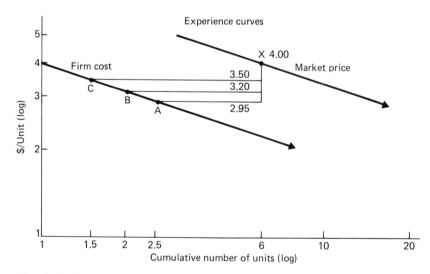

Fig. 3-2   Two Experience Curves

to 10 as it does to get from 10 to 100. So the volumes of A, B, and C really do add up to the volume of X."

"That makes X on the price line," said Bradshaw, "much like the bouncing ball in the old sing-along movies. As you watch the X move you see time passing. Is that right?"

"Yes, that's exactly right," nodded Bates. "And because X is based on the market volume, which is the sum of A, B, and C, X will always lead A, B, and C. Notice that because of their different unit costs, the three firms have different profit margins. You can see that C's is a thin 10 percent, B's is 25 percent, and A's is a whopping 40 percent. That's not unusual for a market leader in some industries."

"As the market growth slows A will let the price be whatever it needs to be to keep enough competitors in the game to keep the antitrust crowd off its back. Because of its large advantage in both number of units produced and profit per unit, it can defend itself against all comers."

"So what you're saying," summarized Bradshaw, "is that whoever controls the market makes a lot of money. Let's slow down for a minute. This experience curve helps explain why the big companies have the lowest costs and make the most money. Fine. Now how does this help us with our product lines? We have always wanted our products to be leaders in their markets."

"But are they?" asked Bates.

"Most of them," said Bradshaw, "have a pretty good market share."

"That's what I looked at," said Peter Bates. "It's hard to know what our costs are compared to our competitors, but market share seems to be a good rough cut. I also looked at whether the markets were new and growing or old and stable. It's better to gain share in a small, new market than in a large, old one. After the market slows, positions tend to freeze. That's not a consequence of the experience curve; it's a consequence of inertia in distribution, sales, and customer preference."

"So what did you find?" Bradshaw asked.

"Have a look at this table.

PRODUCT LINE	SHARE	BIGGEST/ NEAREST	MKT GWTH	REL SHARE
TOASTER OVEN	0.40	0.25	0.15	1.60
TOASTER	0.10	0.20	0.12	0.50
FOOD PROCESR	0.20	0.10	0.40	2.00
JUICER	0.35	0.40	0.35	0.88
BLENDER	0.50	0.15	0.23	3.33
CAN OPENER	0.25	0.45	0.30	0.56
STEAM IRON	0.30	0.25	0.35	1.20
HAIR CURLER	0.30	0.22	0.45	1.36
PENCIL SHRPN	0.05	0.20	0.12	0.25

"Because each product line has a different market share with a different number of competitors with different magnitudes of shares, I needed a measure that would allow me to compare one product line to another. Relative share seems to work pretty well. Let me explain how I arrived at relative share. If we are the leader, then the relative share is our advantage over our nearest competitor; if we are back in the pack, then relative share is how we compare to the leader. If we can't beat the leader, or be a significant number two or three, then we should think about getting out of the race."

"Does that mean," asked Bradshaw, "that if we were tied for first place with another company we would have a relative share of 1.0?"

"Yes, that's right," agreed Bates. "The relative market share spreads our products out from leaders to followers. If we want to see how they look in their markets, we can place them on a second scale of market growth. Low growth corresponds to an old market; high growth to a new market. I used 25 percent as a middle rate. One market is exploding at 45 percent a year and two old ones are just keeping pace with inflation at about 12 percent. Here's what it all looks like" (Fig. 3.3).

Frank Bradshaw did not say anything. He studied the chart. "The bad place to be is low share in an old market. I would say that your analysis confirms our initial product x-ray. Toaster and Pencil Sharpener are losers. But it shows that Hair Curler is something we should look at. And we're going to have to push Can Opener and Juicer if they are going to do well." He studied the graph some more. "You didn't draw this graph on the computer? Why not?"

Peter Bates grinned. "Didn't have a little program all done, so I did it by hand. Nine numbers isn't too bad to do by hand. I did the table on the computer only because I was able to borrow a copy of a program somebody in Wolf Division wrote. I modified it to give me the table of values I showed you."

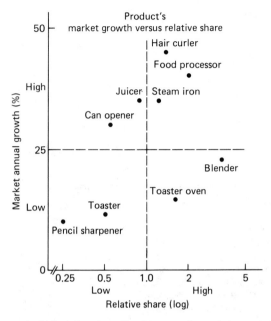

Fig. 3-3 Product Positions—Growth versus Market Share

THE PROGRAM SHARE

```
100 REM    SHARE    20 JANUARY 1981    PETER BATES
102 '
104 REM    © COPYRIGHT 1980 JOHN M. NEVISON ASSOCIATES
105 '
110 REM    MODIFIED FROM TABLE (25 OCT 1980) BY GEORGE LEE
115 '
120 REM    A PROGRAM TO READ MARKET SHARE, THE BIGGEST OR
125 REM    NEAREST COMPETITOR, AND THE MARKET GROWTH.
130 '
135 REM    THE PROGRAM COMPUTES THE RELATIVE MARKET SHARE
140 REM    AND PRINTS OUT THE RESULTS.
145 '
150 REM    VARIABLES:
155 REM       C . . . . . . . . . . . COLUMN COUNTER
160 REM       N . . . . . . . . . . . NUMBER OF ROWS
165 REM       R . . . . . . . . . . . ROW COUNTER
170 REM       R$() . . . . . . . . ROW NAME
175 REM       T() . . . . . . . . . . TABLE OF VALUES
180 '
```

```
185 REM    DIMENSIONS:
190        DIM T(50,5)
195 '
200 REM    READ IN THE TABLE
205 '
210        LET N = 9
215        FOR R = 1 TO N
220            READ R$(R)
225            FOR C = 1 TO 3
230                READ T(R,C)
240            NEXT C
245        NEXT R
250 '
255 REM NAME      SHARE, BIGGEST OR NEAREST, MARKET GROWTH
260        DATA "TOASTER OVEN ", 40, 25, 15
265        DATA "TOASTER       ", 10, 20, 12
270        DATA "FOOD PROCESR", 20, 10, 40
275        DATA "JUICER        ", 35, 40, 35
280        DATA "BLENDER       ", 50, 15, 23
285        DATA "CAN OPENER    ", 25, 45, 30
290        DATA "STEAM IRON    ", 30, 25, 35
295        DATA "HAIR CURLER   ", 30, 22, 45
300        DATA "PENCIL SHRPN ", 5,   20, 12
305 '
310 REM    CONVERT PERCENTAGE TO DECIMAL AND CALCULATE
315 REM    BIGGEST OR US VERSUS THE NEAREST COMPETITOR.
320 REM    RELATIVE MARKET SHARE.
325        FOR R = 1 TO N
330            FOR C = 1 TO 3
335                LET T(R,C) = T(R,C)/100
340            NEXT C
350            LET T(R,4) = T(R,1)/T(R,2)
360        NEXT R
365 '
370 REM    PRINT OUT THE TABLE
372 REM    ***THE PRINT USING STATEMENT MAY BE DIFFERENT
374 REM    ***IN YOUR BASIC. PLEASE CHECK.
375 '
380        PRINT "          PRODUCT LINE   SHARE   BIGGEST/";
385        PRINT " MKT GWTH    REL SHARE"
387        PRINT "                                NEAREST "
390        PRINT
395        FOR R = 1 TO N
400            PRINT R$(R);
405            FOR C = 1 TO 4
410                PRINT USING "   #.##";T(R,C);
415            NEXT C
420            PRINT
425        NEXT R
430 '
435        END
```

The program SHARE is a modified version of TABLE. It reads different values, calculates different results, and prints out a different final picture. In fact, what remains of TABLE is the fundamental tripartite idea: read in a table, do some calculations on it, and print out the final table.

If Lee's initial program had been badly written, Bates probably would have chosen to write his own. But because the initial program was neatly broken into three distinct functions, Bates modified the original more quickly than he could have written the program from scratch.

Bates's experience highlights the value of George Lee's effort to write a clear, easy-to-read program. Because Lee did things correctly the first time, he saved Bates time and effort.

Exercises

1. Modify the data in SHARE to do a set of your own products.
2. Read about the PRINT USING statement in your BASIC and modify the program to work on your computer.

COMPETITIVE GROWTH

One week later Peter Bates met for a fourth time with Frank Bradshaw. After they positioned Bear product lines in their markets with their relative market shares, they wanted to know what the cost would be to build share for those that needed it. To answer that question they needed a detailed look at the market, the competitors, and how they all were moving. It had been a very busy week for Bates.

Bradshaw was sympathetic. He knew Bates was working half way between hard data and industry rumor. Bates was a numbers man, and that was reassuring to Bradshaw. Bates would boil down everything he could to numbers. It was just the right instinct for this part of the job.

"You're going to love this," Bates said. "I've got yet another computer toy."

"Toy?" Bradshaw looked surprised. "You had time to play on the computer with all the other stuff going on last week? How did you manage that?"

"Well, I had this toy already built. I used it to analyze our financial possibilities against my idea of the market realities. Truth be known, without the model, I couldn't have completed all the analysis in one week.

"Before I show you some of the details," continued Bates, "I would like to walk you through a simple case to get the feel of the model."

"Fire away," said Bradshaw. He leaned back in his chair.

"Imagine a simple market with three competing firms. While all three firms grow, the market itself is growing. Suppose that we watch how one firm will gain share, one will preserve share, and one, through inattention or ignorance, will lose share.

"The first year had all three firms exactly even. Each produced 3000 units. The cost to each was $10.00 per unit. The price of all 9000 units in the market was $15.00 apiece. The first year established the starting points for two experience curves: the cost curve for the individual firms and the price curve for the market. The price curve is a convenient fiction that I will discard a little later. I assumed both curves were 80 percent curves."

"80 percent curves?" asked Bradshaw. "What are they?"

"It means that when the cumulative volume doubles, the dollars per unit drops to 80 percent of its initial value. A 90 percent curve hardly drops at all. A 70 percent curve has a lot of drop. Choosing an 80 percent curve for this example is right in the middle. Besides, most of Bear's product lines are on this curve.

"At any rate, after choosing the initial points on both curves and the 80 percent slope for both curves, I sketched out a scenario for the market and our three competitors. The data statements show how the market grows and what the market shares are for each firm.

```
360     READ G, M(1), M(2), M(3)
365     DATA 1.00, .33, .33, .33
370     DATA 1.40, .43, .33, .24
375     DATA 1.40, .50, .33, .17
380     DATA 1.30, .50, .33, .17
385     DATA 1.20, .50, .33, .17
390     DATA 1.20, .50, .33, .17
395     DATA 1.20, .50, .33, .17
400     DATA 1.20, .50, .33, .17
405     DATA 1.20, .50, .33, .17
410     DATA 1.20, .50, .33, .17
415     DATA 1.20, .50, .33, .17
420 '
```

"The first year is our initial start-up. All three have a third of the market. The next year, the market grows 40 percent (1.40). Firm A goes for .43 of the market, Firm B for .33, and Firm C gets left with .24.

"In the second year the market again grows at 1.40. Firm A claims .50 of the market, Firm B preserves its .33, and Firm C is left with .17.

"In the third year the market begins to slow (1.30) and the firms hold their shares. In the fourth year the market slows to its long-term steady growth of 1.20.

"By altering this initial data, you can try out any pattern you wish. In fact, that's exactly what I did when I reviewed each product line to arrive at my recommendations.

"The number of units produced in any given year will be the annual growth times the number produced in the previous year."

```
LET U(0) = G * U(0)
```

"The total number of units in the market is U(0). Each firm must manufacture its share of these units:"

```
LET U(1) = M(1) * U(0)
LET U(2) = M(2) * U(0)
LET U(3) = M(3) * U(0)
```

"Wait," said Bradshaw, "Doesn't that assume the firms will sell all their units?"

"Yes, it does. The way we make that happen is by pricing those gaining market share lower than their competitors. But before we get into pricing our products we must first finance their production. We do this in a conservative way. We pay our current costs to produce the coming year's units. We will earn the end-of-the-year prices, so our profits will be understated if our costs drop over the course of the year as we expect them to.

"I called the financing F(). The first year it is computed as the cost per unit times the number of units times the interest rate.

```
– U(1) * C(1) * I9
```

"I assumed that all the sales from the first year are reinvested in the second year's growth. The new financing is the old financing plus the sales from the previous year minus the current debt necessary to finance the current annual production.

```
LET F(1) = (F(1) + S(1) – U(1)*C(1)) * I9
LET F(2) = (F(2) + S(2) – U(2)*C(2)) * I9
LET F(3) = (F(3) + S(3) – U(3)*C(3)) * I9
```

"After a while, if sales grow large, the financing will turn positive. It then earns the same interest for the company that was being charged against the company."

"That's conservative, too," interjected Bradshaw. "If we can't beat the interest rate we're in bad shape."

"Yes," agreed Bates, "it is conservative, so again it will understate profits. I like to make everything pay its way.

"After we finance our annual production, we build our cumulative volumes for the industry (for price) and for the three firms (for costs).

```
LET V(0) = V(0) + U(0)
LET V(1) = V(1) + U(1)
LET V(2) = V(2) + U(2)
LET V(3) = V(3) + U(3)
```

"The individual unit costs are computed from each firm's cumulative volume on the cost-experience curve.

```
LET C(1) = 10 * (V(1)/3000) ^X
LET C(2) = 10 * (V(2)/3000) ^X
LET C(3) = 10 * (V(3)/3000) ^X
```

"X is the experience factor for the 80 percent curve. The mathematics is pretty dull. Do you want me to go over it?"

"I'll take your word for it, thanks," said Bradshaw. Just because Bates was a numbers man did not mean he, Bradshaw, had to become one.

"The industry price is computed using the price-experience curve," continued Bates.

```
LET P(0) = 15 * (V(0)/9000) ^X
```

"Each firm's price is computed as a weighted average of the initial shares and then later as an average of the annual change in market share. The equations are a little tricky, but they have two desirable properties. First, if you want to build share, you must price below your competitors. Second, if you wish to preserve share, you must drop your price every year. The weighted average of the different prices is the industry price. Prices, like all the other figures, are expressed in current dollars.

```
525      LET P(0) = 15 * (V(0)/9000)^(X)
530      IF Y <= 0 THEN 535 ELSE 555
535        LET P(1) = .33/M(1) * P(0)
540        LET P(2) = .33/M(2) * P(0)
545        LET P(3) = .33/M(3) * P(0)
550        GOTO 575          'IFEND
555 '    ELSE
560        LET P(1) = L(1)/M(1) * P(0)
565        LET P(2) = L(2)/M(2) * P(0)
570        LET P(3) = (P(1) * M(1) + P(2) * M(2) − P(0))/(−M(3))
575 '    IFEND
580 '
```

"At the end of the year, the firms' sales are the number of units sold times their price.

```
LET S(1) = U(1) * P(1)
LET S(2) = U(2) * P(2)
LET S(3) = U(3) * P(3)
```

"At this point we have all the information necessary to print out a year's worth of results, so we go to a subroutine that does just that. Finally, before we return to begin the next year, we stash the values of the current market shares for later use.

```
LET L(1) = M(1)
LET L(2) = M(2)
LET L(3) = M(3)
```

"Next year, when we will need to refer to last year's market shares, the values will be in the L()'s."

"When do we do that?" asked Bradshaw.

"When we figure a firm's price. The price is a function of the change in market share. To get the change, you need to know the old value as well as the current value."

"Okay, right, you just explained that," nodded Bradshaw. "If the firm is increasing its share, it prices below the competitors."

"Well, you have it all," said Bates. "You can see what the results look like on these experience curves" (Fig. 3.4).

"You can see how after five years the firm with .50 of the market has a .41 profit margin, while the .17 market share had a .20 profit margin. Remember both started at the end of the initial year with a .33 profit margin."

"That's really something." Bradshaw shook his head. "If they had started with a narrower margin, Firm C would be hurting to stay in the game. It's clear that A controls the show by year five."

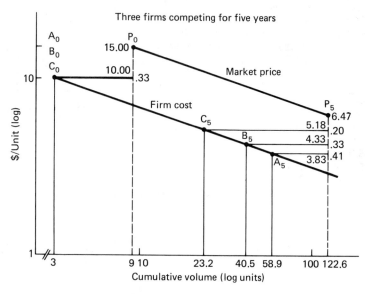

Fig. 3-4   Three Firms Competing over Five Years

"I've got one more detail to add to our example," said Peter Bates. "The financial position. It's the reason that not everyone goes for market share. Here is what A, B, and C look like as time goes by" (Fig. 3.5).

"The three firms' cash positions show that building share is expensive in the short run and very profitable in the long run. The risk is that you have to be willing to plan out a few years ahead of where you start. Not everyone is willing to do that."

"Now we have a simple model that understates our profits, if anything," said Bradshaw. "How did you use this to look over our product lines?"

"It was a little tricky," answered Bates. "In real life there is no industry price curve. This means that in our initial assumptions each market-share goal must be accompanied by an estimated price that will achieve the goal. I derived these prices from interviews with the product-line managers. For example, the real READ and DATA statements might look like this:

READ G,   M(1), P(1),   M(2), P(2),   M(3), P(3)

.
.
.

DATA 1.4,   .50, 8.40,   .33, 9.50,   .17, 14.00

.
.
.

"After that it was straightforward," Bates continued. "I altered the cost curve to reflect each product's history. I took a look at the competitors and set up some alternative futures. One lesson you learn quickly is that you want to achieve share as early as possible. So I tried to get a product line into a leadership position in no more than five years, three years if possible. I compared the costs of doing this for each product. What GROWTH made possible was a rapid evaluation of the alternatives after I had collected the necessary information."

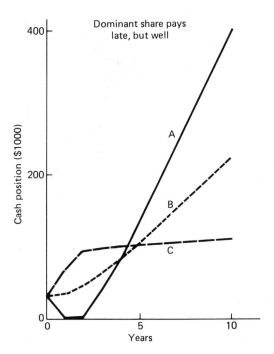

Fig. 3-5   How Market Share Pays Off

THE PROGRAM GROWTH

```
100 REM    GROWTH    15 JANUARY 1981    PETER BATES
105 '
110 REM    © COPYRIGHT 1980 JOHN M. NEVISON ASSOCIATES
115 '
120 REM    MODEL AN INDUSTRY WITH THREE FIRMS COMPETING.
125 '
126 REM    REFERENCE;  JOHN M. NEVISON, "EXECUTIVE
127 REM                COMPUTING," READING, MASS:
128 REM                ADDISON-WESLEY PUBLISHING CO. 1981.
129 '
130 REM    VARIABLES:
135 REM       C() .......... FIRM'S COST PER UNIT
140 REM       F().......... FINANCING (DEBT  OR CASH)
145 REM       G ........... MARKET ANNUAL GROWTH RATE
150 REM       L().......... LAST YEAR'S MARKET SHARES
155 REM       M() ......... MARKET SHARES
157 REM       P$ .......... PRINT TEMPLATE
160 REM       P(0)......... MARKET PRICE PER UNIT
165 REM       P().......... FIRM'S PRICE PER UNIT
170 REM       S().......... SALES FOR THE YEAR
175 REM       U(0) ........ MARKET ANNUAL UNITS
180 REM       U() ......... FIRM'S ANNUAL UNITS
185 REM       V(0)......... MARKET CUMULATIVE VOLUME
190 REM       V()......... FIRM'S CUMULATIVE VOLUME
195 REM       Y ........... YEAR INDEX VARIABLE
205 REM    CONSTANTS:
210        LET I9 = 1.10       'INTEREST RATE ON DEBT OR CASH
215        LET X = LOG(.80)/LOG(2)   'EXPERIENCE FACTOR
217 REM                              FOR 80% CURVE
220 '
225 REM    MAIN PROGRAM
230 '
235 REM    INITIALIZED VARIABLES
240 '
245        FOR I = 0 TO 3
250            LET C(I) = 10
255            LET F(I) = 0
260            LET S(I) = 0
265            LET V(I) = 0
270            LET U(I) = 0
275        NEXT I
280 '
285        LET U(0) = 9000
290 '
```

```
295 REM    YEARLY LOOP
300 '
305 REM    READ THE MARKET GROWTH, G, AND THE FIRMS' MARKET
310 REM    SHARE GOALS, M(). FIND THE NEW ANNUAL MARKET,
315 REM    U(0), AND THE FIRMS' PRODUCTION, U().
320 REM    COMPUTE THE NECESSARY FINANCING,
325 REM    F(). TALLY THE CUMULATIVE VOLUMES, V(). COMPUTE
330 REM    THE FIRMS' COSTS, C(), AND PRICES, P(). FIGURE
335 REM    THE SALES, S(), AND PRINT OUT WHATEVER IS
340 REM    INTERESTING. SET ASIDE MARGINS AND GO ON TO THE
345 REM    NEXT YEAR.
350 '
355        FOR Y = 0 TO 10
360            READ G, M(1), M(2), M(3)
365            DATA 1.00, .33, .33, .33
370            DATA 1.40, .43, .33, .24
375            DATA 1.40, .50, .33, .17
380            DATA 1.30, .50, .33, .17
385            DATA 1.20, .50, .33, .17
390            DATA 1.20, .50, .33, .17
395            DATA 1.20, .50, .33, .17
400            DATA 1.20, .50, .33, .17
405            DATA 1.20, .50, .33, .17
410            DATA 1.20, .50, .33, .17
415            DATA 1.20, .50, .33, .17
420 '
425            LET U(0) = G * U(0)
430 '
435            LET U(1) = M(1) * U(0)
440            LET U(2) = M(2) * U(0)
445            LET U(3) = M(3) * U(0)
450 '
455            LET F(1) = (F(1) + S(1) − U(1) * C(1)) * I9
460            LET F(2) = (F(2) + S(2) − U(2) * C(2)) * I9
465            LET F(3) = (F(3) + S(3) − U(3) * C(3)) * I9
470 '
475            LET V(0) = V(0) + U(0)
480 '
485            LET V(1) = V(1) + U(1)
490            LET V(2) = V(2) + U(2)
495            LET V(3) = V(3) + U(3)
500 '
505            LET C(1) = 10 * (V(1)/3000)^(X)
510            LET C(2) = 10 * (V(2)/3000)^(X)
515            LET C(3) = 10 * (V(3)/3000)^(X)
520 '
525            LET P(0) = 15 * (V(0)/9000)^(X)
```

```
530          IF Y <= 0 THEN 535 ELSE 555
535             LET P(1) = .33/M(1) * P(0)
540             LET P(2) = .33/M(2) * P(0)
545             LET P(3) = .33/M(3) * P(0)
550             GOTO 575    'IFEND
555 '     ELSE
560             LET P(1) = L(1)/M(1) * P(0)
565             LET P(2) = L(2)/M(2) * P(0)
570             LET P(3) = (P(1) * M(1) + P(2) * M(2) - P(0))/(-M(3))
575 '     IFEND
580 '
585             LET S(1) = U(1) * P(1)
590                LET S(2) = U(2) * P(2)
595             LET S(3) = U(3) * P(3)
600 '
605 '

610             GOSUB 655    'PRINT A YEAR
615 '
620             LET L(1) = M(1)
625             LET L(2) = M(2)
630             LET L(3) = M(3)
635       NEXT Y
640       STOP
645 '
650 '
655 REM    SUBROUTINE:  PRINT A YEAR
660 REM       IN: C(), F(), G, M(), P(), S(), U(), V(), Y
665 REM    OUT: --
670 '
675 REM    ***THE PRINT USING STATEMENT MAY BE DIFFERENT
680 REM    ***IN YOUR BASIC.  PLEASE CHECK.
685 '
690       PRINT
695       PRINT
700       LET P$ = "%       %  ###,###.##  ###,###.##
                                              ###,###.##"
705       PRINT "YEAR ";Y;"  MARKET GROWTH: ";G;"  MARKET: ";U(0)
710       PRINT "MARKET CUMULATIVE VOLUME";V(0)
715       PRINT
720       PRINT "            A        B        C"
725       PRINT USING P$; "MKT SHARE", M(1), M(2), M(3)
730       PRINT
735       PRINT USING P$; "ANNUAL UNITS", U(1), U(2), U3
740       PRINT USING P$; "CUM VOLUME", V(1), V(2), V(3)
745       PRINT USING P$; "PRICE/UNIT", P(1),P(2),P(3)
750       PRINT USING P$; "COST/UNIT",C(1),C(2),C(3)
755       PRINT USING P$; "MARGIN", (P(1)-C(1))/P(1),
                             (P(2)-C(2))/P(2),(P(3)-C(3))/P(3)
760       PRINT
```

```
765     PRINT USING P$; "DEBT", F(1), F(2), F(3)
770     PRINT USING P$; "SALES",  S(1), S(2), S(3)
775     PRINT USING P$; "NET CASH", S(1)+F(1), S(2)+F(2), S(3)+F(3)
780 '
825     RETURN
830     END
```

YEAR 0 MARKET GROWTH: 1 MARKET: 9000
MARKET CUMULATIVE VOLUME 9000

	A	B	C
MKT SHARE	0.33	0.33	0.33
ANNUAL UNIT	2,970.00	2,970.00	2,970.00
CUM VOLUME	2,970.00	2,970.00	2,970.00
PRICE/UNIT	15.00	15.00	15.00
COST/UNIT	10.03	10.03	10.03
MARGIN	0.33	0.33	0.33
DEBT	−32,670.00	−32,670.00	−32,670.00
SALES	44,550.00	44,550.00	44,550.00
NET CASH	11,880.00	11,880.00	11,880.00

YEAR 1   MARKET GROWTH: 1.4   MARKET: 12600
MARKET CUMULATIVE VOLUME 21600

	A	B	C
MKT SHARE	0.43	0.33	0.24
ANNUAL UNIT	5,418.00	4,158.00	3,024.00
CUM VOLUME	8,388.00	7,128.00	5,994.00
PRICE/UNIT	8.68	11.32	16.03
COST/UNIT	7.18	7.57	8.00
MARGIN	0.17	0.33	0.50
DEBT	−46,723.14	−32,818.22	−20,303.80
SALES	47,051.67	47,051.67	48,477.48
NET CASH	328.53	14,233.45	28,173.68

YEAR 2   MARKET GROWTH: 1.4   MARKET: 17640
MARKET CUMULATIVE VOLUME 39240

	A	B	C
MKT SHARE	0.50	0.33	0.17
ANNUAL UNIT	8,820.00	5,821.20	2,998.80
CUM VOLUME	17,208.00	12,949.20	8,992.80
PRICE/UNIT	8.03	9.34	13.18
COST/UNIT	5.70	6.25	7.02
MARGIN	0.29	0.33	0.47
DEBT	−69,318.66	−32,806.14	4,593.11
SALES	70,825.50	54,354.45	39,530.51
NET CASH	1,506.84	21,548.31	44,123.62

YEAR 3 MARKET GROWTH: 1.3 MARKET: 22932
MARKET CUMULATIVE VOLUME 62172

	A	B	C
MKT SHARE	0.50	0.33	0.17
ANNUAL UNIT	11,466.00	7,567.56	3,898.44
CUM VOLUME	28,674.00	20,516.76	12,891.24
PRICE/UNIT	8.05	8.05	8.05
COST/UNIT	4.83	5.39	6.25
MARGIN	0.40	0.33	0.22
DEBT	−70,218.99	−28,282.69	18,420.02
SALES	92,319.21	60,930.68	31,388.53
NET CASH	22,100.22	32,647.99	49,808.55

YEAR 4 MARKET GROWTH: 1.2 MARKET: 27518.4
MARKET CUMULATIVE VOLUME 89690.4

	A	B	C
MKT SHARE	0.50	0.33	0.17
ANNUAL UNIT	13,759.20	9,081.07	4,678.13
CUM VOLUME	42,433.20	29,597.83	17,569.37
PRICE/UNIT	7.16	7.16	7.16
COST/UNIT	4.26	4.79	5.66
MARGIN	0.40	0.33	0.21
DEBT	−48,867.36	−17,879.98	22,606.26
SALES	98,455.08	64,980.35	33,474.73
NET CASH	49,587.72	47,100.38	56,080.99

YEAR 5   MARKET GROWTH: 1.2   MARKET: 33022.1
MARKET CUMULATIVE VOLUME 122712.

	A	B	C
MKT SHARE	0.50	0.33	0.17
ANNUAL UNIT	16,511.04	10,897.29	5,613.75
CUM VOLUME	58,944.24	40,495.12	23,183.12
PRICE/UNIT	6.47	6.47	6.47
COST/UNIT	3.83	4.33	5.18
MARGIN	0.41	0.33	0.20
DEBT	−22,857.19	−5,557.61	26,733.01
SALES	106,804.90	70,491.24	36,313.67
NET CASH	83,947.71	64,933.63	63,046.67

YEAR 6   MARKET GROWTH: 1.2   MARKET: 39626.5
MARKET CUMULATIVE VOLUME 162339.

	A	B	C
MKT SHARE	0.50	0.33	0.17
ANNUAL UNIT	19,813.25	13,076.74	6,736.50
CUM VOLUME	78,757.49	53,571.86	29,919.63
PRICE/UNIT	5.91	5.91	5.91
COST/UNIT	3.49	3.95	4.77
MARGIN	0.41	0.33	0.19
DEBT	8,783.67	9,193.67	30,986.02
SALES	117,124.35	77,302.07	39,822.28
NET CASH	125,908.02	86,495.74	70,808.30

YEAR 7   MARKET GROWTH: 1.2   MARKET: 47551.8
MARKET CUMULATIVE VOLUME 209891.

	A	B	C
MKT SHARE	0.50	0.33	0.17
ANNUAL UNIT	23,775.90	15,692.09	8,083.81
CUM VOLUME	102,533.39	69,263.96	38,003.43
PRICE/UNIT	5.44	5.44	5.44
COST/UNIT	3.21	3.64	4.42
MARGIN	0.41	0.33	0.19
DEBT	47,159.30	26,899.04	35,480.38
SALES	129,392.99	85,399.37	43,993.62
NET CASH	176,552.29	112,298.42	79,474.00

YEAR 8   MARKET GROWTH: 1.2   MARKET: 57062.2
MARKET CUMULATIVE VOLUME 266953.

	A	B	C
MKT SHARE	0.50	0.33	0.17
ANNUAL UNIT	28,531.08	18,830.51	9,700.57
CUM VOLUME	131,064.46	88,094.47	47,704.00
PRICE/UNIT	5.04	5.04	5.04
COST/UNIT	2.96	3.37	4.10
MARGIN	0.41	0.33	0.19
DEBT	93,524.66	48,133.26	40,302.06
SALES	143,704.18	94,844.76	48,859.42
NET CASH	237,228.84	142,978.02	89,161.48

YEAR 9   MARKET GROWTH: 1.2   MARKET: 68474.6
MARKET CUMULATIVE VOLUME 335428.

	A	B	C
MKT SHARE	0.50	0.33	0.17
ANNUAL UNIT	34,237.29	22,596.61	11,640.68
CUM VOLUME	165,301.76	110,691.08	59,344.68
PRICE/UNIT	4.68	4.68	4.68
COST/UNIT	2.75	3.13	3.83
MARGIN	0.41	0.33	0.18
DEBT	149,313.50	73,541.95	45,524.84
SALES	160,223.78	105,747.70	54,476.09
NET CASH	309,537.28	179,289.65	100,000.92

YEAR 10   MARKET GROWTH: 1.2   MARKET: 82169.5
MARKET CUMULATIVE VOLUME 417597.

	A	B	C
ANNUAL UNIT	41,084.75	27,115.94	13,968.82
CUM VOLUME	206,386.51	137,807.02	73,313.49
PRICE/UNIT	4.36	4.36	4.36
COST/UNIT	2.56	2.92	3.57
MARGIN	0.41	0.33	0.18
DEBT	216,169.50	103,859.07	51,218.31
SALES	179,173.58	118,254.56	60,919.02
NET CASH	395,343.08	222,113.62	112,137.32

The program begins with a reference to the discussion in this book. For you, the reference is superfluous. For someone who happens upon a stray copy of the program, the reference is critical. Too many assumptions are hidden in this program to be understood without an extended explanation. This book is where that explanation appears.

After the list of variables, we see a couple of constants. In our program these are the two variables that will not change during the run of the program. Several numbers embedded in the program can also be thought of as constants. For example, 9000, 3000, and the .33's in the price equations.

The details of the program's calculations are discussed in the text earlier.

The new programming wrinkle in GROWTH is the GOSUB statement. When the computer hits this GOSUB, it goes to the subroutine that begins on the line number that follows the command. The computer continues on until it encounters a RETURN statement, at which point it returns to the next line number after the GOSUB statement. If there are several GOSUBs to the subroutine from different places in the main program, the RETURN is smart enough to remember to go back to the statement that called it. Subroutines are discussed in Appendix A.

_____ *Exercises* _____

1. What difference does the slope of the experience curve make on the timing and value of gaining share? At 70 percent? At 90 percent?
2. What effect does a 1.20 interest factor have on the value of gaining share?
3. Try a different schedule of market shares. Is is better to gain share earlier or later?
4. Is it easy or difficult to gain share in a slow-growing market?
5. Modify the print section to show only those variables you are interested in.
6. What is the effect of having five initial competitors instead of three? Can you reduce the size of GROWTH and at the same time change the program to accommodate five competitors?
7. Find an assumption in GROWTH that you don't like. Figure out a way to improve it. Modify the program to reflect your improvement.
8. Insert three constants for 3000, 9000, and .33. Call them C9, P9, and M9. Label the constants at the right place at the top of the program. Check to be sure the program still gives the same results when you run it. Do you like your change?

FINAL RESULTS

The final decisions on Bear's nine product lines were relatively easy to make. One line was dissolved as quickly as possible. Two were sold. Two were pushed harder than they had ever been. Peter Bates was impressed. The changes were not quite the ones he would have made based just on the numbers alone. Frank Bradshaw contributed some insights on the particular strengths and weaknesses of the different product lines. Bradshaw had also revised Bates's estimates for some of the market's futures. The net result was a stronger product mix and much higher profits projected for the next two years.

Toaster Oven would continue to maintain market share. It needed cost controls, so Bradshaw transferred some good managers from Toaster and gave them a job where cost control would make a difference.

Toaster raised its price to generate some short-term profits. Its equipment was scheduled to be moved into Toaster Oven's production. The product line would be phased out in 24 months.

Food Processor was recognized as the new future for the whole division. It would be pushed to claim an overwhelming share of its expanding market.

Juicer was going to make an effort to achieve market leadership within 18 months. If it failed, it would reevaluated at that time.

Blender was the ideally positioned product. It would hold its share and generate cash for the growing Food Processor and Juicer.

Can Opener would be sold. There were not enough financial resources within the division to give it the push it would need to achieve share in its maturing market.

Steam Iron would hold its share.

Hair Curler was the long-term hope of the division. Marketing predicted that Hair Curler's future market might exceed Toaster Oven's present one. Hair Curler would be ferociously pushed to achieve a 60 percent share in the next three years.

Pencil Sharpener would be sold immediately.

References

1. Allen, George B., Note on the Use of Experience Curves in Competitive Decision Making, Boston, MA: Intercollegiate Case Clearing House, Soldiers Field, #9-175-174, President and Fellows of Harvard College, 1975.

2. Allen, George B., A Note on the Boston Consulting Group Concept of Corporate Analysis and Corporate Strategy, Boston, MA: Intercollegiate Case Clearing House, Soldiers Field, #9-175-175, President and Fellows of Harvard College, 1975.

3. Dearden, John, *Cost Accounting and Financial Control Systems*, Reading, MA: Addison-Wesley, 1973.

4. Drucker, Peter F., *Managing For Results*, New York: Harper & Row, 1964.

5. Hirshmann, Winfred B., "Profit From the Learning Curve," *Harvard Business Review*, Jan.-Feb., 1964.

6. *Perspectives on Experience*, Boston, MA: The Boston Consulting Group, 1972.

Present Value
and Future Risk

*I sometimes despair of getting anything quite simple and
honest done in this world by the help of men. They would
have to be passed through a powerful press first, to squeeze
their old notions out of them.*

Henry David Thoreau

"I would like you to help me design a corporate-wide capital-budgeting policy, one that will let us plan and control our capital spending," said John Saltman.

Saltman was the Vice President of Finance for Chordata Corporation. He was describing a new project to Harriet DeAngelo, his staff assistant of three years.

"To get where we want to be, we need to begin where people are today. Right now we have a different method of capital planning for each of the four divisions. What we need is a new system that will serve each division and will also work corporate-wide.

"Our problem is that we have a mixed bag of talent out there in the divisions. Just selling them a simple idea like net present value will take time, never mind any complicated techniques. Even the sophisticated divisions are too busy fighting fires to pay much attention to us until they need something. Then they stampede over here to get approval as soon as possible, yesterday if you please, and gallop off with their approval to get on with their work.

"In order to get them thinking about a change, you will visit each division's finance director and find out what he or she is currently doing and would recommend in order to coordinate all our capital spending across the corporation.

"Come back, assemble the pieces, and make your own synthesis. I'd like a report in a week."

FOUR METHODS

One week later DeAngelo walked in with a file folder under her arm to report on her trip.

"It's a real circus out there. Only Wolf Division uses the net present value, but even there they have to come up with their own estimate of the cost of capital. Bear Division uses the internal rate of return. Deer Division uses the accounting rate of return, and Hawk Division uses payback period.

"Even though the Hawk Division makes state-of-the-art aviation-guidance systems, their financial people are old timers. They have always done things that way and they see no reason to change. One guy actually suggested that everyone adopt payback period analysis!

"In order to get the discussion focused, I took along a little example and asked them to show how they would decide between two projects."

"What was the example?" Saltman asked.

"Two projects, A and B. Which one do you choose to fund? Here's my table." DeAngelo opened her file folder and showed Saltman a small table:

YEAR	A	B
0	−10000	−10000
1	1000	2000
2	2000	3000
3	3000	5000
4	4000	5000
5	15000	8000

"The accounting rate of return is the average of the after-tax profits divided by the initial investment. For simplicity, I told Deer Division that all the figures are after-tax profits. They made their calculations like this:

ARR of A = (−10000 + 1000 + 2000 + 3000 + 4000 + 15000)/5/10000
$\qquad$ = 30 percent

ARR of B = (−10000 + 2000 + 3000 + 5000 + 5000 + 8000)/5/10000
$\qquad$ = 26 percent

"So A is the preferred scheme when you visit Deer Division. Not too surprising when you remember they are a retail chain of leisure apparel.

"I told every other division to consider these figures as cash flows. So when you show these same two proposals to the Hawk Division, you get payback periods that look like this:

A—payback period is 4 years.
B—payback period is 3 years.

"So B is the preferred investment when you talk to Hawk.

"Actually, one of their people had the decency to squirm a little. He did not like the fact that they were missing that $15,000 payment in the fifth year of A."

"That's two of four divisions using antiquated methods of comparing projects," Saltman shook his head. "We've got a problem there. How are the other two?"

"Everyone else understands the idea of discounted cash flow," DeAngelo answered. "So when I showed them the table and told them the cost of capital was 13 percent they began with a table like this:

YEAR	A	B	P. V. FACTOR
0	−10000	−10000	1.0
1	1000	2000	.88
2	2000	3000	.78
3	3000	5000	.69
4	4000	5000	.61
5	15000	8000	.54

"Wolf Division did it right. They compared the net present value of the future stream of payments and compared the results like so:

YR	PAYMENT	FACTOR	PRESENT VALUE
0	−10,000	1.00	−10,000
1	1,000	0.88	885
2	2,000	0.78	1,566
3	3,000	0.69	2,079
4	4,000	0.61	2,453
5	15,000	0.54	8,141

THE NET PRESENT VALUE IS : 5125.07
THE COST OF CAPITAL IS: 0.13

YR	PAYMENT	FACTOR	PRESENT VALUE
0	−10,000	1.00	−10,000
1	2,000	0.88	1,770
2	3,000	0.78	2,349
3	5,000	0.69	3,465
4	5,000	0.61	3,067
5	8,000	0.54	4,342

THE NET PRESENT VALUE IS : 4993.27
THE COST OF CAPITAL IS: 0.13

"So A is preferred at Wolf Division."

"How did you make these tables?" asked Saltman. He was surprised to find out that DeAngelo knew how to program.

"I used one of the little computers," said DeAngelo. "The equations were very straightforward. You begin with a cost of capital, C, and compute the discount factor:

```
LET C = .13
LET F = 1/(1+C)
```

"Then for a payment, P, in year Y the calculation is:

```
LET V = F^Y * P
PRINT Y; P, F^Y, V
LET T = T + V
```

"The little symbols F^Y mean F to the Yth power.

"For the year 0 through year 5, the full loop looks like this:

```
260      FOR Y = 0 TO 5
270          READ P
280          DATA −10000, 2000, 3000, 5000, 5000, 8000
290          LET V = F^Y * P
300          PRINT Y; P, F^Y, V
310          LET T = T + V
320      NEXT Y
325 '
```

"The neat feature is that you can do any stream of payments you want by simply varying the data. It can also be used to find an internal rate of return, that is, the cost of capital that makes the net present value zero."

"I know what the IRR is," said Saltman, "but how do you get it with that program?"

"By guessing an answer and running the program," said DeAngelo. "It sounds time-consuming but it's really a very quick method of finding the IRR. After a couple of rounds of guesses, you have it to two decimal places. When you do that for my projects A and B you get 25.5 percent for A and 27.9 percent for B.

"So B is the choice at Bear Division.

"Now the people at Bear Division who came up with these figures had a hard time telling me how they were going to compare two small projects with a third large one when each had a different IRR. They also dimly sensed that in order to pick a group of projects they should check all possible combinations, but of course none of them did that.

"The IRR people are analytical enough to be easy to convert to the net-present-value method. The payback-period folks felt uncomfortable because they were ignoring some of the payments. The accounting-rate-of-return crowd knew they were failing to take any notice of inflation and the time value of money. Everyone was willing to talk about making a change.

"Right now, Wolf Division uses public figures on our debt, equity, and market risk to get the cost of capital for their net-present-value calculations. We should set one corporate cost of capital and make sure they all know what it is."

DeAngelo saw line management's point of view. Her visit had shown her how hard the divisions worked just to keep everything under control.

"And another thing," continued DeAngelo. "Almost every one of of these people complained about the $5000 ceiling on local capital-planning decisions. They all said this was a real nuisance. One person said clearing a $5000 capital-budget item with Corporate was like asking for a hall pass to go to the bathroom."

"I happen to agree that it's too restrictive," said Saltman. "The ceiling is a leftover from an old attempt to control everything from the top. No one can do anything now with five grand. If we give them a new limit of $25,000, we ought to be okay and it ought to make them happy."

"A reasonable amount of space," agreed DeAngelo, "will probably increase their efficiency."

"Good," said Saltman. "We have enough to run with now. Anything else?"

"No, that's about it. Here's a written summary of my interviews."

"Thank you," said Saltman. "I would like to ask you to be the liaison to the divisions with the new system. Is that okay with you?"

DeAngelo smiled broadly. She had enjoyed meeting the divisions' financial managers. What they did day-to-day made the corporate headquarters look tranquil by comparison. She liked the idea of getting out to the divisions.

"Yes, thank you, I would be happy to help put the new plan into effect."

"One final question," said Saltman, "Where did you learn to program a computer?"

"I made the mistake of asking Peter Bates about the TV screen in his office. He gave me a crash course one afternoon. What really clinched it was when he loaned me the computer for the week-end. Now I use it when things get too big to handle easily on my calculator."

THE NEW POLICY

Saltman wrote up the corporate cost of capital. The market was expected to be up about 24 percent in the next year. The prime was going to settle down around 13 percent. Chordata's systematic risk in the market was .4. (See Reference 1 for further details on risk and beta coefficients.) Saltman calculated the cost of equity capital was:

$$\text{Cost of Equity Capital} = .13 + (.24 - .13)*.4$$
$$= .13 + .044$$
$$= .174$$

The firm's tax rate was 48 percent. Total capital broke into 42 percent debt, 58 percent stockholders' equity. So the weighted average cost of capital was:

$$\text{Weighted Average Cost of Capital} = (1 - .48)*.13*(.42)$$
$$+ .174*(.58)$$
$$= .028 + .101$$
$$= .129$$

Saltman met with the division financial managers and described the new system. After much discussion they agreed that it would work. A week later he issued the memo that made it official:

> At the request of the board of directors this office initiated an effort to formulate a consistent policy on capital-budgeting decisions. Recently Harriet DeAngelo visited you to solicit your suggestions for improvement. These efforts have resulted in the following changes in policy:
>
> 1. All decisions on capital spending will be based on the net-present-value (NPV) method.

2. Any project of less than $25,000 may be authorized at the division level.

We hope these two changes will improve the speed and flexibility of every division's decision making while unifying the Corporation's approach to capital spending.

As before, all capital-spending decisions must be reported to this office within five days of their authorization. As before, the present notification forms will continue to be used.

To compute NPV you will need to know the coporate cost of capital. Chordata's current figure is 12.9 percent and should be used effective immediately. If sudden changes in the markets dictate a revision, we will let you know promptly. The 12.9 percent figure includes our best estimate of our present position in the market, our debt, and tax considerations. It is the only figure that may be used to compute NPV.

The NPV method was chosen because of several factors:

1. It works with real cash flow, not accounting figures.
2. It includes all payments.
3. It includes the time value of money.
4. It is anchored in the coporation's real cost of capital.
5. It allows projects to be compared and grouped.
6. It seeks to maximize the shareholders' equity.

Should anyone have troubles changing methods, this office is ready and willing to help. Please contact me or Harriet DeAngelo for assistance.

I would like to thank all of you for your advice and suggestions. Our new system is a direct result of everyone's work. Should you have any suggestions for additional improvements, please let me know.

John Saltman
Vice President for Finance

THE PROGRAM PRESENT

```
100 REM    PRESENT    5 FEBRUARY 1981    HARRIET DEANGELO
102 '
105 REM    © COPYRIGHT 1980 JOHN M. NEVISON ASSOCIATES
110 '
120 REM    PRINT A TABLE OF THE NET PRESENT VALUE OF A SERIES
130 REM    OF FUTURE PAYMENTS.  IF THE RESULT IS POSITIVE,
140 REM    THEN THE INVESTMENT IS A GOOD ONE.
150 '
```

```
160 REM    VARIABLES:
170 REM       C . . . . . . . . . . . . COST OF CAPITAL (DECIMAL)
180 REM       F . . . . . . . . . . . . DISCOUNT FACTOR
190 REM       P . . . . . . . . . . . . THE PAYMENT
200 REM       T . . . . . . . . . . . . TOTAL NET PRESENT VALUE
210 REM       V . . . . . . . . . . . . PRESENT VALUE OF PAYMENT
220 REM       Y . . . . . . . . . . . . YEAR INDEX
222 '
224 '
226 REM    MAIN PROGRAM
227 '
230        LET C = .13
240        LET F = 1/(1+C)
245 '
250        PRINT "YR  PAYMENT", "FACTOR","PRESENT VALUE"
260        FOR Y = 0 TO 5
270           READ P
280           DATA −10000, 2000, 3000, 5000, 5000, 8000
290           LET V = F^Y * P
300           PRINT Y; P, F^Y, V
310           LET T = T + V
320        NEXT Y
325 '
327        PRINT
330        PRINT "THE NET PRESENT VALUE IS : ";T
340        PRINT "THE COST OF CAPITAL IS: ";C
350        END
```

This program does just what DeAngelo said it did. By altering the
data on number of years and stream of payments, the user can do
another present-value problem.

_____ *Exercises* _____

1. If a real estate developer has two investments, A and B, whose stream
   of payments are given below, which project should the investor choose
   if the cost of capital is 12 percent? If the cost of capital is 18 percent?
   Discuss.
   A: −100,000 10,000 20,000 10,000 10,000 160,000
   B: −110,000 20,000 20,000 20,000 20,000 130,000

2. Use PRESENT to find the internal rate of return of A and B. Do some
   further reading to find out why this is not a good way to make capital-
   budgeting decisions.

RISK

John Saltman noticed that Harriet DeAngelo was doodling at the staff meeting. Some of the doodles looked like a computer program. After the meeting he asked her what she was doing.

"I'll show you in a couple of days," she answered. "Right now it's just a hunch."

Saltman agreed to wait and three days later DeAngelo walked into his office smiling broadly. "Have a look at these diagrams, " she said.

The first figure was simple. It showed three possible outcomes and their probabilities (Fig. 4.1).

"So?" Saltman asked. "What's new?"

"Well a couple of things, actually," said DeAngelo. "First notice that we have three possible outcomes and their different possibilities."

"What's so unusual about that?" said Saltman, still puzzled.

"They are realistic estimates," said DeAngelo. "They are not symmetric. They are not pretty numbers. They are the three possible outcomes that we can estimate. We could even refine it to more outcomes with finer probabilities."

"I still don't see what you are driving at," said Saltman.

"Here's the same information in a different way," said DeAngelo handing him another diagram (Fig. 4.2).

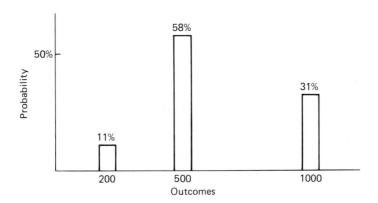

Fig. 4-1   Alternative Outcomes

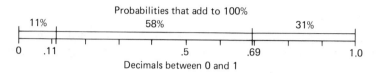

Fig. 4-2   Probabilities and Random Numbers between 0 and 1

"It shows the three probabilities laid out in the interval from zero to one. It is interesting because BASIC has a random-number generator that gives you a random number between zero and one. So we can simulate what will happen with our investment decision with a computer program like this:

```
200     LET R = RND(0)
210     IF R <= .11 THEN 220 ELSE 240
220        LET S = 200
230        GOTO 300
240 '   IFEND
250     IF R <=.69 THEN 260 ELSE 280
260        LET S = 500
270        GOTO 300
280 '   IFEND
290     LET S = 1000
300 '
310     PRINT S
```

"So we can see what happens when we play this set of odds."

Saltman understood why she was so pleased. "That means," he said, "that we could play it a hundred times and take the average to see what this is really worth."

"Yes, you sure could," nodded DeAngelo.

"How would that look in the program?" asked Saltman.

"Probably something like this." DeAngelo added a few lines to her earlier example.

```
180        LET S = 0
190        FOR  T = 1 TO 100
200            LET R = RND(0)
210            IF R <= .11 THEN 220 ELSE 240
220              LET S = S + 200
230              GOTO 300
240 '          IFEND
250            IF R <= .69 THEN 260 ELSE 280
260              LET S = S + 500
270              GOTO 300
280 '          IFEND
290            IF R <= 1.0 THEN 292 ELSE 296
292              LET S = S + 1000
294              GOTO 300
296 '          IFEND
298            PRINT "ERROR IN PROGRAM"
299            STOP
300 '
310        NEXT T
320        PRINT "SELECTED VALUE AVERAGES "; S/100
```

"That's very nice," said Saltman. "What you've just said is that we have a way of handling the risky alternatives. Is that why you are doing this?"

"Even better," said DeAngelo. "We could have done this investment problem by hand, but now we have a way to model risky situations that are extremely difficult to do by hand. For example, where the outcome of one event can affect the next or where the outcome of one event can lead to stopping at an odd point in time.

"As an example of abrupt stopping, consider the stock price of a company with four chance elements in its future: the economy, takeover bids, competitive effects, and government legislation. For each of the next three years all four elements will affect the stock's price.

"The economy can grow normally and give the stock a 1.10 (10 percent) growth. The economy could falter and hold the growth to 1.04. The economy could boom and push the price up at a rate of 1.25. The chances are 60 percent for normal growth, 30 percent for a recession, and 10 percent for a boom.

"If we start our stock price, P1, at 10, our first section would look like this:

```
2215       LET P = 10
2220       FOR I = 1 TO 3
2225 REM   ECONOMIC BEHAVOUR
2230           DATA .60,1.10,   .30, 1.04,   .10, 1.20,   1,1
2232           GOSUB 4000 'SELECT A VALUE
2234           LET P = S * P
2236 '
```

"The second element is a take-over bid. A bid has a 20 percent chance of succeeding in any given year. If it succeeds, the stock price will be up 1.30 (30 percent), but will cease to perform at that moment. It will stop abruptly. The program will look like this:

```
2240 REM    TAKE-OVER
2242        DATA .20, 1,   .80, 0,   1,1
2244        GOSUB 4000 'SELECT A VALUE
2246        IF S = 1 THEN 2247 ELSE 2249
2247          LET P = 1.30 * P
2248          GOTO 2315 'END OF TRIAL
2249 '        IFEND
2250 '
```

"The third element is what the competition does. If things go along normally, they will have no effect (1.00). There's a 40 percent chance the weak competitor may drop out and boost the stock price at a rate of 1.09. There's a small, 20 percent chance that both competitors will sell out to our firm. A sell-out would boost the stock price a lot (1.50). The program could look like this:

```
2260 REM    COMPETITION
2262        DATA .40, 1.00,   .40, 1.09,   .20, 1.50,   1,1
2264        GOSUB 4000 'SELECT A VALUE
2266        LET P = S * P
2268 '
```

"The government could pass favorable tariff legislation that would boost the price (1.30), or do nothing (1.00), or pass regulatory legislation that would put the company out of business. The stock price at bankruptcy would be 50 percent of its current price. This is a second abrupt stop. The program might look like this:

```
2270 REM    LEGISLATION
2272        DATA .10, 1.30,   .86, 1.00,   .04, .50,   1,1
2274        GOSUB 4000 'SELECT A VALUE
2276        LET P = S * P
2278        IF S = .50 THEN 2280 ELSE 2282
2280          GOTO 2315 'END OF TRIAL
2282 '        IFEND
2284 '
2286        RESTORE
2310    NEXT I
2315 '
```

"The nice feature of this program is that we tailor our distributions to our best guess at the real world. Also, we have taken into account two kinds of abrupt interruptions that make calculating the risk by hand almost impossible. By repeating the whole three-year procedure 1000 times we get a good estimate not only for the value of the stock—the average—but also for the risk associated with it—the standard deviation.

"As a matter of fact, this program could be the outline for a whole series of programs. The I loop could be any situation with some distributions in it. That whole section could be replaced with another situation. At each point within the situation where a distribution was known we could insert the appropriate lines of program."

```
2000 REM    RISKY    21 FEBRUARY 1981    HARRIET DEANGELO
2010 '
2020 REM    © COPYRIGHT 1980 JOHN M. NEVISON ASSOCIATES
2030'
2040 REM    COMPUTE THE AVERAGE AND STANDARD DEVIATION
2050 REM    (THE RISK) OF ONE THOUSAND TRIALS
2055 REM    A RISKY SITUATION.
2060'
2070 REM    IN THIS PROGRAM THE SITUATION IS THE STOCK PRICE,
2080 REM    P, PROBLEM DESCRIBED IN CHAPTER FOUR OF
2082 REM    "EXECUTIVE COMPUTING" (JOHN M. NEVISON,
2084 REM    ADDISON-WESLEY PUBLISHING COMPANY,1981).
2090 '
2100 REM    VARIABLES:
2105 REM        D . . . . . . . . . . THE DEVIATION OF THE RESULTS, R()
2110 REM        I . . . . . . . . . . . INDEX OF YEARS
2115 REM        M . . . . . . . . . . THE MEAN (AVERAGE) OF THE RESULTS
2120 REM        P . . . . . . . . . . THE PRICE OF THE STOCK
2122 REM        R() . . . . . . . . THE RESULTS OF THE TRIALS
2124 REM        R(0) . . . . . . . . THE SUM OF THE RESULTS
2125 REM        S . . . . . . . . . . THE SELECTED VALUE FOR A GIVEN YEAR
2126 REM        T . . . . . . . . . . INDEX OF TRIALS
2127 REM        V . . . . . . . . . . THE VARIANCE OF THE RESULTS
2150 '
2190 REM    DIMENSION:
2194        DIM R(1000)
2200 '
```

```
2210        FOR T = 1 TO 1000
2215            LET P = 10
2220            FOR I = 1 TO 3
2225 REM    ECONOMIC BEHAVOUR
2230                DATA .60,1.10,   .30, 1.04,  .10, 1.20,   1,1
2232                GOSUB 4000      'SELECT A VALUE
2234                LET P = S * P
2236 '
2240 REM    TAKE-OVER
2242                DATA .20, 1,   .80, 0,   1,1
2244                GOSUB 4000      'SELECT A VALUE
2246                IF S = 1 THEN 2247 ELSE 2249
2247                  LET P = 1.30 * P
2248                  GOTO 2315      'END OF TRIAL
2249 '                IFEND
2250 '
2260 REM    COMPETITION
2262                DATA .40, 1.00,  .40, 1.09,  .20, 1.50,   1,1
2264                GOSUB 4000      'SELECT A VALUE
2266                LET P = S * P
2268 '
2270 REM    LEGISLATION
2272                DATA .10, 1.30,   .86, 1.00,   .04, .50,   1,1
2274                GOSUB 4000      'SELECT A VALUE
2276                LET P = S * P
2278                IF S = .50 THEN 2280 ELSE 2282
2280                  GOTO 2315      'END OF TRIAL
2282 '                IFEND
2284 '
2286                RESTORE
2310            NEXT I
2315 '
2320            RESTORE
2330            LET R(T) = P
2340            LET R(0) = R(0) + P
2350        NEXT T
2360 '
2370        LET M = R(0)/1000
2375 '
2380        FOR T = 1 TO 1000
2390            LET V = V + (R(T)-M)^2
2400        NEXT T
2410 '
2420        LET D = SQR(V/1000)
2430 '
2440        PRINT "AVERAGE RESULT IS ";M
2450        PRINT "STD. DEVIATION IS "; D
2460 '
2470        STOP
2480 '
2490 '
```

```
4000 REM    SUBROUTINE: SELECT A VALUE
4010 REM      IN: <DATA FROM THE MAIN PROGRAM>
4020 REM    OUT: S
4030 '
4040 REM    READS A LIST OF NUMBERS THAT REPRESENT A
4050 REM    DISTRIBUTION OF POSSIBLE OUTCOMES.  THE LIST
4060 REM    MIGHT LOOK LIKE THIS:
4070 REM       DATA .10,300, .60,500, .30,900, 1,1
4080 REM    EACH PAIR REPRESENTS A PROBABILITY, P3, AND A
4090 REM    VALUE, V3.  THE PROBABILITIES SHOULD NOT EXCEED
4100 REM    1.00 IN TOTAL.  THE LAST PAIR, (1,1), FORCES THE
4110 REM    SUBROUTINE TO STOP READING DATA.
4120'
4125 REM    VARIABLES:
4130 REM       P3.......... A VALUE'S PROBABILITY
4140 REM       P4.......... THE CUMULATIVE PROBABILITY OF
4150 REM                         THE DISTRIBUTION
4160 REM       R3.......... A RANDOM NUMBER BETWEEN ZERO AND
4162 REM                         ONE
4165 REM       S .......... THE VALUE SELECTED BY THE SUBROUTINE
4170 REM       V3.......... A VALUE IN THE DISTRIBUTION
4180 '
4190 REM    INITIALIZE VARIABLES, SELECT A VALUE, S,
4200 REM    FROM THE DISTRIBUTION. FINISH READING THE
4210 REM    DISTRIBUTION. CHECK TO BE SURE S WAS GIVEN A VALUE.
4220'
4300       LET P4 = 0
4305       LET S = -.999999
4310       LET R3 = RND(0)
4320       READ P3, V3       'LOOP
4330          LET P4 = P4 + P3
4340          IF P4 > 1.00 THEN 4450      'READ BOTTOM
4350          IF R3 <= P4 THEN 4360 ELSE 4380
4360             LET S = V3
4370             GOTO 4400      'LOOP EXIT
4380 '          IFEND
4390       GOTO 4320          'LOOP
4400 '
4410       READ P3, V3       'LOOP
4420          LET P4 = P4 + P3
4430          IF P4 > 1.00 THEN 4450      'READ BOTTOM
4440       GOTO 4410          'LOOP
4450 '
4460       IF S = -.999999 THEN 4470 ELSE 4500
4470        PRINT "SUBROUTINE: SELECT A VALUE FAILED."
4480        PRINT "PLEASE CHECK DATA NEAR ";P3;V3
4490        STOP
4500 '    IFEND
4510 RETURN
4515 '
4530 '
4540          END
```

AVERAGE RESULT IS 18.3111
STANDARD DEVIATION IS 7.17227

"What does the subroutine 'select a value' do?" asked Saltman. "Pick a number from the distribution?"

"Right," said DeAngelo. "I wrote a subroutine that can take a long distribution with lots of detail or a short distribution with only one value. The only requirement is that the odds add up to no more than 1.00. The last pair, the one-one pair, tells the subroutine it has completed reading the distribution.

"By using 'select a value' whenever we need to, we can model most random situations where we are able to estimate the distribution of the events. By running the whole situation 1000 times with the T loop, we can get sufficient results to get good averages."

"So we have," said Saltman, "a tool for handling risky situations of whatever shape or size. Is that right?"

"Yes, sir," said DeAngelo.

"That's quite remarkable for such a small program," said Saltman. "It's really hard to believe."

"It is surprising," agreed DeAngelo. "I set out to write a simple routine to evaluate a distribution and I ended up with a tool for doing a large class of simulations to determine the future's risk.

"Speaking of risk," DeAngelo continued, "the result of the stock-price question was 18.3 with a standard deviation (risk) of 7.2. It was also interesting to see how the results were distributed. The results clustered near 16 with failures around 6 and successes stretching out to 40" (Fig. 4.3).

THE PROGRAM RISKY

(Program appears earlier in text.)

This program has an immediate and a long-term advantage. Its immediate advantage is that it models the stock-price situation where future outcomes are imperfectly known. Its long-term advantage is that, as De Angelo explained to Saltman, it can serve as a harness to exercise any imperfectly known situation where different outcomes have different likelihoods.

To do another situation you can replace the whole section of code from lines 2215 to 2315 and the outcome variable (now P). The new outcome variable should be worked into the trial loop. For example, if the new variable were X, then the code might read:

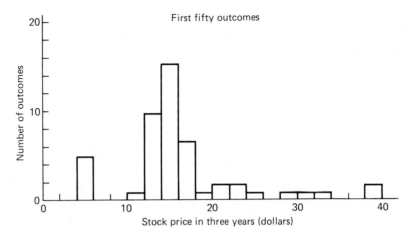

Fig. 4-3   A Distribution of Results

```
LET R(T) = X
LET R(0) = R(0) + X
LET X = 0
```

R(0) is the grand total of the results. It leads to computing the mean, M.

```
LET M = R(0) /1000

FOR T = 1 TO 1000
    LET V = V + (R(T)−M)^2
NEXT T
LET D = SQR(V/1000)
```

The section that builds a total, V, leads into the computation of the standard deviation of the results. Any elementary statistics text can explain the calculations done here.

The subroutine "select a value" is a generalized version of DeAngelo's earlier efforts. The subroutine picks a random number, keeps reading from the distribution until it finds the interval in which the random number fits, and then selects that value for an answer. But before the routine can quit, it must read the rest of the distribution so the data will be out of the way of future READ statements.

If for some reason the variable S does not get a value assigned to it in the course of the subroutine, the last IF ... THEN statement catches the error and stops the program.

NOTE: Simulation has many subtle features and should not be used to make real business decisions without the advice of a competent professional.

_____ *Exercises* _____

1. Modify RISKY by changing the DATA statements to a stock-price problem of your own.
2. Hafer drills oilwells. Each well has a 10 percent chance of making $1,000,000, a 20 percent chance of making $500,000, a 60 percent chance of losing the full cost of the oil rig ($−140,000), and a 10 percent chance of losing half the cost of the rig ($−70,000). Set up Hafer's problem with RISKY and see how he will do if he starts with $500,000.
3. Modify the program HIST in Appendix B and add it as a subroutine to RISKY to plot the results.

References

1. Copeland, Thomas E., and Weston, J. Fred, *Financial Theory and Corporate Policy*, Reading, MA: Addison-Wesley, 1979.
2. Helfert, Erich A., *Techniques of Financial Analysis*, Fourth Edition, Homewood, IL: Richard D. Irwin, 1977.
3. Parzen, Emanuel, *Modern Probability Theory and Its Applications*, New York: Wiley, 1966.
4. Weston, J. Fred, and Brigham, Eugene F., *Managerial Finance*, New York: Holt, Rinehart and Winston, 1972.

5

The Corporation's Data

Where is this division of labor to end? and what object does it finally serve? No doubt another may also think for me; but it is not therefore desirable that he should do so to the exclusion of my thinking for myself.

Henry David Thoreau

Simon Wilson was a lean, six-foot-five-inch tall Ph.D. in Computer Science who had been in data processing for fifteen years and was Director of Data Processing at Chordata. Few knew he had any academic degrees. He still cultivated the Oklahoma twang of his childhood and was known to all as "Slim."

Wilson had recognized early that everyone was going to own a microcomputer, like it or not. He moved to control the stampede: he researched the available models, obtained a volume discount on a good model, and advertised that he could help anyone buy a machine at a discount. The result of this move was that Wilson knew where most of the little computers were in his organization.

Managing the small machines' use was possible only in the most informal way. Wilson tried to pick up information whenever he could. He met Peter Bates at the coffee pot one morning and immediately began to draw Bates out.

"Hello, Peter. You seem to be doing more computer work in the Planning Office than we are in the Data Processing shop."

"Hi, Slim," Bates grinned. "Not really doing that much. But a little bit in the right place can go a long way. I had a very good month working with Frank Bradshaw. We built a couple of different kinds of programs to explore his product mix. Actually, one of them grew rather large."

"More than a page long?"

"Yeah, a couple pages, maybe three."

"It sounds," said Wilson, "Like you are ready for some structured programming."

"Hey!" said Bates, "I'm just a corporate planner, not a programmer."

"Don't let the words scare you," said Wilson. "Structured programming is just a fancy term for some commonsense ideas about how to keep your programs from growing so big you lose control of them."

"Lose control?" Bates frowned. "I don't understand what you mean."

"I mean your program gets so tricky that you can no longer figure out what it does. When you reuse it later and make a few changes, you find you have some new bugs. By following some simple rules when you write programs, you can avoid a lot of of these headaches. Stop by my office, and I'll give you a handout we use with some of our trainees." (See "Style and Structure" and "The Larger Program" in Appendix A.)

STRUCTURE

Two weeks later Peter Bates met Slim Wilson at the coffee pot.

"I finally read that hand-out on structured programming, Slim. I was embarrassed when I reread some of my old programs."

"No need for that, Pete. I've broken every rule at least a dozen times myself. We computer people were real slow to apply some tricks that every good manager has known for years."

"How's that?"

"Well, look," Wilson drew a diagram on a napkin:

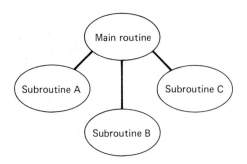

Fig. 5-1   Work Divided into Subroutines

"That's the idea, right? You have a major routine pass down work to a subroutine. You could also say you are a manager and you delegate a task to one of your subordinates. And the other ideas also have parallels. You pass down enough information to get the job done and your subordinate works on it and then passes you the results. You give it to him or her so that you can coordinate several tasks. The main routine in a computer program does the same thing. It wants to receive only the results from its subroutine. Based on the result, the main routine can decide which other routines to call, and so on.

"The subroutine can in turn call sub-subroutines. What this does for a computer program is to push functions together into subroutines and limit the number of variables that get passed back and forth."

"Why is that so important?" asked Bates.

"Well, when your language restricts what can enter or leave a subroutine to specified variables, and some BASICs have this feature, then you can limit the roads on which an error can travel out of a subroutine. In short, it helps to contain errors where they occur."

"That's a fairly obvious advantage," agreed Bates.

"If you are confronted with a 10,000 line computer program that is misbehaving, it's a big advantage. Most organizations of people are much more richly connected than the sparse connections in a computer program's subroutine calls, but there is one organization in the real world that actually is as frugally connected as our structure chart."

"What's that?"

"A spy network. The lines of communication are restricted for the same reason: to limit the damage if someone goes bad."

"I see," said Bates. "Because no one is sure who will go bad, you have to restrict what each person knows in order to minimize damage."

"Right," said Wilson. "Well, in that big malfunctioning program I mentioned it's a whole lot easier to track a bug systematically from subroutine to subroutine. Once, before I learned to program this way, I had a big program to correct and it took me three weeks to trace the mistake back from the output to one of the very first parts of the program."

"That sounds like it was a horrible three weeks. Why are you so concerned with changing programs and correcting them? I find that I spend most of my time trying to write the program, not trying to modify it."

"That's because you are relatively new at the game and because your programs are for your own personal use," said Wilson. "How much of the total work on a program would you guess is modification?"

"After it has been officially completed?"

"Yes. Completely tested and put into use."

"Oh," said Bates, "maybe 10 or 15 percent more time."

"The industry figure," said Wilson, "is about 80 percent. Eighty percent of the work on a program is modification."

Bates whistled. "Wow. It's easy to see how you can get concerned about making programs that are easy to modify."

"Amen, brother," said Wilson.

"Thanks for the tips," said Bates. "I'll try to go and sin no more."

THE CORPORATE DATA BASE

Several of the owners of the small microcomputers had asked Wilson how they might be tied to the Corporation's big computer and, if they were connected, what they could do. Wilson decided to hold a meeting to brief everyone on what the Data Processing department was doing and what it might mean to those who needed data from the big computer's files.

"Several of you have asked what we mean when we say we are converting our files system to a data-base system. This morning I am going to try and answer that question.

"We are consolidating the corporate-wide accounting operations: accounts payable, order entry, accounts receivable, general ledger, and payroll. That we are doing the accounting functions now is not really as important as how we are doing them.

"In the past it has been possible with data stored in files to have several copies of the same information in the system at the same time. For example, three of our programs that write reports about accounts receivable each have a copy of the receivables file. A problem arises when a mistake is corrected or a new entry is made to one file and not to all three. After the transaction has occurred, two of the three files are out of date or wrong. If a new column is inserted in a row of data (each row is an individual record), then every program that reads that file must be revised to account for the shifting column structure. If the new column is inserted at three, column four has become column five, and so on.

"The way to avoid these problems is to put all your information in one data base, one large library whose stacks are closed to the public. At the front desk sits a clerk with a public dictionary of terms and a private card catalogue. You may use the dictionary to find out what is in the library, but the clerk is the only one who can check the card catalogue and retrieve the information you wish.

"If you want to add new information (or alter or delete information) you must show the clerk your special pass. You may have to show it just to read certain sensitive data.

"The clerk in the real computer is a system that surrounds the data base and is called the data-base management system. By restricting access to the data to only this 'manager,' the system uncouples the information (what is in the dictionary) from where it is stored (what is in the card catalogue). A user can read the dictionary to see what's available, say last month's receivables by department, but the user does not need to know where it is located because the 'manager' will fetch it on request.

"The data base's first advantage is that it solves the multiple-copy problem that we currently have with files. One and only one authorized copy of the data exists in the data base. All alterations are performed on that one copy and all programs use only that copy if they wish to remain current. Because the dictionary gives each column a specific name, the data is referred to by name, not by column number, and our second big problem of data reorganization is solved.

"Folks on both sides of the counter enjoy advantages they never had before. The users don't have to know anything but the datum's name. They no longer have to be concerned about where or how it is stored in the library. On the other side of the counter, the technical people can organize the stacks in the library in any fashion they wish— even in a way that is efficient, but difficult to understand. The technical people can also buy new equipment, and as long as they update the card catalogue for the clerk, the system will remain undisturbed from the user's perspective.

"The natural consequence of life getting simpler on both sides of the counter is that it gets much more complicated at the counter. The clerk is a very busy person who must maintain the dictionary for public use and the card catalogue for private use while satisfying all requests brought to the counter.

"So life grows quite complicated for the data-base management system, but because it is a computer program written to do this job, it functions with sufficient speed to keep everyone happy."

DATA-BASE USERS

"Now it is time to spend a few minutes looking at the different kinds of users of our data-base system. The most common user right now is a computer program; for example, the three programs that generate those accounts receivable reports. Each of these programs, instead of reading its data from a file, will make a 'call' to the data base with a new command that has been added to its language. That call tells the data-base manager to retrieve the information and give it to the program.

"The most important operating implication of this behavior is that the programs no longer need to be modified every time the data base is changed. Sure, when a piece of information has been deleted and the program tries to read it, we will find out that the program must be modified. But when changes are made in the world of data that the program never uses, or even changes in the size or storage techniques of an item it does use, the program will continue to work without any modification.

"A second user is the administrator of the data base and the administrator's editing tools. The administrator is a flesh and blood person. His or her responsibilities are many: the security of the system, the integrity of the data, the prompt service to the user, the efficient storage of the data. The integrity of the data is an awesome responsibility. It's as if a library director were responsible for what was written in all the library books.

"This responsibility for data integrity can be delegated by giving other human beings suitable permission to correct the data they know best. In fact, the data-base administrator tries very hard to delegate as much responsibility as possible to the appropriate parties. The continuing work of administering the data base is a sufficient challenge even without this task.

"A third user of some data bases is the query language. Without the query language we have a library where only the knowledgeable — those who know how to write programs like you all do — can make requests of the data. It speeds things up if even a casual user can get direct access to the data. In order to help this casual user, query languages have been written. These languages allow the user to recover information quickly and easily from the data base.

"Look for a moment at this set of data." Wilson flashed a slide on the overhead projector.

```
530      DATA GREEN, COLOR,        37, 30, 39, 23, 24, 20, 33, 23
540      DATA BLUE, COLOR,         32, 62, 44, 69, 58, 63, 49, 25
550      DATA YELLOW, COLOR,       32, 48, 32, 39, 55, 39, 48, 44
560      DATA BROWN, COLOR,        43, 55, 27, 38, 56, 44, 41, 35
570      DATA RED, COLOR,          37, 47, 77, 82, 85, 40, 41, 45
580      DATA DAISY, FLOWER,       70, 72, 63, 35, 60, 54, 56, 57
590      DATA DAFFODIL, FLOWER,    8,  7,  6,  6,  4,  7,  7,  6
600      DATA TULIP, FLOWER,       58, 42, 66, 69, 57, 37, 50, 39
610      DATA HEMLOCK, TREE,       36, 44, 41, 15, 18, 35, 33, 42
620      DATA SPRUCE, TREE,        83, 90, 86, 93, 91, 57, 114, 53
630      DATA PINE, TREE,          26, 29, 46, 49, 29, 50, 37, 31
640      DATA MAPLE, TREE,         10, 10,  8, 10, 14,  9, 11,  8
650      DATA WALNUT, TREE,        60, 41, 44, 71, 64, 28, 20, 45
660      DATA BIRCH, TREE,         39, 31, 24, 22, 27, 47, 43, 22
670      DATA OAK, TREE,           70, 81, 42, 66, 29, 96, 45, 43
680      DATA FLOUNDER, FISH,      9,  8, 13, 12, 10,  5, 12,  9
690      DATA SALMON, FISH,        79, 45, 51, 53, 43, 46, 55, 63
700      DATA HADDOCK, FISH,       5,  4,  4,  4,  4,  5,  4,  3
710      DATA PERCH, FISH,         12, 55, 37, 55, 41, 43, 18, 14
720      DATA TROUT, FISH,         43,  119, 68, 42, 47, 53, 27, 74
730      DATA BASS, FISH,          6,  5,  4,  4,  6,  6,  5,  5
740 '
```

"If the eight numbers in each row represent projected sales, a good query language might allow a couple of direct actions like this." He showed a second slide:

- Define a new column, "Row-sum", as Q5 + Q6 + Q7 + Q8
- Print Product-name, Q5, Q6, Q7, Q8, Row-sum where Row-sum is greater than 200

"Here's a BASIC program that simulates these two commands. I'm showing them to you so you can see what the data base manager will be doing in the back room. I'm also showing them to you so you can use your scattered local files of data that will never get formalized into data bases."

"Why not?" asked Harriet DeAngelo. "Wouldn't they be easier to handle in a data base?"

"Let me give you an answer that's not entirely true for the moment," Wilson grinned. "No. They are easier to handle as files. Especially when they are on your own computers. I'll come back to that question in a minute.

"Here is the BASIC and its corresponding query statement.

```
360 REM    TOTAL SECOND FOUR QUARTERS
370 '
380        FOR R = 1 TO 21
390            LET S(R) = Q(R,5) + Q(R,6) + Q(R,7) + Q(R,8)
400        NEXT R
410 '
```

"Notice how we assign the result to S(R), the sum for the row. This corresponds to our query variable, Row-sum.

"Next, we simulate our query's print command.

```
420 REM    PRINT OUT RESULTS
430 '
440        PRINT "PROD    QTR5 QTR6 QTR7 QTR8 PROD TOTAL"
450        PRINT
460        FOR R = 1 TO 21
470            IF S(R) >= 200 THEN 480 ELSE 500
480                PRINT P$(R);TAB(10); Q(R,5); TAB(15); Q(R,6);
490                PRINT TAB(20); Q(R,7); TAB(25); Q(R,8); TAB(30); S(R)
500 '          IFEND
510        NEXT R
520 '
```

"The printing is done by the four print lines. The restriction to Row-sums of greater than 200 is done by the IF . . . THEN . . . ELSE statement.

"Of course before we can do any of this work, we have to read all our raw data into the computer. So we have an initial piece of code that reads in the data.

```
280 REM    READ IN TABLE
290 '
300        FOR R = 1 TO 21
310            READ P$(R), D$(R), Q(R,1), Q(R,2), Q(R,3), Q(R,4)
320            READ Q(R,5), Q(R,6), Q(R,7), Q(R,8)
330        NEXT R
340 '
```

"The interesting result of this program is that it can be modified to do any table calculations you wish and the results can be printed in any form you desire. So in one small example, you have quite a lot of power, even if you were never to be given a data-base system with a query language."

"Yes?" asked DeAngelo, "And what does that mean?"

"It means what you might have guessed," nodded Wilson. "After the present system is up and running we will hold some training sessions to show you how to define your own data base and query it for whatever information you wish."

"Terrific," said DeAngelo.

"But you all should know that you have already taken the next step by doing a little programming," Wilson continued. "By that I mean that most managers after they get their raw data won't be able to do with it what you can. After you retrieve information from the corporate file you can manipulate it with your own BASIC programs."

"So in learning how to program our little computers we took the second step first," said Peter Bates.

"Yes," said Wilson. "And in doing that you have stolen the march on many of your contemporaries."

THE PROGRAM QUERY

```
100 REM    QUERY      4 APRIL 1981    S. WILSON
111 '
112 REM    © COPYRIGHT 1980 JOHN M. NEVISON ASSOCIATES
120 '
130 REM    READ IN A DATABASE, ADD UP THE SECOND YEAR SALES,
140 REM    AND PRINT OUT SELECTED DIVISIONS.
150 '
160 REM    VARIABLES:
170 REM        C . . . . . . . . . . . COLUMN INDEX
180 REM        D$() . . . . . . . . DIVISION NAME OF PRODUCT
190 REM        P$() . . . . . . . . PRODUCT (OR ROW NAME)
200 REM        Q() . . . . . . . . . QUARTERLY SALES FIGURES
210 REM        R . . . . . . . . . . . ROW INDEX
220 REM        S(). . . . . . . . . . ROW SUMS
230 '
240 REM    DIMENSIONS:
250        DIM P$(25), D$(25), Q(25,8), S(25)
260 '
270 '
```

```
280 REM    READ IN TABLE
290 '
300        FOR R = 1 TO 21
310            READ P$(R), D$(R), Q(R,1), Q(R,2), Q(R,3), Q(R,4)
320            READ Q(R,5), Q(R,6), Q(R,7), Q(R,8)
330        NEXT R
340 '
360 REM    TOTAL SECOND FOUR QUARTERS
370 '
380        FOR R = 1 TO 21
390            LET S(R) = Q(R,5) + Q(R,6) + Q(R,7) + Q(R,8)
400        NEXT R
410 '
420 REM    PRINT OUT RESULTS
430 '
440        PRINT "PROD    QTR5 QTR6 QTR7 QTR8 PROD TOTAL"
450        PRINT
460        FOR R = 1 TO 21
470            IF S(R) > = 200 THEN 480 ELSE 500
480                PRINT P$(R);TAB(10); Q(R,5); TAB(15);Q(R,6);
490                PRINT TAB(20); Q(R,7); TAB(25); Q(R,8); TAB(30); S(R)
500 '          IFEND
510        NEXT R
520 '
530        DATA GREEN, COLOR,      37, 30, 39, 23, 24, 20, 33, 23
540        DATA BLUE, COLOR,       32, 62, 44, 69, 58, 63, 49, 25
550        DATA YELLOW, COLOR,     32, 48, 32, 39, 55, 39, 48, 44
560        DATA BROWN, COLOR,      43, 55, 27, 38, 56, 44, 41, 35
570        DATA RED, COLOR,        37, 47, 77, 82, 85, 40, 41, 45
580        DATA DAISY, FLOWER,     70, 72, 63, 35, 60, 54, 56, 57
590        DATA DAFFODIL, FLOWER,  8,  7,  6,  6,  4,  7,  7,  6
600        DATA TULIP, FLOWER,     58, 42, 66, 69, 57, 37, 50, 39
610        DATA HEMLOCK, TREE,     36, 44, 41, 15, 18, 35, 33, 42
620        DATA SPRUCE, TREE,      83, 90, 86, 93, 91, 57, 114, 53
630        DATA PINE, TREE,        26, 29, 46, 49, 29, 50, 37, 31
640        DATA MAPLE, TREE,       10, 10,  8, 10, 14,  9, 11,  8
650        DATA WALNUT, TREE,      60, 41, 44, 71, 64, 28, 20, 45
660        DATA BIRCH, TREE,       39, 31, 24, 22, 27, 47, 43, 22
670        DATA OAK, TREE,         70, 81, 42, 66, 29, 96, 45, 43
680        DATA FLOUNDER, FISH,    9,  8,  13, 12, 10,  5, 12,  9
690        DATA SALMON, FISH,      79, 45, 51, 53, 43, 46, 55, 63
700        DATA HADDOCK, FISH,     5,  4,  4,  4,  4,  5,  4,  3
710        DATA PERCH, FISH,       12, 55, 37, 55, 41, 43, 18, 14
720        DATA TROUT, FISH,       43,  119, 68, 42, 47, 53, 27, 74
730        DATA BASS, FISH,        6,  5,  4,  4,  6,  6,  5,  5
740 '
750        END
```

PROD	QTR5	QTR6	QTR7	QTR8	PROD TOTAL
RED	85	40	41	45	211
DAISY	60	54	56	57	227
SPRUCE	91	57	114	53	315
OAK	29	96	45	43	213
SALMON	43	46	55	63	207
TROUT	47	53	27	74	201

The program performs the activity described by Wilson in his talk. It has three sections: read in the table, perform the calculations, and print the results. In the print section, TAB's keep the output under control.

_____ *Exercises* _____

1. Find out what kind of data-base abilities your computer center has available. Try to use the query language if one is available.
2. Modify the program QUERY to read data that relates to one of your jobs.
3. Modify your QUERY's output to limit what gets printed.
4. Modify the calculation part of QUERY to do a different calculation.

References

1. Date, C. J., *An Introduction to Database Systems*, Second Edition, Reading, MA: Addison-Wesley, 1977.
2. Martin, James, *Principles of Data Base Management*, Englewood Cliffs, NJ: Prentice-Hall, 1976.
3. Nevison, John M., *The Little Book of BASIC Style: How to write a program you can read*, Reading, MA; Addison-Wesley, 1978.
4. Orr, Kenneth T., *Structured Systems Development*, New York, NY: Yourdon Press, 1977.
5. Yourdon, Edward, *Techniques of Program Structure and Design*, Englewood Cliffs, NJ: Prentice-Hall, 1976.

PART II

LINE MANAGEMENT

6

Project Planning, Scheduling, and Control

*If one advances confidently in the direction of his dreams,
and endeavors to live the life which he has imagined, he will
meet with a success unexpected in common hours.*

Henry David Thoreau

The three product managers of Deer Division, Jean Grant, Robert Grasso, and Martin Graves, had all come up from the sales force. The general manager of the division, Eileen Randall, appreciated their marketing talent but was frustrated by their inability to plan, schedule, and control projects. At the suggestion of Steve Cauldwell, she had arranged for George Lee from the Wolf Division to come over and give a one-day seminar to her three product managers.

Lee had worked hard to prepare his presentation. He knew he would be talking to three senior managers and he wanted his material to flow smoothly. The group met in a small conference room.

"We are going to go over a technique for planning projects that are composed of several parts. I'm going to use a simple example for sake of illustration, but together we are going to build some methods that can be used on much larger projects. Let's keep this informal. Please interrupt at any point with questions. Our first example is the guest-cook problem.

HELP WITH DINNER

"Suppose company is coming to dinner on Saturday night and that one guest always insists on helping in the kitchen. The guest cook

99

usually retards the schedule rather than advancing it. The problem is how to use the help without delaying dinner.

"A good place to begin is with a graphic representation of the project of preparing dinner. The chart that follows is known as a Gantt chart. It's named for Henry Gantt who did quite a bit of work early in this century on how to prepare diagrams that help with project planning and control.

```
                                    TIME (MINUTES)
   JOB      0              50        100         150         200
            +----------+----------+----------+----------+
   SHOP     I XXXXXXXXXXXX
   PREP     I              XXXXX
   SALAD    I              XXXXXX
   COOK     I                    XXXXXXXX
   SERVE    I                           XX
```

LEGEND: XXX PLANNED

"The chart shows five jobs, their lengths and when they happen. The jobs are: shopping for the meal, preparing the meat and vegetables, making the salad, cooking the meat and vegetables, and serving the meal. The longest job is SHOP; the shortest is SERVE. The earliest is SHOP; the latest is SERVE. (Only by coincidence are they also the longest and the shortest.) Two jobs can go on concurrently: SALAD and PREP for example. While nothing explicitly says which job follows which job, we may guess that SHOP precedes SALAD and PREP, PREP precedes COOK, and COOK and SALAD precede SERVE.

"To get a computer program to draw this picture we need to provide it with some information."

"Excuse me," said Grant, "but why do we need a computer to do this? It looks simple enough to do by hand."

"Sure, of course it is," agreed Lee. "But if we can do this small example, then we may apply the same technique to a much larger one later."

"Okay, let's give it a try," Grant shrugged.

"Here's our initial information," said Lee.

```
330      DATA BEGIN,   1,   0
340      DATA SHOP,   12,   1
350      DATA PREP,    6,  13
360      DATA SALAD,   7,  13
370      DATA COOK,    8,  19
380      DATA SERVE,   2,  27
390      DATA END,     0,  29
400 '
```

"The first number is the length of time in five-minute units. The second number is the time at which the job can start. To print out the first line of the Gantt chart we would write the following:

```
480      PRINT J$(J); TAB(11); "I";
500      FOR K = S(J) TO (S(J) + L(J) −1)
510          PRINT TAB(11+K); "X";
530      NEXT K
540 '
```

"This would print out:

```
SHOP     I XXXXXXXXXXXX
```

where each X equals a five-minute unit of time."

"The full program that printed out our complete Gantt chart looks like this:

```
100 REM   GANTT      30 MAY 1981    GEORGE LEE
110 '
120 REM   © COPYRIGHT 1980 JOHN M. NEVISON ASSOCIATES
130 '
140 REM   THIS PROGRAM PRINTS A GANTT CHART OF A SET
150 REM   OF JOBS IN A PROJECT.
160 '
170 REM   VARIABLES:
180 REM       J,K .......... INDEX VARIABLES
190 REM       J$() .......... NAMES OF JOBS
200 REM       L() .......... LENGTH OF JOBS
210 REM       N ............ NUMBER OF JOBS
220 REM       S() .......... STARTING TIMES
230 '
240 REM   READ IN THE JOB NAME, J$(), THE JOB LENGTH,
250 REM   L(), AND THE JOB STARTING TIME, S().
260 '
270      READ N
280      DATA 7
290 '
```

```
300        FOR J = 1 TO N
310            READ J$(J), L(J), S(J)
320        NEXT J
322
325 REM    TIME IS IN 5-MINUTE UNITS
330        DATA BEGIN,   1,   0
340        DATA SHOP,   12,   1
350        DATA PREP,    6,  13
360        DATA SALAD,   7,  13
370        DATA COOK,    8,  19
380        DATA SERVE,   2,  27
390        DATA END,     0,  29
400 '
410 REM    PRINT A GANTT CHART
420 '
430        PRINT TAB(30); "TIME (MINUTES)"
440        PRINT "JOB"; TAB(11); "0        50      100       150";
445        PRINT "      200"
450        PRINT TAB(11); "+---------+---------+";
455        PRINT "---------+---------+"
460 '
470        FOR J = 2 TO N-1
480            PRINT J$(J); TAB(11); "I";
500            FOR K = S(J) TO (S(J) + L(J) -1)
510                PRINT TAB(11+K); "X";
530            NEXT K
542            PRINT
560        NEXT J
570        PRINT
580        PRINT
590        PRINT "LEGEND:   XXX PLANNED"
660 '
670        END
```

"In our case, this Gantt chart is a way of showing someone how to make dinner."

"It doesn't show that," said Grasso. "You don't learn how to cook by looking at it."

"Good point," said Lee. "I was wrong. What the chart shows is how to plan making dinner. It shows the tasks that someone must do. It shows how the components of the project are arranged in time. The shopping must be done first and will take an hour. The salad and the main course may be prepared concurrently. After everything is ready, the meal is served.

"We can also use our chart to track the project, to control it. As each job is done we tick it off on the chart. Or we could draw a second line that represents the actual task, start to finish. We could alter the chart to reflect changes in the plan. New progress could be charted on the revised plan.

"Finally, because an old chart provides a history of the plan and its fulfillment, we can use the chart to improve estimates for the next project. One person takes longer than anticipated to complete a job. Certain supplies arrive sooner than anticipated. Another person does a job in half the estimated time. All of these lessons can be incorporated in the next plan to make it better.

"In fact, by adding the actual start and finish of each task to our table of data, and revising our program slightly, we can get a chart that looks like this:

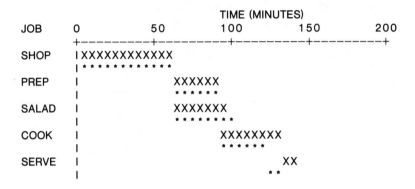

```
                        TIME (MINUTES)
      JOB       0          50          100         150         200
                +----------+----------+----------+----------+
      SHOP      I XXXXXXXXXXXX
                I * * * * * * * * * * * *
      PREP      I                  XXXXX
                I                  * * * * * *
      SALAD     I                  XXXXXX
                I                  * * * * * * * *
      COOK      I                          XXXXXXXX
                I                          * * * * * *
      SERVE     I                                    XX
                I                                    * *

      LEGEND:  XXX PLANNED
               * * * ACTUAL
```

"Looking at the chart, we see that dinner was ready a little early because it did not take as long to cook as was anticipated. Our chart also has given us one part of the answer to our guest-cook question. Because only two jobs go on concurrently, the guest must help with one of them. So the question becomes which one?"

THE PROGRAM GANTT

(Program appears earlier in text.)

_____ *Exercises* _____

1. Revise GANTT to print the actual jobs.

FROM JOBS TO NETWORKS OF JOBS

"To answer this question we need to know exactly how each job relates to the others. We need to sketch a network of jobs. We can draw this network for our dinner" (Fig. 6.1).

"Why are the BEGIN and the END job on the drawing?" asked Graves.

"Because it's possible for projects to blossom into several jobs at the beginning or conclude with several jobs running in parallel. In order to begin and end the network cleanly, it is convenient to have a single entry point and a single exit point. For example, if we were to add a task called POUR-DRINKS, the task might have no predecessor but BEGIN and no successor but END.

"Looking at the network diagram you can figure out how long it will take to go from start to finish. For each job we will set down two numbers, the length of the job and the job's earliest start:

$$\text{BEGIN } (1,0)$$
$$\text{SHOP } (12,1)$$

PREP (6,13)   SALAD (7,13)
COOK (8,19)

$$\text{SERVE } (2,27)$$
$$\text{END } \quad (0,29)$$

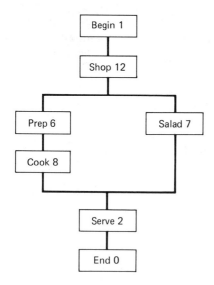

Fig. 6-1   A Network of Jobs

"Computing the early start time is straightforward if you know the length of each job. Notice that SERVE must wait until the last of its predecessors, COOK, is completed. SERVE waits to start until time 27. Again, time is in five-minute intervals."

"Does that mean the whole dinner took 28 units to complete and that everyone can start eating at time 29?" asked Grant.

"Yes, that's exactly right," said Lee. "Thanks for pointing that out."

"Why does BEGIN have a length of one?" asked Grasso.

"It's a trick to make all the first jobs start in interval number one. It doesn't affect anything. Good question."

"Now our example is simple enough," continued Lee, "that the next calculation may look silly, but bear with me. I'm going to start at the end and walk backwards through the network and calculate the latest possible starting time for each task. I'm going to list it as the third number inside the parentheses:

$$\text{END} \quad (0,29,29) \; 0$$
$$\text{SERVE} \; (2,27,27) \; 0$$
$$\text{COOK} \; (8,19,19) \; 0$$
$$\text{PREP} \; (6,13,13) \; 0 \qquad \text{SALAD} \; (7,13,20) \; 7$$
$$\text{SHOP} \; (12,1,1) \; 0$$
$$\text{BEGIN} \; (1,0,0) \; 0$$

"In all but one case the early and the late starts are the same. Only the SALAD has two different starts. Because the other jobs that precede SERVE take so long, SALAD could delay its start until time 20. It could start as early as time 13. The difference in the starting times is called 'slack.' SALAD has seven units of slack. The number indicating the slack is printed to the right of the parentheses.

"All the other jobs have no slack. Notice the zeros on the right of their parentheses. When a job has no slack it is on the slow path of the project. The slow path is the 'critical path' because any job delay on that path delays the whole project. The critical path for our project is SHOP, PREP, COOK, and SERVE.

"If the network of jobs were larger than in our simple example, say several hundred elements, then it would be difficult to keep an eye on all the pieces. The prudent manager pays the most attention to those jobs on the critical path. By making sure they are going well, the manager is making sure the project as a whole is staying on schedule. Of course if another job slips more than its planned slack, it may end up on the critical path also."

"Watching all this," said Graves, "could be tricky with a big project. Things could be all over the place."

THE GANTT CHART REVISITED

"Thank you, Marty," said Lee. "That problem leads us back to our Gantt chart.

"Can we change it somehow to pick up the necessary details of slack time and the critical path? Of course I wouldn't ask the question if the answer were not 'yes.'"

Lee showed them an enhanced Gantt chart:

```
                              TIME (MINUTES)
    JOB    0          50         100        150        200
           +----------+----------+----------+----------+
    SHOP   I CCCCCCCCCCCC
    PREP   I             CCCCCC
    SALAD  I             XXXXXXX.......
    COOK   I                   CCCCCCCC
    SERVE  I                           CC


    TIME OF COMPLETION = 29
```

"Notice how we get this chart to tell us about how our tasks are ordered. We turn any job on the critical path into 'C's. If a job is not critical, it will have some dots after the 'X's to indicate the available slack when it starts as early as possible."

"How did the computer know what was on the critical path?" asked Grasso. "Did we give it some additional information?"

"We gave it some new information and we took out some old information," said Lee. "Most importantly, we wrote a new part of the program to have the computer figure out several things.

"Let's begin at the end. The Gantt chart reveals each job's name, its length, its early start, and its slack."

"That means," said Graves, "that the program has to know the late start as well, because the slack is the early start minus the late start."

"That's right," agreed Lee. "But all we really need to see is the slack. The slack also gives us a clue about the sequence of jobs. The slack extends until it's time for the next job to begin, so we may infer most of the network from the diagram as it stands. We don't need anything else to manage the project. We print the numbers in a table that follows the Gantt chart:

		STARTS		
JOB	LENGTH	EARLY	LATE	SLACK
SHOP	12	1	1	0
PREP	6	13	13	0
SALAD	7	13	20	7
COOK	8	19	19	0
SERVE	2	27	27	0

"The part of the program that prints out the table and the chart will be reviewed later. A more interesting thing to explore is the initial data that the program requires."

THE PREDECESSOR TABLE

"We must tell the program which jobs are connected to which other jobs. One way to do this is to announce the new job's predecessors when we introduce a new job. So the information for our dinner project might look like this:"

```
2200      DATA BEGIN, NO-MORE
2205      DATA SHOP, BEGIN, NO-MORE
2210      DATA PREP, SHOP, NO-MORE
2215      DATA SALAD, SHOP, NO-MORE
2220      DATA COOK, PREP, NO-MORE
2225      DATA SERVE, COOK, SALAD, NO-MORE
2230      DATA END, SERVE, NO-MORE
2255 '
```

"What's that NO-MORE mean?" asked Grant. "There is no job called that."

"It's a way to tell the program that there are no more predecessors for a given job. Because we do not know in advance how many predecessors a job will have, we let the program keep reading predecessors until it finds a NO-MORE, a roadblock that says 'end of the line.'"

"A question," said Grasso. "Look at PREP. It has only SHOP for a predecessor. Why isn't BEGIN there too? It precedes PREP."

"Good question," said Lee. "Notice that BEGIN is not an immediate predecessor. You can travel back from PREP to SHOP and from SHOP to BEGIN, so immediate predecessors are all we really require to compose the network of the project.

"The program takes this information and creates a table that looks like this:

		Job number J =					
		1	2	3	4	5	6	7
Job number I =	1	0	0	0	0	0	0	0
	2	1	0	0	0	0	0	0
	3	0	1	0	0	0	0	0
	4	0	1	0	0	0	0	0
	5	0	0	1	0	0	0	0
	6	0	0	0	1	1	0	0
	7	0	0	0	0	0	1	0

Fig. 6-2   A Predecessor Table

"A '1' indicates that for a job, I, the job J comes before it. So if the table is called P( ), the program can look at all the Js for a given I and find the P(I,J)s that are '1' and know that job J precedes job I."

"I don't think I understood that," said Graves. "Would you go over that again?"

"Sure," said Lee. "If you start with a row, a job, then you can look across the row and find which columns have 1s and know what the immediate predecessors of the job are."

"Okay, if that's all there is to it, then I understand," said Graves. "But let me check. Does what you just said mean that if I pick a column, I can search down it and find the jobs that follow?"

"Took the words right out of my mouth," said Lee. "That's right. So what this table gives you is an easy way, if you are a computer program, to crawl around the network.

"One advantage of having the network in the program is that we can let the program figure out the starting times. We no longer need to provide that information. The only other necessary information besides the predecessors is the length of each job. We can enter that on one line of data like this:

```
2085      FOR J = 1 TO N
2090          READ L(J)
2095      NEXT J
2100      DATA 1, 12, 6, 7, 8, 2, 0
2105 '
```

"The program itself then does what we did by hand. It computes the early starts, the late starts, and the slack. When it has this information in hand, it prints out the enhanced Gantt chart and the table."

"That program," asked Grasso, "can we get a copy of it?"

"Sure," said Lee. "As a matter of fact, we're going to spend a little while working with this program right now. Each of you should sketch out a project by jobs, with the network of predecessors and the length of each job. After you get it roughed out on paper we will type it into the program and see what the results look like.

"By the way, our enhanced Gantt chart solves the guest-cook problem: we want dinner on time so we keep the guest off the critical path. Our guest cook will help by making the salad."

THE PROGRAM CPM-I

```
1000 REM    CPM-I    5 JUNE 1981    GEORGE LEE
1002 REM    CRITICAL PATH METHOD (I)
1003 '
1004 REM    © COPYRIGHT 1980 BY JOHN M. NEVISON ASSOCIATES
1005 '
1006 REM    THIS PROGRAM MAY BE USED TO FIND THE CRITICAL
1007 REM    PATH AND THE EARLIEST POSSIBLE STARTING TIMES FOR
1008 REM    A NETWORK OF JOBS.
1009 '
1010 REM    GIVEN A LIST OF JOBS, THEIR LENGTHS, AND THEIR
1015 REM    PREDECESSORS, PRINT A GANTT CHART THAT SHOWS
1020 REM    EACH JOB, "XXX"S, ANY SLACK, "..."S, AND WHETHER
1025 REM    THE JOB IS ON THE CRITICAL PATH, "CCC"S, OF THE
1026 REM    PROJECT.
1030 '
1035 REM    VARIABLES:
1040 REM        C..........COMPLETION TIME FOR THE WHOLE
1042 REM                        PROJECT
1045 REM        E..........GREATEST (LATEST) END TIME
1050 REM        E() ........END TIME FOR JOBS
1055 REM        E$.........ERROR FLAG
1060 REM        I,J,K ......INDEX VARIABLES
1065 REM        J$() .......NAMES OF JOBS
1070 REM        L..........LITTLEST (EARLIEST) LATE START
1075 REM        L().........LENGTH OF JOBS
1080 REM        N..........NUMBER OF JOBS
1085 REM        P$.........NAME OF PREDECESSOR
1090 REM        P() ........PREDECESSOR TABLE
1095 REM        S() ........STARTING TIMES
1100 '
1105 REM        DIMENSIONS:
1110        DIM E(12), J$(12), L(12), P(12,12), S(12,2)
1115 '
1120 '
```

```
1125 REM    MAIN PROGRAM
1130 '
1135        GOSUB 2000       'READ IN DATA
1140        IF E$ <> "OKAY" THEN 1142 ELSE 1144
1142          GOTO 1180      'STOP
1144 '      IFEND
1145        GOSUB 3000       'COMPUTE EARLY STARTS
1150        LET C = S(N,1) + L(N)
1155        GOSUB 4000       'COMPUTE LATE STARTS
1160        GOSUB 7000       'PRINT GANTT CHART
1165        GOSUB 8000       'PRINT TABLE OF VALUES
1170 '
1175 '
1180        STOP
1185 '
1190 '
2000 REM    SUBROUTINE: READ IN DATA
2005 REM      IN: --
2010 REM      OUT: J$(), L(), N, P()
2015 '
2020 REM    READ IN THE NUMBER OF JOBS, C, THE JOB LENGTHS,
2025 REM    L(J), AND THE JOB NAMES WITH THE NAMES OF IMMED-
2030 REM    IATELY PRECEDING JOBS.  MARK THE PREDECESSOR
2035 REM    TABLE WITH A 1 FOR EVERY COLUMN JOB, K, THAT
2040 REM    PRECEDES A GIVEN ROW JOB, I.
2045 '
2050 REM    THE READER MIGHT TRY AND FILL IN THE TABLE
2055 REM    P() FOR THE FEW CASES TO SEE HOW IT LOOKS.
2060 '
2065        LET E$ = "OKAY"
2070        READ N
2075        DATA 7
2080 '
2085        FOR J = 1 TO N
2090            READ L(J)
2095        NEXT J
2096 '
2097 REM    TIME IN 5-MINUTE UNITS
2100        DATA 1, 12, 6, 7, 8, 2, 0
2105 '
```

```
2110        FOR J = 1 TO N
2115            READ J$(J), P$
2120            IF P$ = "NO-MORE" THEN 2160        'LOOP
2125                GOSUB 2280      'CHECK NAME
2130                IF E$ <> "OKAY" THEN 2135 ELSE 2140
2135                    GOTO 2265      'RETURN
2140 '              IFEND
2145                LET P(J,K) = 1
2150                READ P$
2155            GOTO 2120      'LOOP
2160 '
2165        NEXT J
2170 '
2175        IF J$(N) <> "END" THEN 2180 ELSE 2190
2180          PRINT "NO END JOB"
2185          LET E$ = "NOT-OKAY"
2190 '      IFEND
2195 '
2200        DATA BEGIN, NO-MORE
2205        DATA SHOP, BEGIN, NO-MORE
2210        DATA PREP, SHOP, NO-MORE
2215        DATA SALAD, SHOP, NO-MORE
2220        DATA COOK, PREP, NO-MORE
2225        DATA SERVE, COOK, SALAD, NO-MORE
2230        DATA END, SERVE, NO-MORE
2255 '
2260 '
2265 RETURN
2270 '
2275 '
2280 REM     SUBROUTINE:  CHECK NAME
2285 REM        IN:  J, J$(), P$
2290 REM     OUT:  E$, K
2295 '
2300        LET E$ = "OKAY"
2305        FOR K = 1 TO J - 1
2310            IF P$ = J$(K) THEN 2330      'LOOP EXIT
2315        NEXT K
2320        PRINT P$; " DOES NOT PRECEDE "; J$(K)
2325        LET E$ = "NOT-OKAY"
2330 '
2335 RETURN
2340 '
2345 '
```

```
3000 REM      SUBROUTINE: COMPUTE EARLY STARTS
3005 REM        IN: L(), N, P()
3010 REM      OUT: S(J,1)
3015 '
3020 REM      THE JOB'S EARLIEST START, S(J,1) IS JUST AFTER
3025 REM      THE SLOWEST OF IT'S PREDECESSORS HAS BEEN
3030 REM      COMPLETED.
3035 '
3040 REM      L(J)........... LENGTH OF JOB J
3045 REM      S(J,1)........ EARLY START TIME
3050 REM      E(J) .......... END TIME
3055 REM      E............. GREATEST (LATEST) END TIME
3060 '
3065          FOR J = 1 TO N
3070            LET E = 0
3075            FOR K = 1 TO N
3080              IF P(J,K) = 1 AND E < E(K) THEN 3090 ELSE 3095
3090                LET E = E(K)
3095 '              IFEND
3100            NEXT K
3105            LET S(J,1) = E
3110            LET E(J) = E + L(J)
3115          NEXT J
3120 '
3125 RETURN
3130 '
3135 '
4000 REM      SUBROUTINE: COMPUTE LATE STARTS
4005 REM        IN: L(), N, P(), C
4010 REM      OUT: S(J,2)
4015 '
4020 '
4025 REM      THE LATEST A JOB CAN BE COMPLETED IS JUST BEFORE
4030 REM      ITS SUCCESSOR MUST.
4035 '
4040 REM      S(J,2)........ LATE START OF JOB J
4045 REM      L............. EARLIEST LATE START
4050 '
4055          FOR K = N TO 1 STEP −1
4060            LET L = C
4065            FOR J = 1 TO N
4070              IF P(J,K) <> 0 AND L > S(J,2) THEN 4080 ELSE 4085
4080                LET L = S(J,2)
4085 '              IFEND
4090            NEXT J
4095            LET S(K,2) = L −L(K)
4100          NEXT K
4105 '
4110 RETURN
4115 '
4120 '
```

```
7000 REM    SUBROUTINE: PRINT GANTT CHART
7005 REM      IN: J$(), L(), N, S()
7010 REM    OUT: --
7015 '
7020 REM    PRINT OUT A GANTT CHART THAT SHOWS REGULAR JOBS
7025 REM    AS "X"S, CRITICAL JOBS AS "C"S, AND SLACK ON
7026 REM    REGULAR JOBS AS "."S.
7030 '
7035        PRINT TAB(35); "TIME (MINUTES) "
7040        PRINT
7045        PRINT "JOB"; TAB(11); "0       50      100";
7046        PRINT "      150      200"
7050        PRINT TAB(11); "+---------+---------+";
7052        PRINT "---------+---------+"
7055        FOR J = 2 TO N - 1
7060            PRINT J$(J); TAB(11); "I" ;
7065            LET K = S(J,1)
7070            IF S(J,1) - S(J,2) < > 0 THEN 7075 ELSE 7130
7075                IF K > S(J,1) + L(J) - 1 THEN 7095      'LOOP
7080                    PRINT TAB(11+K); "X";
7085                    LET K = K + 1
7090                GOTO 7075 'LOOP
7095 '
7100                IF K > S(J,2) + L(J) - 1 THEN 7120      'LOOP
7105                    PRINT TAB(11+K); ".";
7110                    LET K = K + 1
7115                GOTO 7100 'LOOP
7120 '
7125                GOTO 7160 'IFEND
7130 '          ELSE
7135                IF K > S(J,1) + L(J) - 1 THEN 7155      'LOOP
7140                    PRINT TAB(11+K); "C";
7145                    LET K = K + 1
7150                GOTO 7135 'LOOP
7155 '
7160 '          IFEND
7165                PRINT
7170        NEXT J
7175        PRINT
7180        PRINT
7185 RETURN
7190 '
8000 REM    SUBROUTINE: PRINT TABLE OF VALUES
8005 REM      IN: C, J$(), L(), N, S()
8010 REM    OUT: --
8015 '
8020 '
```

```
8025      PRINT "TIME OF COMPLETION = " ; C*5
8030      PRINT
8034      PRINT "                      STARTS"
8035      PRINT "JOB    LENGTH       EARLY ";
8036      PRINT "LATE    SLACK"
8040      PRINT
8045      FOR J = 2 TO N − 1
8050          PRINT J$(J); TAB(10);L(J); TAB(25);S(J,1);
8052          PRINT TAB(30); S(J,2); TAB(40); S(J,2) − S(J,1)
8055      NEXT J
8060 '
8065 RETURN
8070 '
8075 '
8080      END
```

The gross outline of the program is revealed by the subroutines that the main routine invokes. Each subroutine performs a task in a fashion similar to the discussion in the text. To discover the details of how any piece of code works, the reader must finally take a close look at it one line at a time. Anyone who wishes to explore the workings of these subroutines should get a piece of scrap paper and do just that: work through the code and take notes.

_____ *Exercises* _____

1. Run CPM-I on your computer and verify that the results are the same as in the example in the text.
2. Draw up a network for a project of your own and enter the predecessor table and job lengths in CPM-I. Try a run.

SCHEDULING WITH A SCARCE RESOURCE

By lunch time everyone had successfully used the computer to produce an enhanced Gantt chart of a project for a Deer Division product line. All three product managers were enthusiastic about their new plans. After lunch they reassembled in the conference room.

"This afternoon," began George Lee, "we are going to help two trolls named Tread and Truss build a bridge to live under. Their problem is the same one we had this morning but with one extra feature: they have a scarce resource. The enhanced Gantt chart for their project looks like this:

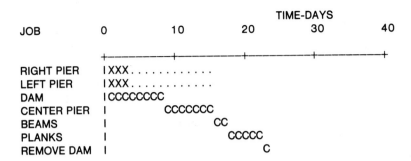

```
                                          TIME-DAYS
JOB            0           10        20        30        40

              +-----------+---------+---------+---------+
RIGHT PIER    I XXX. . . . . . . . . . .
LEFT PIER     I XXX. . . . . . . . . . .
DAM           I CCCCCCCC
CENTER PIER   I           CCCCCCC
BEAMS         I                     CC
PLANKS        I                       CCCCC
REMOVE DAM    I                         C
```

"So far the project looks feasible. But here's the problem. It takes two trolls to dam the stream. It takes only one troll to build a bridge pier. It takes two trolls to lay the log beams on the piers and it takes two trolls to plank the log beams. One troll can remove the dam. Their scarce resource is trolls. All of what has been said can be summed up in the following data:

JOB	LENGTH OF JOB	RESOURCE USED	START	SLACK
RIGHT PIER	3	1	1	12
LEFT PIER	3	1	1	12
DAM	8	2	1	0
CENTER PIER	7	1	9	0
BEAMS	2	2	16	0
PLANKS	5	2	18	0
REMOVE DAM	1	1	23	0

"The resource histogram that accompanies the above data looks like this:

RESOURCE USED

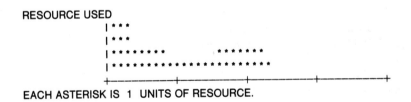

```
              I * * *
              I * * *
              I * * * * * * * *         . * * * * * *
              I * * * * * * * * * * * * * * * * * * * * * *
              +-----------+---------+---------+---------+
```

EACH ASTERISK IS 1 UNITS OF RESOURCE.

"The present plan requires four trolls for times 1 to 3. Only two trolls exist. They are the scarce resource. Tread and Truss looked at this situation and they delayed the start of their left and right piers to 9 and 12.

"When they ran CPM-II a second time they saw they had solved their problem:

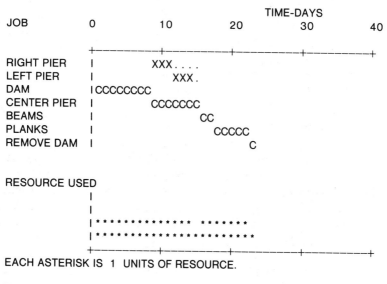

```
                                          TIME-DAYS
   JOB            0          10         20         30         40

                  +————————+————————+————————+————————+
   RIGHT PIER     I         XXX....
   LEFT PIER      I          XXX.
   DAM            ICCCCCCCC
   CENTER PIER    I         CCCCCCC
   BEAMS          I              CC
   PLANKS         I               CCCCC
   REMOVE DAM     I                    C


   RESOURCE USED
                  I
                  I
                  I * * * * * * * * * * * * * *  * * * * * * *
                  I * * * * * * * * * * * * * * * * * * * * *
                  +————————+————————+————————+————————+
   EACH ASTERISK IS  1  UNITS OF RESOURCE.

   TIME OF COMPLETION =  24
```

JOB	LENGTH OF JOB	RESOURCE USED	START	SLACK
RIGHT PIER	3	1	9	4
LEFT PIER	3	1	12	1
DAM	8	2	1	0
CENTER PIER	7	1	9	0
BEAMS	2	2	16	0
PLANKS	5	2	18	0
REMOVE DAM	1	1	23	0

"This time their resource requirements stayed within their limits. At no time did the plan require more than the two trolls they had available. The plan was a workable solution given their scarce resource. They set to work."

"What happens," asked Grant, "if part of a job takes two trolls and part of a job takes only one troll?"

"There are two ways to handle that contingency," said Lee. "First, you can say the job takes 1.5 people. If you don't like that approach, you break the job into two jobs, one with two people and one with one person."

"Is it correct to say," asked Grasso, "that you plan to run the program several times before you get it right?"

"Yes," nodded Lee.

"Then why don't you have the program do the adjusting?" Grasso continued.

"It's possible," agreed Lee, "but the program is more flexible when you stay in charge. You lose a few minutes juggling jobs, but you gain a solution that is exactly the one you want. The trolls might have a friend and decide to invite her over if they wanted to speed up the project. If she could come, they might want to shorten the length of some jobs and increase their resources to three. For example, the planking could be finished faster. The point is that the trolls retain a great deal of flexibility by using a program that keeps them in control."

"I think I hear you saying, 'Stay loose,'" said Grasso. "I'm willing to give it a try. Maybe it's not such a bad idea. I know my plans are always a balancing act. I can see how I would cycle around several times before I had just the right solution."

"We are going to do that right now," said Lee. "Each of the plans we made this morning has to be revised to include a resource. It can be dollars per week, man-days, man-hours, or anything else you wish. You have to tie some resource to each job, put in the length and start time, and look at the results. If you exceed some reasonable resource limits, reschedule some jobs and rerun CPM-II until things work."

THE PROGRAM CPM-II

```
1000 REM   CPM-II   5 JUNE 1981    GEORGE LEE
1010 REM   CRITICAL PATH METHOD (II)
1020 '
1021 REM   © COPYRIGHT 1980 BY JOHN M. NEVISON ASSOCIATES
1022 '
1030 REM   THIS PROGRAM MAY BE USED TO
1040 REM   BALANCE RESOURCE USE OF A CRITICAL PATH NETWORK
1050 REM   BY ADJUSTING THE STARTING TIMES.
1060 '
1070 REM   GIVEN A LIST OF JOBS, THEIR LENGTHS, THEIR
1080 REM   STARTING TIMES, THEIR REQUIRED RESOURCES, AND
1090 REM   THEIR PREDECESSORS, PRINT A GANTT CHART, A
1100 REM   RESOURCE HISTOGRAM, AND A TABLE OF VALUES FOR
1110 REM   THE NETWORK.
1140 '
```

```
1150 REM    VARIABLES:
1160 REM        A . . . . . . . . . . VALUE OF EACH ASTERISK IN HISTOGRAM
1170 REM        C . . . . . . . . . . COMPLETION TIME FOR THE WHOLE
1175 REM                  PROJECT
1180 REM        E . . . . . . . . . . GREATEST (LATEST) END TIME
1190 REM        E() . . . . . . . . END TIME FOR JOBS
1200 REM        E$ . . . . . . . . . ERROR FLAG
1210 REM        G$() . . . . . . . . GRAPH FOR HISTOGRAM
1220 REM        H() . . . . . . . . HISTOGRAM STEPS
1230 REM        I,J,K . . . . . . . INDEX VARIABLES
1240 REM        J$() . . . . . . . NAMES OF JOBS
1250 REM        L . . . . . . . . . . LITTLEST (EARLIEST) LATE START
1260 REM        L() . . . . . . . . LENGTH OF JOBS
1270 REM        M. . . . . . . . . . MAXIMUM HISTOGRAM STEP
1280 REM        N. . . . . . . . . . NUMBER OF JOBS
1290 REM        P$. . . . . . . . . NAME OF PREDECESSOR
1300 REM        P() . . . . . . . . PREDECESSOR TABLE
1310 REM        R() . . . . . . . . RESOURCE REQUIRED
1320 REM        S() . . . . . . . . STARTING TIMES
1330 REM        X . . . . . . . . . . DUMMY DATA VARIABLE
1340 '
1350 REM    CONSTANTS:
1360        LET H9 = 4          'HEIGHT OF RESOURCE HISTOGRAM
1370        LET S9 = 11         'SPACES TO LEFT EDGE OF CHARTS
1380        LET T9 = 40         'SPACES ACROSS CHARTS (TIME UNITS)
1390        LET T$ = "DAYS"     'TIME LABEL
1400 '
1410 REM    DIMENSIONS:
1420        DIM E(25), H(40), G$(10,40), J$(25)
1430        DIM L(25), P(25,25), R(25), S(25,2)
1440 '
1450 REM    MAIN PROGRAM
1460 '
1470        GOSUB 2000          'READ IN DATA
1480        IF E$ <> "OKAY" THEN 1482 ELSE 1484
1482          GOTO 1580         'STOP
1484 '       IFEND
1490        GOSUB 3000          'COMPUTE EARLY STARTS
1500        IF E$ <> "OKAY" THEN 1502 ELSE 1504
1502          GOTO 1580         'STOP
1504 '       IFEND
1510        LET C = S(N,1) + L(N)
1520        GOSUB 4000          'COMPUTE LATE STARTS
1530        GOSUB 7000          'PRINT GANTT CHART
1540        GOSUB 7200          'PRINT RESOURCE HISTOGRAM
1550        GOSUB 8000          'PRINTTABLE OF VALUES
1560 '
1570 '
1580        STOP
1590 '
1600 '
```

```
2000 REM    SUBROUTINE: READ IN DATA
2005 REM      IN: --
2010 REM    OUT: E$, J$(), L(), N, R(), P(), S()
2015 '
2020 REM    READ IN THE NUMBER OF JOBS, N, THE JOB LENGTHS,
2025 REM    L(J), AND THE JOB NAMES WITH THE NAMES OF IMMED-
2030 REM    IATELY PRECEDING JOBS.  MARK THE PREDECESSOR
2035 REM    TABLE WITH A 1 FOR EVERY COLUMN JOB, K, THAT
2040 REM    PRECEDES A GIVEN ROW JOB, I.
2045 '
2050 REM    THE READER MIGHT TRY AND FILL IN THE TABLE
2055 REM    P() FOR THE FEW CASES TO SEE HOW IT LOOKS.
2060 '
2065        LET E$ = "OKAY"
2070        READ N
2075        DATA 9
2080 '
2085        FOR J = 1 TO N
2087            READ X$, S(J,1), L(J), R(J)
2088        NEXT J
2090        DATA BEGIN, 0, 1, 0
2091        DATA RIGHT PIER, 9, 3, 1
2092        DATA LEFT PIER, 12, 3, 1
2093        DATA DAM, 1, 8, 2
2094        DATA CENTER PIER, 9, 7, 1
2095        DATA BEAMS, 16, 2, 2
2096        DATA PLANKS, 18, 5, 2
2097        DATA REMOVE DAM, 23, 1, 1
2098        DATA END, 24, 0, 0
2101 '
2102        READ X
2103        DATA −.9999
2104        IF X < > −.9999 THEN 2105 ELSE 2109
2105          PRINT "WRONG NUMBER OF DATA FOR STARTING DATA."
2106          PRINT "BE SURE TO INCLUDE STARTING DATA FOR THE"
2107          PRINT "'BEGIN' JOB AND THE 'END' JOB."
2108          LET E$ = "NOT-OKAY"
2109 '      IFEND
2110        FOR J = 1 TO N
2115            READ J$(J), P$
2120          IF P$ = "NO-MORE" THEN 2160      'LOOP
2125              GOSUB 2280     'CHECK NAME
2130              IF E$ < > "OKAY" THEN 2135 ELSE 2140
2135                GOTO 2265     'RETURN
2140 '            IFEND
2145              LET P(J,K) = 1
2150              READ P$
2155          GOTO 2120    'LOOP
2160 '
2165        NEXT J
2170 '
```

```
2175      IF J$(N) < > "END" THEN 2180 ELSE 2190
2180        PRINT "NO END JOB"
2185        LET E$ = "NOT-OKAY"
2190 '    IFEND
2195 '
2200      DATA BEGIN, NO-MORE
2205      DATA RIGHT PIER, BEGIN, NO-MORE
2210      DATA LEFT PIER, BEGIN, NO-MORE
2215      DATA DAM, BEGIN, NO-MORE
2220      DATA CENTER PIER, DAM, NO-MORE
2225      DATA BEAMS, LEFT PIER, RIGHT PIER, CENTER PIER, NO-MORE
2230      DATA PLANKS, BEAMS, NO-MORE
2235      DATA REMOVE DAM, PLANKS, NO-MORE
2240      DATA END, PLANKS, NO-MORE
2255 '
2260 '
2265 RETURN
2270 '
2275 '
2280 REM    SUBROUTINE:  CHECK NAME AND FIND PREDECESSOR
2285 REM      IN: E$, J, J$(), P$
2290 REM     OUT: E$, K
2295 '             .
2305      FOR K = 1 TO J − 1
2310        IF J$(K) = P$ THEN 2330      'LOOP EXIT
2315      NEXT K
2320      PRINT P$; " DOES NOT PRECEDE "; J$(K)
2325      LET E$ = "NOT-OKAY"
2330 '
2335 RETURN
2340 '
2345 '
3000 REM    SUBROUTINE:  CHECK STARTS
3005 REM      IN: E$, L(), N, P(), S(J,1)
3010 REM     OUT: E$
3015 '
3020 REM    THE JOB'S START, D(J,1), MUST BE AFTER THE
3025 REM    SLOWEST OF ITS PREDECESSORS HAS BEEN
3030 REM    COMPLETED.
3035 '
3040 REM    L(J). . . . . . . . . . LENGTH OF JOB J
3045 REM    S(J,1). . . . . . . . EARLY START TIME
3050 REM    E(J) . . . . . . . . . END TIME
3055 REM    E. . . . . . . . . . . . GREATEST (LATEST) END TIME
3060 '
```

```
3065       FOR J = 1 TO N
3070          LET E = 0
3075          FOR K = 1 TO N
3085             IF P(J,K) = 1 AND E < E(K) THEN 3090 ELSE 3095
3090                LET E = E(K)
3095 '           IFEND
3100          NEXT K
3102          IF S(J,1) < E THEN 3103 ELSE 3109
3103             PRINT "STARTING TIME"; S(J,1); " OF JOB #";
3104             PRINT J; " MUST BE LATER THAN "; E; "."
3105             PRINT "PLEASE RETYPE THE STARTING TIMES."
3106             PRINT
3107             LET E$ = "NOT-OKAY"
3108             GOTO 3125 'RETURN
3109 '           IFEND
3110          LET E(J) = S(J,1) + L(J)
3115       NEXT J
3120 '
3125 RETURN
3130 '
3135 '
4000 REM    SUBROUTINE: COMPUTE LATE STARTS
4005 REM       IN: L(), N, P(), C
4010 REM    OUT: S(J,2)
4015 '
4020 '
4025 REM    THE LATEST A JOB CAN BE COMPLETED IS JUST BEFORE
4030 REM    ITS SUCCESSOR MUST START.
4035 '
4040 REM    S(J,2) . . . . . . . . LATE START OF JOB J
4045 REM    L . . . . . . . . . . . . EARLIEST LATE START
4050 '
4055       FOR K = N TO 1 STEP −1
4060          LET L = C
4065          FOR J = 1 TO N
4070             IF P(J,K) = 1 AND L > S(J,2) THEN 4080 ELSE 4085
4080                LET L = S(J,2)
4085 '           IFEND
4090          NEXT J
4095          LET S(K,2) = L −L(K)
4100       NEXT K
4105 '
4110 RETURN
4115 '
4120 '
```

```
7000 REM      SUBROUTINE:  PRINT GANTT CHART
7005 REM        IN: J$(), L(), N, S()
7010 REM      OUT: --
7015 '
7020 REM      PRINT OUT A GANTT CHART THAT SHOWS REGULAR JOBS
7025 REM      AS "X"S, CRITICAL JOBS AS "C"s, AND SLACK ON
7026 REM      REGULAR JOBS AS "."S.  FOR EACH TIME, K,
7027 REM      ACCUMULATE THE JOB'S RESOURCE, R(J), IN THE
7028 REM      HISTOGRAM STEP, H(K).
7029 '
7030      FOR K = 1 TO T9
7031          LET H(K) = 0
7032      NEXT K
7033 '
7035      PRINT TAB(35); "TIME-"; T$
7045      PRINT "JOB"; TAB(S9); "0       10      20";
7046      PRINT "     30      40"
7050      PRINT TAB(11); "+----------+----------+";
7051      PRINT "----------+----------+"
7052 '
7055      FOR J = 2 TO N − 1
7060          PRINT J$(J); TAB(S9); "I";
7065          LET K = S(J,1)
7070          IF S(J,1) − S(J,2) <> 0 THEN 7075 ELSE 7130
7075              IF K > S(J,1) + L(J) − 1 THEN 7095    'LOOP
7080                  PRINT TAB(S9+K); "X";
7083                  LET H(K) = H(K) + R(J)
7085                  LET K = K + 1
7090              GOTO 7075 'LOOP
7095 '
7100              IF K > S(J,2) + L(J) − 1 THEN 7120      'LOOP
7105                  PRINT TAB(S9+K); ".";
7110                  LET K = K + 1
7115              GOTO 7100 'LOOP
7120 '
7125              GOTO 7160 'IFEND
7130 '        ELSE
7135              IF K > S(J,1) + L(J) − 1 THEN 7155      'LOOP
7140                  PRINT TAB(S9+K); "C";
7143                  LET H(K) = H(K) + R(J)
7145                  LET K = K + 1
7150              GOTO 7135 'LOOP
7155 '
7160 '        IFEND
7165              PRINT
7170      NEXT J
7175      PRINT
7180      PRINT
7185 RETURN
7190 '
```

```
7200 REM    SUBROUTINE:  PRINT RESOURCE HISTOGRAM
7202 REM      IN: H()
7204 REM    OUT: --
7205 '
7206 REM    PRINT OUT A HISTOGRAM THAT IS T9 TIME UNITS
7208 REM    ACROSS AND H9 UNITS HIGH.
7210 '
7211       FOR I = 1 TO H9
7212          FOR K = 1 TO T9
7213             LET G$(I,K) = " "
7214          NEXT K
7215       NEXT I
7216 '
7218 REM   FIND MAXIMUM, M, OF THE HISTOGRAM STEPS, H(K).
7220       LET M = H(1)
7225       FOR K = 2 TO T9
7230          IF H(K) > H9 THEN 7235 ELSE 7240
7235             LET M = H(K)
7240 '          IFEND
7245       NEXT K
7247 '
7250 REM   SCALE HISTOGRAM IF MAXIMUM IS LARGER THAN H9.
7251       LET A = 1
7252       IF M > H9 THEN 7253 ELSE 7254
7253          LET A = M/H9
7254 '     IFEND
7255 REM   MARK OUTPUT GRAPH G$(), WITH ASTERISKS.
7258       FOR K = 1 TO T9
7260          FOR I = 1 TO H9
7265             IF I*A <= H(K) THEN 7270 ELSE 7275
7270                LET G$(I,K) = "*"
7275 '             IFEND
7280          NEXT I
7283 '
7285       NEXT K
7287 '
```

```
7288 REM    PRINT OUT THE ACTUAL HISTOGRAM ON THE GRAPH, G$()
7290        PRINT "RESOURCE USED"
7295        FOR I = H9 TO 1 STEP -1
7300            PRINT TAB(S9); "I";
7305            FOR K = 1 TO T9
7310                PRINT TAB(S9+K); G$(I,K);
7315            NEXT K
7317            PRINT
7320        NEXT I
7325        PRINT TAB(S9); "+----------+----------+";
7326        PRINT "----------+----------+"
7330        PRINT "EACH ASTERISK IS "; A; " UNITS OF RESOURCE."
7335        PRINT
7340 '
7345 RETURN
7350 '
7355 '
8000 REM    SUBROUTINE: PRINT TABLE OF VALUES
8005 REM      IN: C, J$(), L(), N, S()
8010 REM      OUT: --
8015 '
8020 '
8025        PRINT "TIME OF COMPLETION = " ; C
8030        PRINT
8035        PRINT "JOB    LENGTH OF JOB    RESOURCE USED";
8036        PRINT "    START    SLACK"
8040        PRINT
8045        FOR J = 2 TO N - 1
8050            PRINT J$(J); TAB(15);L(J); TAB(30); R(J);
8052            PRINT TAB(47); S(J,1); TAB(58); S(J,2) - S(J,1)
8055        NEXT J
8060 '
8065 RETURN
8070 '
8075 '
8080        END
```

The second critical-path program works very much like the first program in its various subroutines. It does differ, however, in some ways from the first program. The most obvious difference is that a resource is associated with each job. This addition leads to a little new programming logic. The program still figures out the Gantt chart as before. But now, after the chart is drawn, the program adds down the page in each time unit to see what the total resource being used at a given time is. The results of this calculation are graphed in the resource histogram, sometimes called a resource density chart, which appears right below the Gantt chart.

The second way this program differs from its predecessor is that the user enters the starting times. Starting times must be under the user's control if he or she is to be able to delay selected projects to make the resource histogram stay within bounds. The portion of the program that computed starting times in CPM-I has been converted to checking starting times in CPM-II. The program checks starts now because a user can make a mistake and start a new job before its predecessors have finished.

_____ *Exercises* _____

1. Modify your project from CPM-I to include both a resource and a starting time for each job. Try it with CPM-II.
2. Sometimes it is interesting to see how the resources accumulate as the project proceeds. Write an additional subroutine to print the cumulative resource used. Try to make the graph square—from 0 to 100 percent of the schedule on the horizontal axis and 0 to 100 percent of the resource on the vertical axis.

   (HINT: See the utility program PLOT in Appendix B for some ideas on making graphs in BASIC.)

_____

CONTROLLING THE PROJECT

Jean Grant, Robert Grasso, and Martin Graves completed their revised schedules and looked pleased with their results as they assembled for the last session of the afternoon. Lee was relieved that they had taken so enthusiastically to the little computers.

"You were right, George," said Grasso. "I had to adjust a job length as well as juggle the starting times and resources to make things work. It was a tricky mix. I liked being able to control how the final schedule shaped up."

"Glad you liked it," said Lee, "because now we're going to take the final step in this project plan. We're going to carry out the plan.

"Our two trolls set to work, and a few days later they paused to take stock. They had begun to lay the beams. Most of the early work had gone well, but the beams had been hard to find and they had delayed the start of setting them in place for two days. As the jobs progressed, they had recorded the actual starts and finishes of each task:

```
3240 REM    SUBROUTINE: READ ACTUAL TIMES
3250 REM      IN:  N
3260 REM      OUT:  A(), F(), T1
3270 '
3290 REM    READ ACTUAL START, A(J,1), AND ACTUAL FINISH,
3300 REM    F(J), FOR JOBS WHERE THIS HAS HAPPENED.
3310 '
3320 REM    READ PRESENT TIME, T1.
3330          READ T1
3340          DATA 19
3350 '
3360          FOR J = 1 TO N
3370              READ X$, A(J,1), F(1)
3380          NEXT J
3390          DATA BEGIN, 0, 0
3400          DATA RIGHT PIER, 9, 11
3410          DATA LEFT PIER, 12, 14
3420          DATA DAM, 1, 8
3430          DATA CENTER PIER, 9, 14
3440          DATA BEAMS, 18, 0
3450          DATA PLANKS, 0, 0
3460          DATA REMOVE DAM, 0,0
3465          DATA END, 0, 0
3470 '
```

"A chart that compared their final plan with their actual work looked like this:

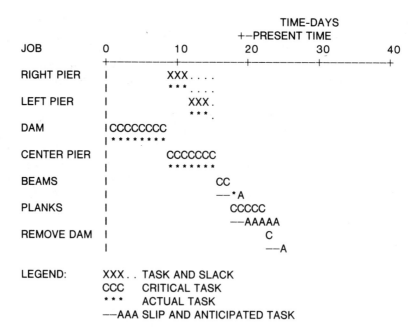

```
                                              TIME-DAYS
                                            +–PRESENT TIME
        JOB          0            10         20          30          40
                     +———————————+———————————+———————————+———————————+
        RIGHT PIER   I           XXX . . . .
                     I            * * * . . . .
        LEFT PIER    I             XXX .
                     I              * * * .
        DAM          I CCCCCCCC
                     I * * * * * * * *
        CENTER PIER  I           CCCCCCC
                     I           * * * * * * *
        BEAMS        I                   CC
                     I                  ——*A
        PLANKS       I                   CCCCC
                     I                  ——AAAAA
        REMOVE DAM   I                     C
                     I                    ——A

        LEGEND:      XXX . . TASK AND SLACK
                     CCC    CRITICAL TASK
                     * * *     ACTUAL TASK
                     ——AAA SLIP AND ANTICIPATED TASK
```

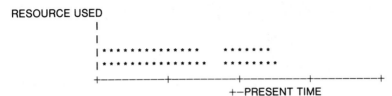

```
RESOURCE USED
     |
     |
     | * * * * * * * * * * * * *    * * * * * * *
     | * * * * * * * * * * * * *    * * * * * * * *
     +———————————+———————————+———————————+———————————+
                             +—PRESENT TIME
EACH ASTERISK IS 1  UNITS OF RESOURCE.
```

JOB	LENGTH OF JOB	ALL FIGURES ACTUAL (OR ANTICIPATED) RESOURCE USED	START	SLACK
RIGHT PIER	3	1	9	4
LEFT PIER	3	1	12	1
DAM	8	2	1	0
CENTER PIER	7	1	9	0
BEAMS	2	2	18	−2
PLANKS	5	2	20	−2
REMOVE DAM	1	1	25	−2

PRESENT TIME IS 19
ESTIMATED TIME TO COMPLETE PROJECT IS 24 DAYS

"Truss and Tread reviewed their progress and were pleased to see that they had stayed on schedule until the beams were delayed. The delay in the beams' arrival made the new completion date lag behind the planned completion, but they saw exactly what the new date was, so they did not worry much about the delay."

"That output looks like it requires a lot of figuring in the program," interjected Graves. "Is it as hard as it looks?"

"Not really," answered Lee. "The planning part gets done the way it was in CPM-II, off the starting times. The actual start and finish make possible the actual work history on the second line of each job. The present forecast is built off the actual work to date."

"What if you want to compare the actual work with a revised plan?" asked Grant.

"Then you redo your planning data and rerun the program. Only please be sure to label the output clearly as 'revised plan,'" said Lee.

"So we only have one plan at a time?" she confirmed.

"Yes, one plan and one actual work history," said Lee. "If you get fancy, experience shows that things tend to get very confused."

"Okay," said Graves, "CPM-II convinced me of that. Can we give this a try now?"

"Sure can," said Lee. "CPM-III is the last assignment for the day. You should imagine you are part way through your projects and have completed a few tasks. If there are no further questions, let's go to work. What we are doing now is controlling the project."

THE PROGRAM CPM-III

```
1000 REM    CPM-III    5 JUNE 1981    GEORGE LEE
1010 REM    CRITICAL PATH METHOD (III)
1020 '
1030 REM    © COPYRIGHT 1980 BY JOHN M. NEVISON ASSOCIATES
1040 '
1050 REM    THIS PROGRAM MAY BE USED TO SEE HOW AN ACTUAL
1052 REM    PROJECT, PLANNED USING CPM-I AND CPM-II, IS
1054 REM    WORKING.  THE PROGRAM READS IN THE PRESENT
1056 REM    TIME, T1, AND THE ACTUAL STARTS, A(J,1), AND
1058 REM    ACTUAL FINISHES, F(J), OF JOBS.
1060 '
1062 REM    THE PROGRAM PRINTS A GANTT CHART THAT COMPARES
1064 REM    THE PLANNED JOB TO THE ACTUAL (OR ANTICIPATED)
1066 REM    JOB.
1068 '
1070 REM    THE RESOURCE HISTOGRAM SHOWS THE ACTUAL (OR
1072 REM    ANTICIPATED) RESOURCE USE.
1074 '
1076 REM    THE TABLE DETAILS THE NUMBERS BEHIND THE PICTURES.
1078 '
1080 REM    VARIABLES:
1082 REM        A() ........ ACTUAL (OR ANTICIPATED) STARTING TIMES
1170 REM        A .......... VALUE OF EACH ASTERISK IN HISTOGRAM
1180 REM        C .......... COMPLETION TIME FOR THE WHOLE
1185 REM                        PROJECT
1190 REM        E .......... GREATEST (LATEST) END TIME
1200 REM        E() ........ END TIME FOR JOBS
1210 REM        E$ ........ ERROR FLAG
1220 REM        F() ........ ACTUAL FINISH TIMES
1230 REM        G$() ....... GRAPH FOR HISTOGRAM
1240 REM        H() ........ HISTOGRAM STEPS
1250 REM        I,J,K ....... INDEX VARIABLES
1260 REM        J$() ....... NAMES OF JOBS
1270 REM        L .......... LITTLEST (EARLIEST) LATE START
1280 REM        L(). ........ LENGTH OF JOBS
1290 REM        M .......... MAXIMUM HISTOGRAM STEP
1300 REM        N .......... NUMBER OF JOBS
1310 REM        P$ ........ NAME OF PREDECESSOR
1320 REM        P() ........ PREDECESSOR TABLE
1330 REM        R() ........ RESOURCES FOR JOBS
1340 REM        S() ........ STARTING TIMES
1350 REM        T1 ......... PRESENT TIME
1360 REM        X .......... DUMMY DATA VARIABLE
1370 '
```

```
1380 REM    CONSTANTS:
1390        LET H9 = 4          'HEIGHT OF RESOURCE HISTOGRAM
1395        LET N = 11          'NUMBER OF JOBS
1400        LET S9 = 11         'SPACES TO LEFT EDGE OF CHARTS
1410        LET T9 = 40         'SPACES ACROSS CHARTS (TIME)
1420        LET T$ = "DAYS"     'TIME UNIT LABEL
1430 '
1440 REM    DIMENSIONS:
1450        DIM A(12,2), E(12), F(12),  G$(4,40), H(40)
1460        DIM J$(12), L(12), P(12,12), R(12), S(12,2)
1470 '
1490 REM    MAIN PROGRAM
1500 '
1510        GOSUB 1680          'READ DATA
1520        IF E$ <> "OKAY" THEN 1522 ELSE 1524
1522          GOTO 1640         'BOTTOM OF PROGRAM
1524 '      IFEND
1530        GOSUB 2610          'CHECK STARTS
1540        IF E$ <> "OKAY" THEN 1542 ELSE 1544
1542          GOTO 1680         'BOTTOM OF PROGRAM
1544 '      IFEND
1550        LET C = S(N,1) + L(N) −1
1560        GOSUB 2990          'COMPUTE LATE STARTS
1570        GOSUB 3240          'READ ACTUAL TIMES
1580        GOSUB 3510          'CHECK ACTUAL AND COMPUTE
1582                            'ANTICIPATED STARTS
1590        GOSUB 4170          'COMPUTE ACTUAL LATE STARTS
1600        GOSUB 4420          'PRINT GANTT CHART
1610        GOSUB 4690          'PRINT RESOURCE HISTOGRAM
1620        GOSUB 5220          'PRINT TABLE OF VALUES
1640 '
1650        STOP
1660 '
1670 '
1680 REM    SUBROUTINE:  READ DATA
1690 REM       IN: --
1700 REM      OUT: F$, J$(), L(), N, P(), R(), S()
1710 '
1720 REM    SEE REMARKS IN PROGRAM CPM-II.
1780 '
1800 REM    FOR THE FIRST FEW CASES TO SEE HOW IT WORKS.
1810 '
1820        LET E$ = "OKAY"
1830        READ N
1840        DATA 9
1850 '
```

```
1860      FOR J = 1 TO N
1870          READ X$, S(J,1), L(J), R(J)
1880      NEXT J
1890      DATA BEGIN, 0, 1, 0
1900      DATA RIGHT PIER, 9, 3, 1
1910      DATA LEFT PIER, 12, 3, 1
1920      DATA DAM, 1, 8, 2
1930      DATA CENTER PIER, 9, 7, 1
1940      DATA BEAMS, 16, 2, 2
1950      DATA PLANKS, 18, 5, 2
1960      DATA REMOVE DAM, 23, 1, 1
1970      DATA END, 24, 0, 0
2000 '
2010      READ X
2020      DATA -.9999
2030      IF X <> -.9999 THEN 2040 ELSE 2080
2040        PRINT "WRONG NUMBER OF DATA.  BE SURE TO INCLUDE";
2050        PRINT "A DATA SET FOR THE 'BEGIN' JOB AND THE ";
2060        PRINT "'END' JOB."
2065        LET E$ = "NOT-OKAY"
2070        GOTO 2410     'RETURN
2080 '    IFEND
2085 '
2090      FOR J = 1 TO N
2100          READ J$(J), P$
2110          IF P$ = "NO-MORE" THEN 2190    'LOOP
2120              GOSUB 2440     'FIND  PREDECESSOR AND
2125                             'CHECK NAME
2130              IF E$ <> "OKAY" THEN 2140 ELSE 2150
2140                GOTO 2410    'RETURN
2150 '            IFEND
2160                LET P(J,K) = 1
2170                READ P$
2180          GOTO 2110    'LOOP
2190 '
2200      NEXT J
2210 '
2220      IF J$(N) <> "END" THEN 2230 ELSE 2260
2230        PRINT "NO END JOB"
2240        LET E$ = "NOT-OKAY"
2250        GOTO 2410       'RETURN
2260 '    IFEND
2270 '
```

```
2280      DATA BEGIN, NO-MORE
2290      DATA RIGHT PIER, BEGIN, NO-MORE
2300      DATA LEFT PIER, BEGIN, NO-MORE
2310      DATA DAM, BEGIN, NO-MORE
2320      DATA CENTER PIER, DAM, NO-MORE
2340      DATA BEAMS, LEFT PIER, RIGHT PIER, CENTER PIER, NO-MORE
2350      DATA PLANKS, BEAMS, NO-MORE
2360      DATA REMOVE DAM, PLANKS, NO-MORE
2370      DATA END, PLANKS, NO-MORE
2390 '
2410 RETURN
2420 '
2430 '
2440 REM    SUBROUTINE: FIND PREDECESSOR AND CHECK NAME
2450 REM       IN: E$, J, J$(), P$
2460 REM    OUT: E$, K
2470 '
2480      FOR K = 1 TO J−1
2490         IF J$(K) = P$ THEN 2500 ELSE 2510
2500            GOTO 2550 'LOOP EXIT (OKAY)
2510 '           IFEND
2520      NEXT K
2530      PRINT P$; " DOES NOT PRECEDE "; J$(K)
2540      LET E$ = "NOT-OKAY"
2550 '
2560 RETURN
2570 '
2580 '
2610 REM    SUBROUTINE:  CHECK STARTS
2620 REM       IN: E$, L(), N, P(), S(J,1)
2630 REM    OUT: E$
2640 '
2650 REM    SEE REMARKS IN CPM-II.
2720 '
2730      FOR J = 1 TO N
2740         LET E(J) = 0
2750      NEXT J
2760 '
```

```
2770        FOR J = 1 TO N
2780          LET E = −1
2790          FOR K = 1 TO N
2800            IF P(J,K) < > 0 AND E(K) > E THEN 2810 ELSE 2820
2810              LET E = E(K)
2820 '           IFEND
2830          NEXT K
2840          IF S(J,1) < = E THEN 2850 ELSE 2920
2850            PRINT "STARTING TIME "; S(J,1); " OF JOB #";
2870            PRINT J; " MUST BE LATER THAN "; E; "."
2880            PRINT "PLEASE RETYPE THE STARTING TIMES."
2890            PRINT
2900            LET E$ = "NOT-OKAY"
2910            GOTO 2960 'RETURN
2920 '         IFEND
2930            LET E(J) = S(J,1) + L(J) − 1
2940        NEXT J
2950 '
2960 RETURN
2970 '
2980 '
2990 REM    SUBROUTINE:  COMPUTE LATE STARTS
3000 REM      IN:  L(), N, P(), C
3010 REM    OUT:  S(J,2)
3020 '
3040 REM    SEE REMARKS IN CPM-II.
3090 '
3100        FOR K = N TO 1 STEP −1
3110          LET L = C + 1
3120          FOR J = 1 TO N
3130            IF P(J,K) < > 0 AND S(J,2) < L THEN 3140 ELSE 3150
3140              LET L = S(J,2)
3150 '           IFEND
3170          NEXT J
3180          LET S(K,2) = L − L(K)
3190        NEXT K
3200 '
3210 RETURN
3220 '
3230 '
3240 REM    SUBROUTINE: READ ACTUAL TIMES
3250 REM      IN:  N
3260 REM    OUT:  A(), F(), T1
3270 '
3290 REM    READ ACTUAL START, A(J,1), AND ACTUAL FINISH,
3300 REM    F(J), FOR JOBS WHERE THIS HAS HAPPENED.
3310 '
3320 REM    READ PRESENT TIME, T1.
3330        READ T1
3340        DATA 19
3350 '
```

```
3360        FOR J = 1 TO N
3370            READ X$, A(J,1), F(1)
3380        NEXT J
3390        DATA BEGIN, 0, 0
3400        DATA RIGHT PIER, 9, 11
3410        DATA LEFT PIER, 12, 14
3420        DATA DAM, 1, 8
3430        DATA CENTER PIER, 9, 14
3440        DATA BEAMS, 18, 0
3450        DATA PLANKS, 0, 0
3460        DATA REMOVE DAM, 0,0
3465        DATA END, 0, 0
3470 '
3480 RETURN
3490 '
3500 '
3510 REM    SUBROUTINE: CHECK ACTUAL AND COMPUTE ANTICIPATED
3520 REM               STARTS
3530 REM    IN: A(), E$, F(), L(), N, P()
3540 REM    OUT: A(), E$, F()
3545 '
3550 REM    THE JOB'S START, A(J,1), MUST BE AFTER THE LATEST
3560 REM    OF ITS PREDECESSORS HAS BEEN COMPLETED.
3570 '
3580 REM    A(J,1) ......... ACTUAL (AND ANTICIPATED) START TIME
3590 REM    E(J) ........... END TIME
3600 REM    F(J) ........... ACTUAL (OR ANTICIPATED) FINISH TIME
3610 REM    E ............. GREATEST (LATEST) END TIME
3620 '
3630        FOR J = 1 TO N
3640            LET E(J) — 0
3650        NEXT J
3660 '
3670        FOR J = 1 TO N
3680            LET E = -1
3690            FOR K = 1 TO N
3700                IF P(J,K) = 1 AND E(K) > E THEN 3710 ELSE 3730
3710                    LET E = E(K)
3730 '              IFEND
3740            NEXT K
3750        IF A(J,1) <> 0 AND A(J,1) <= E THEN 3760 ELSE 3800
3760            PRINT "ACTUAL START"; A(J,1); " OF JOB # ";
3770            PRINT J; " WAS STARTED BEFORE ONE OF ITS "
3780            PRINT "PREDECESSORS WAS FINISHED, PLEASE"
3790            PRINT "CHECK."
3800 '          IFEND
3805 '
```

```
3810 REM    AFTER HAVING FOUND THE LATEST OF THE PREDECES-
3820 REM    SORS, TIME E, AND CHECKED FOR MISTAKES,  COMPUTE
3830 REM    ANTICIPATED STARTS AND FINISHES FOR THE FUTURE
3840 REM    'ACTUAL'S (NOW WITH VALUES OF ZERO).
3845 '
3850            IF A(J,1) <> 0 AND F(J) = 0 THEN 3860 ELSE 3900
3860              LET E(J) = A(J,1) + L(J) − 1
3870              LET F(J) = A(J,1) + L(J) − 1
3880              GOTO 4100 'BOTTOM OF CASES
3900 '          IFEND
3910            IF A(J,1) <> 0 AND F(J) <> 0 THEN 3920 ELSE 3950
3920              LET E(J) = F(J)
3930              GOTO 4100 'BOTTOM OF CASES
3950 '          IFEND
3960            IF A(J,1) = 0 AND F(J) = 0 THEN 3970 ELSE 4020
3970              LET A(J,1) = E + 1
3990              LET E(J) = A(J,1) + L(J) − 1
4000              LET F(J) = A(J,1) + L(J) − 1
4010              GOTO 4100 'BOTTOM OF CASES
4020 '          IFEND
4030            IF A(J,1) = 0 AND F(J) <> 0 THEN 4040 ELSE 4090
4040              PRINT "FINISH TIME, "; F(J); " FOR JOB ";
4050              PRINT J; " DOES NOT HAVE A STARTING TIME."
4060              PRINT "PLEASE CORRECT DATA."
4070              LET E$ = "NOT-OKAY"
4080              GOTO 4100 'BOTTOM OF CASES
4090 '          IFEND
4100'
4110            IF E$ <> "OKAY" THEN 4130      'LOOP EXIT
4120        NEXT J
4130 '
4140 RETURN
4150 '
4160 '
4170 REM    SUBROUTINE:  COMPUTE ACTUAL LATE STARTS
4180 REM      IN:  L(), N, P(), C
4190 REM    OUT:  A(J,2)
4200 '
4220 REM    THE LATEST  A JOB CAN BE COMPLETED IS JUST BEFORE
4230 REM    ITS SUCCESSOR MUST START
4240 '
4250 REM    A(J,2) . . . . . . . . LATE START OF JOB J
4260 REM    L . . . . . . . . . . . . . EARLIEST LATE START
4270 '
```

```
4280        FOR K = N TO 1 STEP −1
4290            LET L = C + 1
4300            FOR J = 1 TO N
4310                IF P(J,K) = 1 AND A(J,2) < L THEN 4320 ELSE 4330
4320                    LET L = A(J,2)
4330 '              IFEND
4340            NEXT J
4350            LET A(K,2) = L − (F(K) − A(K,1) + 1)
4360        NEXT K
4380 '
4390 RETURN
4400 '
4410 '
4420 REM    SUBROUTINE:  PRINT GANTT CHART
4430 REM      IN:  J(), L(), N, R(), S(), T1
4440 REM    OUT:  H()
4450 '
4460 REM    PRINT OUT A GANTT CHART THAT SHOWS REGULAR JOBS
4470 REM    AS "X"S, CRITICAL JOBS AS "C"S, AND SLACK ON
4480 REM    REGULAR JOBS AS "."S.  PRINT THE ACTUAL JOB WITH
4490 REM    "*"S OR "C"S.
4491 '
4492 REM    WHILE PRINTING THE CHART, FOR EACH TIME, K,
4494 REM    ACCUMULATE THE ACTUAL RESOURCE, R(J), IN THE
4496 REM    HISTOGRAM STEP, H(K).
4500 '
4510        FOR K = 1 TO T9
4520            LET H(K) = 0
4530        NEXT K
4540 '
4550        PRINT TAB(35); "TIME-";T$
4560        PRINT TAB(S9 + T1); "+−PRESENT TIME"
4570        PRINT "JOB"; TAB(S9); "0        10        20";
4575        PRINT "       30        40"
4580        PRINT TAB(S9); "+−−−−−−−−−+−−−−−−−−−+";
4585        PRINT "−−−−−−−−−+−−−−−−−−−+"
4590 '
4600        FOR J = 2 TO N−1
4610            GOSUB 5420 'PRINT PLANNED JOB
4620            GOSUB 5700 'PRINT ACTUAL (OR ANT.) JOB
4630        NEXT J
4632        PRINT "LEGEND:"; TAB(15); "XXX.. TASK AND SLACK"
4633        PRINT TAB(15); "CCC   CRITICAL TASK"
4635        PRINT TAB(15); "* * *   ACTUAL TASK"
4637        PRINT TAB(15); "−−AAA SLIP AND ANTICIPATED TASK"
4640        PRINT
4650        PRINT
4660 RETURN
4670 '
4680 '
```

```
4690 REM    SUBROUTINE:  PRINT RESOURCE HISTOGRAM
4700 REM      IN:  H(), T1
4710 REM    OUT: --
4720 '
4730 REM    SEE REMARKS IN CPM-II.
4750 '
4760        FOR I = 1 TO H9
4770            FOR K =1 TO T9
4780                LET G$(I,K) = " "
4790            NEXT K
4800        NEXT I
4810 '
4830        LET M = H(1)
4840        FOR K = 2 TO T9
4850            IF H(K) > M THEN 4860 ELSE 4870
4860              LET N = H(K)
4870 '            IFEND
4880        NEXT K
4910 '
4920        LET A = 1
4930        IF M > H9 THEN 4940 ELSE 4950
4940          LET A = M/H9
4950 '      IFEND
4970        FOR K = 1 TO T9
4980            FOR I = 1 TO H9
4990                IF H(K) >= I*A THEN 5000 ELSE 5010
5000                  LET G$(I,K) = "*"
5010 '              IFEND
5020            NEXT I
5030        NEXT K
5040 '
5060        PRINT "RESOURCE USED"
5070        FOR I = H9 TO 1 STEP −1
5080            PRINT TAB(S9); "I";
5090            FOR K = 1 TO T9
5100                PRINT TAB(S9+K); G$(I,K);
5110            NEXT K
5120            PRINT
5130        NEXT I
5140        PRINT TAB(S9); "+---------+---------+";
5145        PRINT "---------+---------+"
5150        PRINT TAB(S9+T1); "+−PRESENT TIME"
5160        PRINT "EACH ASTERISK IS"; A; " UNITS OF RESOURCE."
5170        PRINT
5190 RETURN
5200 '
5210 '
```

```
5220 REM    SUBROUTINE: PRINT TABLE OF VALUES
5230 REM       IN:  C, J$(), L(), N, S()
5240 REM    OUT: --
5250 '
5260       PRINT
5270       PRINT "       ALL FIGURES ACTUAL (OR ANTICIPATED)"
5280       PRINT "JOB        LENGTH OF JOB   RESOURCE USED";
5290       PRINT " START    SLACK"
5300       PRINT
5310       FOR J = 2 TO N-1
5320          PRINT J$(J), F(J) - A(J,1) + 1, R(J), A(J,1);
5330          PRINT TAB(58); A(J,2) - A(J,1)
5335       NEXT J
5340       PRINT
5345       PRINT "PRESENT TIME IS "; T1
5350       PRINT "ESTIMATED TIME TO COMPLETE PROJECT IS ";
5360       PRINT F(N); " "; T$
5390 RETURN
5400 '
5410 '
5420 REM    SUBROUTINE:  PRINT PLANNED JOB
5430 REM       IN:  J, J$, S(), L()
5440 REM    OUT: --
5445 '
5450       PRINT J$(J); TAB(S9); "I";
5460       LET K = S(J,1)
5470       IF S(J,1) - S(J,2) <> 0 THEN 5480 ELSE 5590
5480          IF K > S(J,1) + L(J) - 1 THEN 5520     'LOOP
5490             PRINT TAB(S9+K); "X";
5500             LET K = K + 1
5510          GOTO 5480      'LOOP
5520 '
5530          IF K > S(J,2) + L(J) - 1 THEN 5570     'LOOP
5540             PRINT TAB(S9+K); ".";
5550             LET K = K + 1
5560          GOTO 5530       'LOOP
5570 '
5580          GOTO 5650       'IFEND
5590 '     ELSE
5600          IF K > S(J,1) + L(J) - 1 THEN 5640     'LOOP
5610             PRINT TAB(S9+K); "C";
5620             LET K = K + 1
5630          GOTO 5600       'LOOP
5640 '
5650 '     IFEND
5660       PRINT
5670 RETURN
5680 '
5690 '
```

```
5700 REM    SUBROUTINE:  PRINT ACTUAL (OR ANTICIPATED) JOB
5710 REM      IN:  J, J$(), S(), A(), F(), T1
5720 REM    OUT:  H()
5730 '
5750        PRINT TAB(S9); "I";
5760        LET K = S(J,1)
5770        IF A(J,2) − A(J,1) > 0 THEN 5780 ELSE 6020
5780          IF K > F(J) THEN 5950    'LOOP
5790            IF K >= A(J,1) THEN 5830    'LOOP
5800              PRINT TAB(S9+K); "−";
5810              LET K = K + 1
5820            GOTO 5790 'LOOP
5830 '
5840            IF K < T1 THEN 5850 ELSE 5890
5850              PRINT TAB(S9+K); "*";
5860              LET H(K) = H(K) + R(J)
5870              LET K = K + 1
5880              GOTO 5930IFEND
5890 '            ELSE
5900              PRINT TAB(S9+K); "A";
5910              LET H(K) = H(K) + R(J)
5920              LET K = K + 1
5930 '          IFEND
5940          GOTO 5780    'LOOP
5950 '
5960          IF K > A(J,2) + F(J) − A(J,1) THEN 6000    'LOOP
5970            PRINT TAB(S9+K); ".";
5980            LET K = K + 1
5990          GOTO 5960    'LOOP
6000 '
6010          GOTO 6140    'IFEND
6020 '      ELSE
6030          IF K > F(J) THEN 6130    'LOOP
6040            IF K >= A(J,1) THEN 6080    'LOOP
6050              PRINT TAB(S9+K); "−";
6060              LET K = K + 1
6070            GOTO 6040 'LOOP
6080 '
6081            IF K < T1 THEN 6082 ELSE 6089
6082              PRINT TAB(S9+K); "*";
6083              LET H(K) = H(K) + R(J)
6084              LET K = K +1
6085              GOTO 6115IFEND
6089 '            ELSE
6090              PRINT TAB(S9+K); "A";
6100              LET H(K) = H(K) + R(J)
6110              LET K = K + 1
6115 '          IFEND
6120          GOTO 6030    'LOOP
6130 '
6140 '      IFEND
```

```
6150      PRINT
6160 RETURN
6170 '
6190      END
```

The third critical-path program helps the busy manager actually control the project after it has been planned. In order to do this the actual start and finish for each job are required. In addition, the current date is needed. The results are printed for all to see.

The actual logic of the Gantt chart subroutine is a bit more complex, but not overwhelmingly so. The resource histogram is drawn for the actual, not the planned, activity. So is the table of values.

_____ *Exercises* _____

1. Modify your project as the product managers are doing and try it out with CPM-III.
2. Notice that the data for all three CPM programs could be read from the same file if CPM-I and CPM-II ignored some of the data. Create such a file of data and modify all three programs to read the same file. (Warning: This exercise will require that you learn how to input data from a file on your computer. Consult your local BASIC manual for details.)

   (HINT: For CPM-I the new read line will read and not use a lot of the data. Use the variable X or X$ to do this. For example, the new line might be

   READ #1: X$, X, L(J), X, X, X

   where the only variable you need is L( ).)

TIMELY ESTIMATES

Martin Graves found the project-planning course helped him plan and control his projects. A few months later he saw a lecture on time estimation advertised in the company newsletter and decided to attend. The speaker was a senior scientist in the Hawk Divison's laboratory. His group usually had several research projects going on at once, and over the years he had tried many of the available techniques for scheduling. His talk was just what Graves had been looking for. The lecture hall was crowded.

"Thank you all for coming. Today I'm going to try to answer one of the hardest questions you get asked: 'When can I have that?' You know that if your guess is short, you will be camped in the office all night getting it done. If your guess is too long, you make yourself look like a bumbling dolt. What's the right answer?

"Like most projects your current one is made up of several smaller pieces, some of which are highly unpredictable. This compounds the problem. If you have no way of knowing how long any of the components will take, how can you estimate the whole project with anything but a seat-of-the-pants guess? The answer is three things: the beta distribution, a fundamental theorem of statistics, and a small computer program to make them work for you."

GUESSING THE TASK

"The more steps a project can be split into, the better. Look at each task hard and guess the smallest amount of time this task can reasonably take. Then guess the largest amount of time it could take if everything goes wrong. Finally guess the single most likely amount of time it could take. For example, begin with a job you think might take six days to do. The absolute minimum time if everything went perfectly is four days. If everything goes wrong, you get sick, the equipment breaks, et cetera, the job could stretch out to eighteen days. You reflect on your most likely time and decide it is really eight days.

"If we call the low guess A, the high guess B, and the most likely guess M, we could draw a curve through our three numbers that would look like this" (Fig. 6.3).

"This curve is called a probability-density function. It shows that the likely times range between A and B; in our example, between four and eighteen. The curve also shows that most of the times tend to be

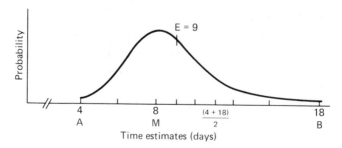

Fig. 6-3 Beta Distribution of Task Completion Time

close to M; in our example, eight. Does that make M the best guess? Not necessarily. Notice that our high estimate is further from the center than our low estimate. In order to get a better estimate of the center we find the midpoint of the extremes, (A + B)/2. The midpoint in our example is (4 + 18)/2 = 11. We average the midpoint with twice the most likely value (2 * M) to arrive at an estimate of the expected value, E. The equation is:

    E = (2*M + (A+B)/2)/3

or, in our example:

    E = (2*8 + (4+18)/2)/3
    E = 9

"Again, E is the expected value. You may assume your density function is a beta distribution and that E is the best estimate of the mean of the distribution."

"Why is the expected value different from the most likely value?" asked someone in the front row.

The speaker nodded, "Good question. The expected value is the better number because it incorporates information about the extremes, A and B, as well as M. So the answer to the apparent paradox is that the expected value is different from the single most likely value because it tries to incorporate all the information into a central value.

"Suppose you repeat your estimates with each of eight additional tasks that compose your project" (Fig. 6.4).

"One of the most interesting theorems in all of statistics assures us that *no matter what the individual distributions are*, the sum of these distributions will tend toward the 'normal,' or Gaussian, bell-shaped distribution. The sum of the above distributions looks like this" (Fig. 6.5).

"This is the curve for the whole project. The expected value, E, is the sum of the E's for the individual tasks, so we know what the expected value for the whole project is. But perhaps the nicest feature about the project's curve is that it has smoothed out the task uncertainties. The times fall off steeply and symmetrically from our expected value. The curve has absorbed the long tails of the individual tasks into a smooth overall estimate. The patron saint of statisticians, Saint Offset, has been at work. The low uncertainties of one task were offset by the high uncertainties of another.

"The calculation of the spread about the expected value is simple. For each task the distance from the low to the high is assumed to be six standard deviations. So:

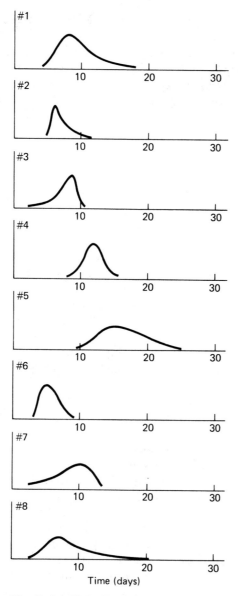

Fig. 6-4   Eight Task Distributions

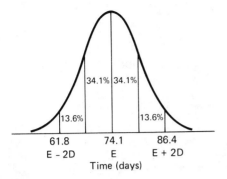

Fig. 6-5   Project Distribution

D = (B − A)/6

in our example:

D = (18 − 4)/6 = 2.333

"The standard deviation is a measure of how spread out the curve is. Task 5 is broad and its standard deviation is large. Task 4 is narrow and its standard deviation is small. The standard deviation of the project as a whole is less than one might expect because of the offsetting effects of adding the individual deviations.

"In fact, you don't add the deviations, you add the square of the deviations. The overall project standard deviation is the square root of the sum of these squares. To illustrate this, I made the following incomplete table:

```
TABLE OF TASKS
#    LOW    LIKELY    HIGH    EXPECTED    D*D
1    4      8         18
2    5      6         12
3    2      9         11
4    8      12        16
5    9      14        32
6    3      4         9
7    2      10        14
8    2      7         18
```

"Notice that two columns are not filled in. In order to fill them in I wrote a small computer program. You can already see what the parts of the program would be.

1. Read in A, B, and M for each task.
2. Compute E and D*D.
3. Tally E and D*D.
4. When everything is complete, print out the results.

"Here's what the program produced:

```
PROJECT EXPECTED TIME IS: 74.1667
STANDARD DEVIATION IS: 6.13505
```

```
                TIME: 61.8966  69.8721  74.1667  78.4612  86.4368
COMPLETION PROB:        2%        24%      50%      76%      98%
```

TABLE OF TASKS

#	LOW	LIKELY	HIGH	EXPECTED	D*D
1	4	8	18	9	5.44444
2	5	6	12	6.83333	1.36111
3	2	9	11	8.16667	2.25
4	8	12	16	12	1.77778
5	9	14	32	16.1667	14.6944
6	3	4	9	4.66667	1
7	2	10	14	9.33333	4
8	2	7	18	8	7.11111

PROJECT TOTALS				74.1667	37.6389

"The heart of the program itself looks like this:

```
310 REM    PERFORM THE COMPUTATIONS
320 '
322        LET S1 = 0
324        LET S2 = 0
330        FOR R = 1 TO R9
340            LET  E = (2*T(R,2) + (T(R,1)+T(R,3))/2) / 3
350            LET T(R,4) = E
360            LET D = (T(R,3) − T(R,1))/6
370            LET T(R,5) = D*D
380            LET S1 = S1 + E
390            LET S2 = S2 + D*D
400        NEXT R
```

"As you can see, I store all my results in a table T(R,C). The first three columns of the table are my low, most likely, and high estimates. The fourth column is my expected value, E. The fifth column is the standard deviation squared."

"What do S1 and S2 do?" asked a person sitting in the back of the room.

"They are my two sums, one for the expected value and one for the deviation squared," explained the speaker.

"Why is the standard deviation squared?" asked someone else.

"Mathematical necessity. I don't want to go into it now, but D must be squared or else the answer will be wrong. That is, you might have a number that estimates the spread but it would not be fair to call it the standard deviation.

"When I have finished working through the tasks, I use the sums to get the two main numbers I am interested in: the project mean or expected value, E, and the project standard deviation, D."

```
410     LET E = S1
420     LET D = SQR(S2)
430 '
```

THE TASKS TOGETHER

"Now let's look at our answer again. We know it's a bell-shaped curve and it has the numbers shown in Fig. 6.5.

"How do we answer management's question, 'When can I have that?' I generally pick the second standard deviation above the mean and say probably before 86 and there's a fifty-fifty chance we will be done by 74. It's surprising how much confidence this can give management, plus, of course, you can sleep nights after you have made a good estimate.

"Figure 6.6 gives a table of values showing how the probability (the area) grows as the standard deviation increases.

"The reason I go high is that I find I still have trouble including every task that needs to be included in my project. Among the tasks that I have forgotten at one time or another are:

- Planning the project
- Meetings to give progress reports
- Training people how to use a new procedure
- Managing and controlling the project

"So I still find my time estimates a little low. However, my last project was 4 percent above the expected value, so I feel that I am finally learning."

Martin Graves took close notes on the meeting. He picked up a copy of the speaker's computer program which was distributed after the talk. He had an idea: he could incorporate these time estimates in his critical-path planning.

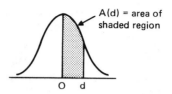

d	A(d)	d	A(d)	d	A(d)	d	A(d)
.0	.000	1.1	.364	2.1	.482	3.1	.4990
.1	.040	1.2	.385	2.2	.486	3.2	.4993
.2	.079	1.3	.403	2.3	.489	3.3	.4995
.3	.118	1.4	.419	2.4	.492	3.4	.4997
.4	.155	1.5	.433	2.5	.494	3.5	.4998
.5	.191	1.6	.445	2.6	.495	3.6	.4998
.6	.226	1.7	.455	2.7	.497	3.7	.4999
.7	.258	1.8	.464	2.8	.497	3.8	.49993
.8	.288	1.9	.471	2.9	.498	3.9	.49995
.9	.316	2.0	.477	3.0	.4987	4.0	.49997
1.0	.341					5.0	.49999997

Area under a normal curve

Fig. 6-6   Area under the Normal Curve*

THE PROGRAM TIMELY

```
100 REM    TIMELY    14 SEPTEMBER 1981    SANDY MCDERMOTT
110 '
120 REM    © COPYRIGHT 1980 JOHN M. NEVISON ASSOCIATES
130 '
140 REM    READ IN A TABLE OF TIME ESTIMATES FOR
150 REM    INDIVIDUAL TASKS. COMPUTE THE TASK MEAN,
160 REM    STANDARD DEVIATION, AND DEVIATION SQUARED.
162 REM    SUM THE MEANS AND THE SQUARED DEVIATIONS.
164 REM    PRINT OUT THE RESULTS.
166 '
```

* Kemeny/Schleifer/Snell/Thompson, *Finite Mathematics with Business Applications*, 2nd edition, © 1972, pp. 131. Reprinted by permission of Prentice-Hall, Inc., Englewood Cliffs, N.J.

```
168 REM    VARIABLES:
170 REM        A . . . . . . . . . . . THE TASK LOW ESTIMATE
174 REM        B . . . . . . . . . . . THE TASK HIGH ESTIMATE
176 REM        C . . . . . . . . . . . THE COLUMN INDEX
178 REM        D . . . . . . . . . . . THE TASK (AND LATER THE PROJECT)
179 REM                          STANDARD DEVIATION
182 REM        E . . . . . . . . . . . THE TASK (AND LATER THE PROJECT)
184 REM                          EXPECTED TIME (THE MEAN)
188 REM        R . . . . . . . . . . . THE ROW INDEX
192 REM        S1,S2 . . . . . . . . SUM VARIABLES
196 REM        T() . . . . . . . . . . THE TABLE OF TASK VALUES
197 '
198 REM    CONSTANT:
199        LET R9 = 8          'NUMBER OF ROWS (TASKS)
200 '
205 REM    READ IN TABLE
210 '
220        FOR R = 1 TO R9
230            READ A, M, B
240            LET T(R,1) = A
250            LET T(R,2) = M
260            LET T(R,3) = B
270        NEXT R
280        DATA 4, 8,  18
282        DATA 5, 6,  12
284        DATA 2, 9,  11
286        DATA 8, 12, 16
288        DATA 9, 14, 32
290        DATA 3, 4,  9
292        DATA 2, 10, 14
294        DATA 2, 7,  18
300 '
310 REM    PERFORM THE COMPUTATIONS
320 '
322        LET S1 = 0
324        LET S2 = 0
330        FOR R = 1 TO R9
340            LET  E = (2*T(R,2) + (T(R,1)+T(R,3))/2) / 3
350            LET T(R,4) = E
360            LET D = (T(R,3) − T(R,1))/6
370            LET T(R,5) = D*D
380            LET S1 = S1 + E
390            LET S2 = S2 + D*D
400        NEXT R
410        LET E = S1
420        LET D = SQR(S2)
430 '
500 REM    PRINT OUT RESULTS
510 '
520        PRINT "PROJECT EXPECTED TIME IS:"; E
530        PRINT "STANDARD DEVIATION IS:"; D
540        PRINT
```

```
550      PRINT "          TIME:";
560      PRINT TAB(12); E−2*D; TAB(18); E−.7*D; TAB(24); E;
570      PRINT TAB(30); E+.7*D; TAB(36); E+2*D
580      PRINT "COMPLETION PROB:   2%   24%    50%    ";
582      PRINT "76%    98%"
590  '
592      PRINT
593      PRINT "TABLE OF TASKS"
595      PRINT " #      LOW     LIKELY   HIGH    EXPECTED D*D"
600      FOR R = 1 TO R9
605          PRINT R;
610          FOR C = 1 TO 5
620              PRINT TAB(C*9); T(R,C);
630          NEXT C
640          PRINT
650      NEXT R
652      PRINT
660      PRINT "PROJECT TOTALS"; TAB(4*9); E;
665      PRINT TAB(5*9); S2
999      END
```

TIMELY neatly separates its three functions into three pieces: read in the data, perform the computations, and print the results. Each piece performs a clear function.

One interesting trick in this program is how the TAB(C*9) function is used to print every 9 spaces. (See the example in "Program Paragraphs" in Appendix A for another version of this trick.)

———— *Exercises* ————————————————————————

1. Use TIMELY to estimate a project of your own by typing in your own data. Do you find the results helpful?
2. Modify the output of TIMELY to print out just the numbers that you personally want to use.

References

1. Daellenbach, Hans G., and George, John A., *Introduction to Operations Research Techniques*, Boston, MA: Allyn and Bacon, 1978.
2. Kemeny, John G., Schleifer, Arthur, Jr., Snell, J. Laurie, and Thompson, Gerald L., *Finite Mathematics with Business Applications*, Second Edition, Englewood Cliffs, NJ: Prentice-Hall, 1972.
3. Levy, F.K., Thompson, G.L., and Wiest, J.D., "The ABC's of the Critical-Path Method," *Harvard Business Review* 41(1963), pp. 98–108.
4. Miller, Robert W., "How to Plan and Control with PERT," *Harvard Business Review*, March–April, 1962.

7

The Model Inventory

Commerce is unexpectedly confident and serene, alert, adventurous and unwearied. It is very natural in its methods withal, far more so than many fantastic enterprises and sentimental experiments, and hence its singular success.

Henry David Thoreau

Louis Mason had been in inventory and materials requirement planning for 20 years. He took great care in training newcomers. During the past five years the materials requirement planning had been completely computerized. Mason had learned the computer side thoroughly. When Simon Wilson offered a small office computer at a discount, Mason was among the first to purchase one. Now he used it to instruct new inventory managers. He found that they learned more when they could experiment first hand with a computer model of inventory. His one-day introduction gave him a chance to stay in touch with the younger crowd and pick up ideas as well as dispense them. His new group had five people in it.

"Inventory accumulates in the interstices of manufacture," he began. "It appears where the raw materials arrive, where the intermediate parts hesitate between processes, and where the finished goods await shipment. Inventory smoothes the whole business's operation; the arrival of raw material, the flow of production, and the departure of finished goods. The problem with inventory is that it seems to grow of its own accord and excess inventory can tie up valuable resources.

"To manage inventory properly you have to know several things about the business: the value of capital, the value of a smooth flow of goods, the value of prompt customer service, and the profit margin of the product. In addition, you must have some idea of the future pattern of supply of raw materials and of demand for finished goods. Finally you must remember that any system you use to gather information and to control inventory will itself cost something to run. So you must know what the system itself will cost.

"While there are likely to be three distinct kinds of inventory in any business—raw material, intermediate products, and finished goods goods—all have similar underlying properties. Each replenishes itself from a supply, each costs something to carry on the shelf, and each incurs a penalty for shortages."

MODEL OF MATERIAL

"The program we will build today will model one inventory. It should prove a simple task for you to build similar models of the various inventories for which you will be responsible. The first problem is to picture what happens with a real inventory. Let's start with an inventory of 55 units:

```
LET I = 55
```

Assume demand will be 5 units a week:

```
LET D = 5
```

Let's have a reorder period of 12 weeks:

```
LET P = 12
```

When we reorder, let's replenish our inventory with 60 units:

```
LET R = 60
```

"So now we begin to see what happens as we run this inventory each week. First, we draw our weekly demand from the inventory:

```
LET I = I − D
```

We check to see if it is time to replenish, and if it is, we replenish our inventory:"

```
IF INT(T/P) = T/P THEN 40 ELSE 50
    LET I = I + R
IFEND
```

"Question," said one of the students. "What is T?"

"T is the current time unit. It goes from week 1 to week 52. The IF . . . THEN . . . ELSE statement asks whether the time, T, is an even multiple of the reorder period, P. If it is, then we reorder.

"Finally we print our current inventory:

```
PRINT I;
```

"We will want to repeat our weekly process 52 times to make a year. So we let time, T, go from 1 to 52 in the program by using two statements:

```
FOR T = 1 TO 52
      .
      .
      .
NEXT T
```

"When we put this all together it looks like this:

```
100      LET I = 55
110      LET D = 5
120      LET P = 12
130      LET R = 60
140      FOR  T = 1 TO 52
150          LET I = I − D
160          IF INT(T/P) = T/P THEN 170 ELSE 180
170              LET I = I + R
180  '      IFEND
190          PRINT I;
200      NEXT T
210      END
```

When we run this program we get a string of numbers that looks like this:

```
50 45 40 35 30 25 20 15 10 5 0 55 50 45 40 35 30 25 20
15 10 5 0 55 50 45 40 35 30 25 20 15 10 5 0 55 50 45
40 35 30 25 20 15 10 5 0 55 50 45 40 35
```

"Now all this is okay, but it might be nice to get a graphic representation of this inventory. If we replace our PRINT I statement with a new piece of code:

```
FOR K = 1 TO I
    PRINT "*";
NEXT K
PRINT
```

We will get a picture of our inventory that looks like this:

```
****************************************************
***************************************************
**********************************************
*******************************************
******************************************
**************************************
*********************************
***************************
*********************
***************
**********
*****


**********************************************************
********************************************************
****************************************************
***********************************************
*****************************************
**************************************
**********************************
*********************
***************
**********
*****


*********************************************************
*****************************************************
***********************************************
******************************************
************************************
*****************************
**************************
*********************
***************
**********
*****
```

```
*********************************************************
****************************************************
**************************************************
**********************************************
**************************************
***********************************
*************************
********************
****************
**********
*****

***********************************************************
*******************************************************
**********************************************************
*******************************************
************************************
```

"A slightly fancier plotting routine will give us this:

```
            +****************************************************
            +************************************************
            +*****************************************
            +*************************************
            +******************************
            +************************
            +********************
            +***************
            +**********
            +*****
            +
        *****+
            +*****************************************************
            +********************************************
            +***************************************
            +**********************************
            +*****************************
            +*************************
            +********************
            +***************
            +**********
            +*****
            +
        *****+
    **********+
```

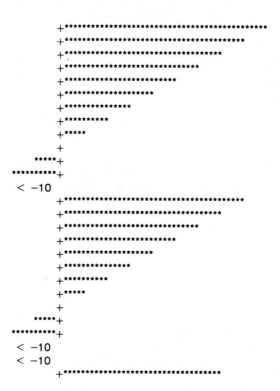

"We can see that on the particular run illustrated above, our inventory fell below zero. We assume here that the stock was back-ordered and the customer was willing to wait until the new shipment came in."

THE PROGRAM INVENTRY

```
100 REM   INVENTRY      17 JULY 1981   LOUIS MASON
110 '
120 REM   © COPYRIGHT 1980 JOHN M. NEVISON ASSOCIATES
130 '
140 '
150 REM   THIS PROGRAM MODELS AN INVENTORY WITH CONSTANT
160 REM   DEMAND AND A REGULAR REORDER PERIOD.
170 '
180 REM   REFERENCE: NEVISON, JOHN M., EXECUTIVE COMPUTING,
190 REM              READING, MA: ADDISON-WESLEY
200 REM              PUBLISHING COMPANY, 1981.
210 '
220 '
```

```
230 REM   VARIABLES:
240 REM       D . . . . . . . . . . . DEMAND (INVENTORY SOLD)
250 REM       I . . . . . . . . . . . . INVENTORY ON HAND
260 REM       K . . . . . . . . . . . INDEX VARIABLE
270 REM       R . . . . . . . . . . . REPLENISHMENT (INVENTORY IN)
280 REM       T . . . . . . . . . . . TIME PERIOD
290 '
300       LET I = 55
310       LET D = 5
320       LET P = 13
330       LET R = 60
340       FOR  T = 1 TO 52
350           LET I = I – D
360           IF INT(T/P) = T/P THEN 370 ELSE 380
370               LET I = I + R
380 '         IFEND
390           GOSUB 440     'PRINT OUT ASTERISKS
400       NEXT T
410       STOP
420 '
430 '
440 REM   SUBROUTINE:  PRINT OUT ASTERISKS
450 REM       IN: I
460 REM       OUT:
470 '
480       IF I < –10 THEN 490 ELSE 510
490         PRINT " < –10"
500         GO TO 680
510 '       IFEND
520       IF I > 50 THEN 530 ELSE 550
530         PRINT " > 50"
540         GO TO 680
550 '       IFEND
560       IF I < 0 THEN 570 ELSE 620
570         FOR K = I TO –1
580             PRINT TAB(10+I);"*";
590         NEXT K
600         PRINT "+"
610         GO TO 680
620 '       IFEND
630       PRINT TAB(10);"+";
640       FOR K = 1 TO I
650           PRINT "*";
660       NEXT K
670       PRINT
680 '
690 RETURN
700 '
710       END
```

The program is built out of the ideas discussed in the text. The IF ... THEN ... ELSE statement sees if it is time to reorder by checking to see if the time in weeks, T, is an even multiple of the reorder period, P. It checks to see if T/P is a whole number:

IF INT(T/P) = T/P THEN . . . ELSE . . .

The fancy printing subroutine displays the inventory between −10 and +50. Note that the printing can be turned off entirely by simply removing the GOSUB statement from the main program.

_____ *Exercises* _____

1. Try INVENTRY with a different initial inventory, a different reorder period or a different reorder amount. Do you see any rules of thumb about how these quantities interact?
2. Modify INVENTRY to reorder an amount that returns inventory to a certain level.
3. Modify INVENTRY to reorder when inventory falls below a certain level.

_____

CARRYING INVENTORY VERSUS REPLENISHING INVENTORY

"Now that we have seen a picture of the raw inventory we can ask the first of a series of questions about how best to handle it. The first question is why we have an annual pattern that lies between these extremes" (Fig. 7.1).

"The answer is that we are trying to strike a balance between two costs, carrying costs and replenishing costs. Carrying costs include such things as the cost of storage, the interest on the money invested in the inventory, the insurance on the goods, the deterioration of some per-

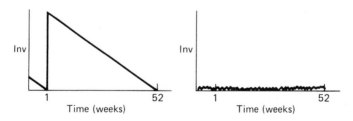

Fig. 7-1   Annual Inventory Extremes

centage of the goods, and the obsolescence of some percentage of the goods. Carrying costs are most frequently computed as a percentage of the dollar value of inventory."

"How many percentages?" another new manager asked.

"All of the percentages are usually averaged together to get one overall figure. Usually the most important of the carrying costs is the cost of the capital invested in inventory. The more money in inventory, the less cash for other parts of the business, the more capital investment in the business, and the less return on investment (ROI) for a given level of return. Keeping the inventory as lean as possible can, in summary:

1. Lower expenses
2. Reduce borrowing
3. Free cash for other business opportunities
4. Lower current assets invested in the business
5. Increase the return on investment of the whole enterprise.

"The other cost is the cost of replenishing the inventory. This cost includes the clerical and handling costs necessary to order and stock a new shipment. It is usual to think of this replenishment cost as a constant. It takes as much ink, paper, and time to write an order for 10 units as it does to write an order for 10,000 units and about as much effort to handle a large order as a small one."

"Is that really true?" asked one of the managers.

"I know it seems difficult to believe at first, but it really does hold true for the great majority of cases. Of course a very large shipment will take longer to unload than a tiny shipment and quality control will be more expensive, but in most cases the bulk of the cost remains overhead. Believe it or not, it is a sound assumption.

"Pushing on now," Mason continued, "we can add these two costs to our inventory model with a little work. The carrying cost, $C1$, is 20 percent of the inventory's annual value, so the weekly carrying cost is .20/52. The cost of each item is $54. We can build up the carrying cost in our program by adding the line:

```
IF I >= 0 THEN ... ELSE ...
    LET C1 = C1 + .20/52 * D1 * I
IFEND
```

where $D1$ is our $54.00 cost of a unit of inventory. The replenishment cost, $C2$, for our example is $80.00. We insert a new line in the program where we reorder:

LET C2 = C2 + 80

"Of course we must begin with C1 at zero and C2 at the inventory's current fraction of replenishment. We need to print out the values each time:

```
LET C1 = 0
LET C2 = I/R * 80
PRINT T; C1; C2,
```

The center of the program now looks like this;

```
435      LET C1 = 0
437      LET C2 = I/R * 80
440      FOR T = 1 TO 52
445         IF I >= 0 THEN 450 ELSE 455
450            LET C1 = C1 + .20/52 * D1 * I
455 '       IFEND
460         LET I = I − D
470         IF T/P − INT(T/P) <= .001 THEN 480 ELSE 500
480            LET C2 = C2 + 80
490               LET I = I + R
500 '          IFEND
510      NEXT T
511      LET C2 = C2 −  (I/R * 80)
515      PRINT T; C1;C2
```

"If we run our program for one year, we find that our costs are:

```
52  313.615  346.667
```

"Now we notice that we can express our initial inventory and our replenishment amount in terms of our replenishment period and the weekly demand:

```
LET D = 5
LET P = 12
LET I = (P−1) * D
LET R = P * D
```

"In fact, we may now find the best reorder period and the related reorder amount, R, by varying P. When we modify the program to do that we get:"

```
100 REM   INV      18 JULY 1981      LOUIS MASON
110 '
120 REM   © COPYRIGHT 1980 JOHN M. NEVISON ASSOCIATES
130 '
140 '
150 REM   THIS PROGRAM EXPLORES WHAT DIFFERENT POLICIES
160 REM   ON INVENTORY WILL COST.
170
180 REM   VARIABLES:
190 REM       C............TOTAL COST
200 REM       C1...........COST OF CARRYING INVENTORY
210 REM       C2...........COST OF REPLENISHING INVENTORY
220 REM       D............DEMAND (INVENTORY SOLD)
230 REM       D1...........THE COST OF AN ITEM OF INVENTORY ($)
240 REM       I............INVENTORY ON HAND
250 REM       K............INDEX VARIABLE
260 REM       P............THE REORDER PERIOD (WEEKS)
270 REM       R............REPLENISHMENT (INVENTORY IN)
280 REM       T............TIME INDEX (WEEKS)
290 '
300 REM   MAIN PROGRAM
310 '
320       PRINT "REPLENISHMENT"
330       PRINT "PERIOD AMOUNT", "CARRYING COST",
340       PRINT "REORDER COST","TOTAL COST"
350       LET D1 = 54
360       LET D = 5
370       FOR P = 9 TO 15
380           LET I = (P−1)* D
390           LET R = P * D
400           LET C1 = 0
410           LET C2 = I/R * 80
420           FOR T = 1 TO 52
430               IF I > = 0 THEN 440 ELSE 450
440                 LET C1 = C1 + .20/52 * D1 * I
450 '             IFEND
460               LET I = I − D
470               IF T/P − INT(T/P) < = .001 THEN 480 ELSE 500
480                 LET C2 = C2 + 80
490                 LET I = I + R
500 '             IFEND
510           NEXT T
520           LET C2 = C2 − (I/R * 80)
530           PRINT P; R, C1, C2, C1+C2
540       NEXT P
550 '
560       END
```

"What do the other two calculations with C2 do?" asked one of the new managers.

"The first equation assigns the portion of the replenishment cost that belongs to the current inventory to the initial value of C2. The second equation takes off the replenishment cost of the inventory left over at the end of the year. The result is that C2 reflects the replenishment costs for exactly the 52-week period."

"A run of the program gives the following results:

REPLENISHMENT PERIOD	AMOUNT	CARRYING COST	REORDER COST	TOTAL COST
5	25	111.115	832	943.115
10	50	251.308	416	667.308
15	75	407.077	277.333	684.41
20	100	562.846	208	770.846
25	125	671.885	166.4	838.285

"We notice that the lowest cost is in the neighborhood of a 15-week reorder period. So we rerun our program FOR P = 9 TO 15 and find:

REPLENISHMENT PERIOD	AMOUNT	CARRYING COST	REORDER COST	TOTAL COST
9	45	223.269	462.222	685.491
10	50	251.308	416	667.308
11	55	282.462	378.182	660.643
12	60	313.615	346.667	660.282
13	65	324	320.	644
14	70	371.769	297.143	668.912
15	75	407.077	277.333	684.41

"Now as we examine the results, we notice when the period is 13 weeks, the lowest total cost occurs. At this point C1 balances C2. This is not an accident. In fact, it makes good sense. We started out trying to balance the reordering cost against the carrying costs.

"So at a known, steady demand of five units a week the inventory can best be managed by reordering at the right time and the right amount to balance the replenishing cost against the carrying costs. The right amount is known as the 'economic order quantity' or EOQ.

"We can draw two conclusions from our discoveries. First, the best replenishment time and amount are 13 weeks and 65 items. Second, that inventory will cost at least $644/year. It cannot be managed for less and still meet demand."

THE PROGRAM INV

(Program appears ealier in text.)

This program illustrates how a simple program can be enhanced to explore new ideas. Especially interesting is the trial-and-error approach to finding the right reorder period, P, by making a loop and trying different values.

_____ *Exercises* _____

1. Begin with INVENTRY and alter it the way Louis Mason did. Run the intermediate versions to be sure you get the same results. When you are finished, your program should look like INV.

_____

REPLENISHMENT DELAY

"Until now our model has assumed that a reorder would get filled at once. If it takes some time to fill an order, we can adjust the program to order ahead. For example, if it takes two weeks to fill an order the program becomes:

```
IF INT ((T+2)/P) = (T+2)/P THEN ... ELSE ...
  LET R$ = "REORDER"
IFEND
 .
 .
 .
IF R$ = "REORDER" AND INT(T/P) = T/P THEN ... ELSE ...
  LET I= I + R
  LET R$ = "WAITING"
IFEND
```

"Now when we run the program it will appear to do everything the same way we have always done it, but the reorder flag, R$, reminds us that the actual reordering will be set up two weeks early."

DEMAND

"The big unknown in inventory is the customer's demand. There are several ways of guessing what the demand will be. If the demand had a pattern last year, then we may assume it will follow a similar pattern this year. For example, suppose the demand looked like this last year:

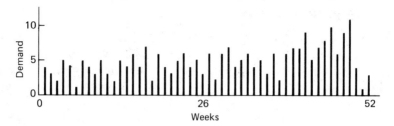

Fig. 7-2   Historical Demand

"We can include this demand history in our program by adding a loop that reads it into the variable D(T):

```
FOR T = 1 TO 52
    READ D(T)
NEXT T
DATA 4, 3, 2, 5, 4, 1, 5, 4, 3, 5
DATA 3, 2, 5, 4, 6, 4, 7, 2, 6, 4
DATA 3, 5, 6, 4, 5, 3, 6, 2, 6, 7
DATA 4, 5, 8, 3, 6, 7, 5, 8, 6, 5
DATA 7, 9, 5, 7, 8, 10, 6, 9, 11, 4
DATA 1, 3
```

"We use this history by moving our demand, D, inside our weekly loop, FOR T = 1 TO 52, and changing it slightly:

```
LET D = D(T)
```

"Now we run our program and we see what our replenishment policy of 65 units every 13 weeks looks like:

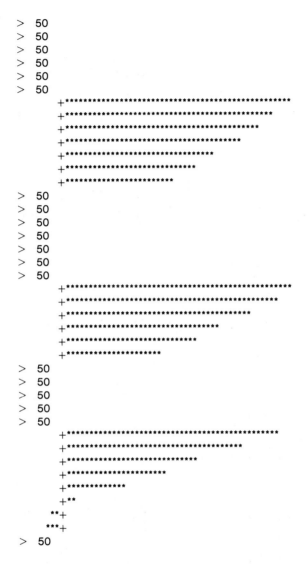

```
>  50
>  50
>  50
>  50
>  50
>  50
        +*****************************************************
        +***************************************************
        +************************************************
        +*********************************************
        +*********************************
        +******************************
        +************************
>  50
>  50
>  50
>  50
>  50
>  50
>  50
        +*******************************************************
        +****************************************************
        +**********************************************
        +**********************************
        +*****************************
        +********************
>  50
>  50
>  50
>  50
>  50
        +*******************************************************
        +*****************************************
        +*****************************
        +*********************
        +*************
        +**
    **+
   ***+
>  50
```

"We could improve our replenishment policy by basing it on last year's demand and ordering what we think will be needed in the next 13 weeks:

LET R = D(T+1) + D(T+2) + D(T+3) ... + D(T+13)

"If we notice that we occasionally run out of stock, we could try reordering 5 percent extra:

```
LET R = D(T+1) + . . . + D(T+13)
LET R = 1.05 * R
```

"Another way of guessing what the customer's demand will be is to assume it is random and make the program reflect that idea. For example, what if the same demands we saw above looked like this:

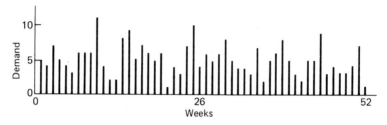

Fig. 7-3   Random Demand

"This random demand can be rearranged to show us the pattern of its distribution:

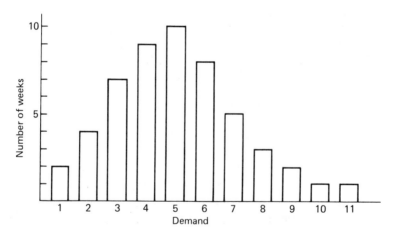

Fig. 7-4   Histogram of the Random Demand

"We could actually arrange our history of demand to reflect our idea of its distribution. We don't need to do this, but it is a way of reminding ourselves that we are thinking of the demand history as a distribution from which we will draw a value at random:

```
FOR T = 1 TO 52
    READ D(T)
NEXT T
DATA 1, 1
DATA 2, 2, 2, 2
DATA 3, 3, 3, 3, 3, 3, 3
DATA 4, 4, 4, 4, 4, 4, 4, 4, 4
DATA 5, 5, 5, 5, 5, 5, 5, 5, 5, 5
DATA 6, 6, 6, 6, 6, 6, 6, 6
DATA 7, 7, 7, 7, 7
DATA 8, 8, 8
DATA 9, 9
DATA 10
DATA 11
```

"If the demand is random like this, we use a random number to pick our demand each time we do a new week:

```
LET R9 = RND(52)
LET D = D(R9)
```

One run of the program using the distribution gave the following result:

```
 >   50
       +*******************************************
       +******************************************
       +************************************
       +******************************
       +***************************
       +********************
       +***************
       +************
       +*
    ***+
 <  −10
```

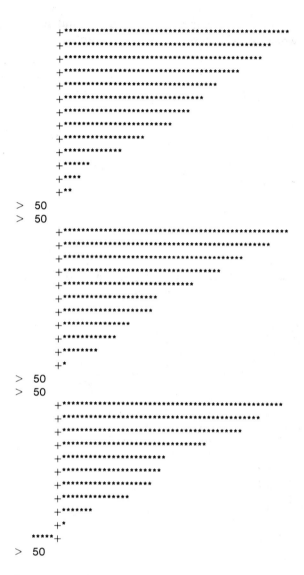

"See that once again we have periods when our inventory has run out. This brings up the important question of how much an out-of-stock item costs the business."

THE PROGRAM INVENT

```
100 REM    INVENT     17 JULY 1981    LOUIS MASON
110 '
120 REM    © COPYRIGHT 1980 JOHN M. NEVISON ASSOCIATES
130 '
140 '
150 REM    THIS PROGRAM MODELS AN INVENTORY WITH RANDOM
160 REM    DEMAND AND A REGULAR REORDER PERIOD.
170 '
180 REM    REFERENCE: NEVISON, JOHN M., EXECUTIVE COMPUTING,
190 REM               READING, MA: ADDISON-WESLEY PUBLISHING
200 REM               COMPANY, 1981.
210 '
220 '
230 REM    VARIABLES:
231 REM        C1 . . . . . . . . . . CARRYING COST
232 REM        C2 . . . . . . . . . . REPLENISHMENT COST
233 REM        C3 . . . . . . . . . . SHORTAGE COST
235 REM        D1 . . . . . . . . . . DOLLAR VALUE OF A UNIT OF INVENTORY
240 REM        D . . . . . . . . . . . DEMAND (INVENTORY SOLD)
245 REM        D() . . . . . . . . . DEMAND DISTRIBUTION
250 REM        I . . . . . . . . . . . . INVENTORY ON HAND
270 REM        P . . . . . . . . . . . REORDER PERIOD
280 REM        R . . . . . . . . . . . REPLENISHMENT (INVENTORY IN)
285 REM        R9 . . . . . . . . . . RANDOM NUMBER
290 REM        T . . . . . . . . . . . TIME PERIOD
300 '
310 REM DIMENSIONS:
320        DIM D(52)
330 '
340 REM READ DEMAND HISTORY
350 '
360        FOR T = 1 TO 52
370            READ D(T)
380        NEXT T
390        DATA 1, 1
392        DATA 2, 2, 2, 2
394        DATA 3, 3, 3, 3, 3, 3, 3
396        DATA 4, 4, 4, 4, 4, 4, 4, 4, 4
398        DATA 5, 5, 5, 5, 5, 5, 5, 5, 5, 5
400        DATA 6, 6, 6, 6, 6, 6, 6, 6
402        DATA 7, 7, 7, 7, 7
404        DATA 8, 8, 8
406        DATA 9, 9
408        DATA 10
410        DATA 11
432 '
```

```
435 REM    INITIALIZE VARIABLES
437 '
440        LET D1 = 54
450        LET P = 13
460        LET R = 65
470        LET I = (P−1)/P * R
480        LET C1 = 0
490        LET C2 = I/R * 80
500        LET C3 = 0
503 '
505 REM    DO THE YEAR'S INVENTORY
507 '
510        FOR  T = 1 TO 52
520            IF I > = 0 THEN 530 ELSE 550
530                LET C1 = C1 + .20/52 * D1 * I
540                GOTO 570
550 '          ELSE
560                LET C3 = C3 + .05 * D1 * (−I)
570 '          IFEND
575            LET R9 = RND(52)
580            LET D = D(R9)
590            LET I = I − D
600            IF INT(T/P) = T/P THEN 610 ELSE 630
610                LET I = I + R
620                LET C2 = C2 + 80
630 '          IFEND
640            GOSUB 700       'PRINT OUT ASTERISKS
650        NEXT T
660        LET C2 = C2 − (I/R*80)
670        STOP
680 '
690 '
```

```
700 REM    SUBROUTINE: PRINT OUT ASTERISKS
710 REM      IN: I
720 REM    OUT:
730 '
740        IF I < -10 THEN 750 ELSE 770
750          PRINT " < -10"
760          GO TO 940
770 '      IFEND
780        IF I > 50 THEN 790 ELSE 810
790          PRINT " > 50"
800          GO TO 940
810 '      IFEND
820        IF I < 0 THEN 830 ELSE 880
830          FOR K = I TO -1
840             PRINT TAB(10+I);"*";
850          NEXT K
860          PRINT "+"
870          GO TO 940
880 '      IFEND
890        PRINT TAB(10);"+";
900        FOR K = 1 TO I
910           PRINT "*";
920        NEXT K
930        PRINT
940 '
950 RETURN
960 '
970        END
```

The program is a revised version of INVENTRY. In it, we use our best reorder period, 13, and amount, 65, to see what happens when the demand, D is distributed in a random fashion with a mean of 5. (The actual distribution in the program approximates a Poisson distribution with a mean of 5.)

By reading any distribution in a fashion similar to the way D(T) is read in the program, and by using a random number the way we do in the program, you can imitate any distribution of demand.

___ *Exercises* ___

1. Run the program a few times to see what different outcomes will look like.
2. Print out the costs associated with different runs. Is it expensive to run out of inventory?

COST OF INCURRING SHORTAGES

"There are many ways of looking at the cost of running out of an item. When an item is out of stock a customer can either back order the item or cancel the order. If the customers cancel their orders, then the cost of shortage is the lost profits plus their ill will. If everyone back orders an item, there remains some ill will generated by the wait for the merchandise. So a shortage is never without a cost.

"A shortage cost can be described as a cost per item or a cost per item per week. If it is a cost per item per week, and if it is calculated as a percentage, it will appear in our program very much like our carrying cost.

560   LET C3 = C3 + .05 * D1 * (−I)

"Here we take our shortage costs to be 5 percent of the cost per item per week."

BALANCING COSTS

"The total cost of the inventory is the sum of the carrying cost, the replacement cost, and the shortage cost. These three costs are always the basic three costs in any inventory problem. The way to find the right level of inventory and the minimum cost is to write the appropriate assumptions into the model of the problem and vary the times and amounts that really can be varied in practice.

"This concludes my remarks for the morning," said Mason. "We are going to spend some time trying out various inventory policies with our model. As you will see, different situations will require different policies."

QUANTITY DISCOUNTS AND CHANGES IN SUPPLY

That afternoon Louis Mason called his new managers together for a brief talk before they resumed work on their inventory models.

"A few of you asked about quantity discounts and the problems of changes in raw material costs. I would like to go over this briefly.

"Frequently a purchasing agent has a chance to buy inventory at quantity discounts. The question arises 'When is the quantity discount a good buy?' The answer is simple. The discount is a good buy if it exceeds the carrying cost of the extra inventory.

"To answer this question in practice, simply add the inventory at its discounted price and check out what the carrying cost on the extra inventory will be. The carrying cost will go up. If the carrying cost goes up by more than the total amount the discount saved, then the discount is not a good deal.

"Another question that frequently confronts an inventory manager is how much to buy now against a future supply price increase. By trying out various possibilities with the inventory model, you can decide when and how much supply to buy as well as what the total projected expense will be.

"I'm done talking now," said Mason. "The rest of the day will be devoted to further work with your inventory models. If you think it is hard to manage the model, you ought to have been here 30 years ago when people learned how to do this by trial and error with the real inventory."

_____ *Exercises* _____

1. Review the first exercises you did with INVENTRY. Try them on INVENT and see if you can find the cheapest way to manage the inventory. (Suggestion: Be sure to change the random distribution to an historical pattern for this work. Refer to the text for a good historical pattern to try.)

2. Figure out how to reorder when half the customers will cancel if an item is out of stock. (Make the shortage cost a percentage of back order per week plus all the profits on the lost sales.)

3. Check the demand history and do a moving check of the average period and reorder the maximum demand.

4. Do a moving check of the past demands in a period and reorder an amount that covers 95 percent of the demands.

5. Work with a limited space for inventory. This limit may increase costs if you must rent additional space to store items.

_____

References

1. Brown, Robert G., *Statistical Forecasting for Inventory Control*, New York: McGraw-Hill, 1959.

2. Magee, John F., "Guides to inventory policy: I. Functions and lot sizes," *Harvard Business Review*, January-February, 1956.

3. Magee, John F., "Guides to inventory policy: II. Problems of uncertainty," *Harvard Business Review*, March-April, 1956.

4. Magee, John F., "Guides to inventory policy: III. Anticipating future needs," *Harvard Business Review*, May-June, 1956.

5. Parzen, Emanuel, *Modern Probability Theory and Its Applications*, New York: Wiley, 1960.

8

The Diet Problem:
Linear Programming

I have always endeavored to acquire strict business habits;
they are indispensable to every man.

Henry David Thoreau

Hawk Division ran a series of one-day seminars for its production managers. Among the topics discussed was linear programming, the mathematical method of scheduling production runs in the plant. The speaker was a young production manager named Helen Anderson.

Five years earlier Anderson had coordinated a project with the data processing department that defined the procedures to control the division's manufacture of military aircraft parts. Her one-day review of the subject was required listening for new production managers.

"The method I am going to discuss today," she began, "can be used to solve problems as diverse as managing a production line, running a national economy, scheduling shipping from warehouses to stores, and assigning people to projects. In order to learn more about this method, we will begin with an everyday version of the question: the diet problem.

"Suppose that instead of all the vitamins, minerals, and nutrients you really need, your diet required only three nutrients: protein, carbohydrate, and fat. Suppose also that there were only five foods you could purchase:

	Grams of Nutrient		
	Protein	Carbohydrate	Fat
Milk (1 qt.)	32	48	40
Hamburger (1 lb.)	112	–	91
Tuna fish (10 oz.)	83	–	21
Potatoes (5 lb.)	45	500	–
Peanut butter (28 oz.)	126	95	262

"Your weekly requirements of these nutrients (in grams) are:

Protein	490
Carbohydrate	1841
Fat	392

"The question is how much of which foods to buy to satisfy your dietary needs.

"The first way to solve this problem is to make a guess and see if it works. With 10 pounds of hamburger, 4 bags of potatoes, and 4 jars of peanut butter, every need in this imaginary diet will be satisfied. So far, however, our solution has ignored a feature that most of us must pay attention to: price. Food costs money.

"For the frugal family, or business, or nation-state, price is a very important consideration. A frequent restatement of the diet problem is: how much of which foods do you buy to satisfy your diet *at the lowest possible price?*

"Recent prices for these foods are (in cents):

1 Quart of Milk	58
1 Pound of Hamburger	139
1 10-Ounce Can of Tuna	189
1 5-Pound Bag of Potatoes	98
1 28-Ounce Jar of Peanut Butter	159

To guess is still possible, but a little harder than before. We now must compare all the nutritionally satisfactory answers to find the cheapest. One way to simplify our guessing is to have a computer program do it for us.

"A computer program to guess the answer will have three equations to figure out what the nutritional value of any particular guess is.

If N1 is protein, N2 is carbohydrate, and N3 is fat, then the equations may look like this:

```
LET N1 = 32*M + 112*H + 83*T + 45*P + 126*B
LET N2 = 48*M + 0*H + 0*T + 500*P + 95*B
LET N3 = 40*M + 91*H + 23*T + 0*P + 262*B
```

"Now we also know that we want a combination only when the protein is more than 490, the carbohydrate is more than 1841, and the fat is more than 392. So we can select our values by using some IF . . . THEN . . . ELSE statements:

```
IF N1 >= 490 AND N2 >= 1841 AND N3 >= 392 THEN . . . ELSE . . .
   LET C = C + 1              'COUNT OKAY CHOICES
IFEND
```

"We decide to try up to 5 quarts of milk, 8 pounds of hamburger, 3 cans of tuna fish, 4 bags of potatoes, and 4 jars of peanut butter. We will try our nutrition check on all the possible combinations of these foods by putting the check in the center of five loops:

```
330        FOR M = 0 TO 5
340          FOR H = 0 TO 8
350            FOR T = 0 TO 3
360              FOR P = 0 TO 4
370                FOR B = 0 TO 4
380                  LET N1 = 32*M + 112*H + 83*T + 45*P + 126 * B
390                  LET N2 = 48*M + 500*P + 95*B
400                  LET N3 = 40*M + 91*H + 23*T + 262*B
410                  IF N1>=490 AND N2>=1841 THEN 420 ELSE 520
420                  IF N3>=392 THEN 431 ELSE 520
431                    LET C = C + 1    'COUNT OKAY CHOICES
520 '                IFEND
530                NEXT B
540              NEXT P
550            NEXT T
560          NEXT H
570        NEXT M
580 '
```

"When this program runs we find that we get 1411 different combinations that will satisfy our minimum requirements. Now we add a little check to see if the current choice is the cheapest, and if it is, we call that our current best choice:

```
440      LET P9 = 58*M+139*H+189*T+98*P+159*B
450      IF P9 < M9 THEN 460 ELSE 515
460        LET M9 = P9
470        LET M1 = M
480        LET H1 = H
490        LET T1 = T
500        LET P1 = P
510        LET B1 = B
515 '    IFEND
```

"When we let this program run and print out the final values for the foods and their total price, we find what we want to buy."

```
OKAY CHOICES: 1411
CHEAPEST CHOICE IS: 8.26
BUY:
 2  QUARTS OF MILK
 0  POUNDS OF HAMBURGER
 0  10-OZ. CANS OF TUNA FISH
 4  5-LB. BAGS OF POTATOES
 2  28-OZ. JARS OF PEANUT BUTTER
```

THE PROGRAM DIET

```
100 REM    DIET    14 SEPTEMBER 1981    HELEN ANDERSON
102 '
104 REM    © COPYRIGHT 1980 BY JOHN M. NEVISON ASSOCIATES
110 '
120 REM    FIND THE AMOUNT OF FOOD THAT WILL
130 REM    MEET MINIMUM NUTRITIONAL NEEDS AS
140 REM    CHEAPLY AS POSSIBLE.
150 '
```

```
160 REM    VARIABLES:
170 REM       B . . . . . . . . . . . PEANUT BUTTER
180 REM       B1 . . . . . . . . . . THE BEST AMOUNT OF  P.B.
185 REM       C . . . . . . . . . . . COUNTER FOR OKAY CHOICES
190 REM       H . . . . . . . . . . . HAMBURGER
200 REM       H1 . . . . . . . . . . THE BEST AMOUNT OF HAMBURGER
210 REM       N1 . . . . . . . . . . THE FIRST NUTRIENT, PROTEIN
220 REM       N2 . . . . . . . . . . THE SECOND NUTRIENT, CARBOHYDRATE
230 REM       N3 . . . . . . . . . . THE THIRD NUTRIENT, FAT
240 REM       M . . . . . . . . . . . MILK
260 REM       M1 . . . . . . . . . . THE BEST AMOUNT OF MILK
261 REM       M9 . . . . . . . . . . THE MINIMUM PRICE
270 REM       P . . . . . . . . . . . POTATOES
290 REM       P1 . . . . . . . . . . THE BEST AMOUNT OF POTATOES
291 REM       P9 . . . . . . . . . . THE PRICE OF THE FOOD
295 REM       T . . . . . . . . . . . TUNA FISH
300 REM       T1 . . . . . . . . . . THE BEST AMOUNT OF TUNA FISH
310 '
320        LET M9 = 10000
325        LET C = 0
327 '
330        FOR M = 0 TO 5
340          FOR H = 0 TO 8
350            FOR T = 0 TO 3
360              FOR P = 0 TO 4
370                FOR B = 0 TO 4
380                  LET N1 = 32*M + 112*H + 83*T + 45*P + 126 * B
390                  LET N2 = 48*M + 500*P + 95*B
400                  LET N3 = 40*M + 91*H + 23*T + 262*B
410                  IF N1>=490 AND N2 >=1841 THEN 420 ELSE 520
420                  IF N3>=392 THEN 431 ELSE 520
431                    LET C = C + 1      'COUNT OKAY CHOICES
440                    LET P9 = 58*M+139*H+189*T+98*P+159*B
450                    IF P9 < M9 THEN 460 ELSE 515
460                      LET M9 = P9
470                      LET M1 = M
480                      LET H1 = H
490                      LET T1 = T
500                      LET P1 = P
510                      LET B1 = B
515 '                  IFEND
520 '                IFEND
530                NEXT B
540              NEXT P
550            NEXT T
560          NEXT H
570        NEXT M
580 '
```

```
590     PRINT "OKAY CHOICES: "; C
600     PRINT "CHEAPEST CHOICE IS: "; M9/100
610     PRINT "BUY:"
620     PRINT M1; " QUARTS OF MILK"
630     PRINT H1; " POUNDS OF HAMBURGER"
640     PRINT T1; " 10-OZ. CANS OF TUNA FISH"
650     PRINT P1; " 5-LB. BAGS OF POTATOES"
660     PRINT B1; " 28-OZ. JARS OF PEANUT BUTTER"
670  '
680     END
```

DIET illustrates how a computer program can apply simple brute force to solve a problem. No one would ever try to calculate these combinations by hand. However, it is easy to state the method in such a way that the computer can do the work for us.

The variable M9 tracks the minimum price so that when we are through we have the minimum price and amount of each food we should buy.

_____ *Exercises* _____

1. Change the upper limit on potatoes to 10 and rerun the program. Did it help?
2. Eliminate potatoes from the diet and see what happens. Is the result much more expensive? Why?

_____

REFLECTION

"Now let's explore what we have done. When we said FOR M = 0 TO 5 quarts we tried six different possibilities for milk. For each of these milk possibilities we tried nine possibilities of hamburger. Between these two foods we tried $(5+1) * (8+1) = 6 * 9 = 54$ possibilities. With all five foods we tried 5400 possibilities.

"The problem with our method is that it only works for a small number of foods and a small number of nutrients. If we add only five more foods and let each of them vary from 0 to 9, we have increased the number of cases from 5000 to 500 million! We might well starve to death waiting for the computer to calculate a diet problem of any significant size."

THE TUCKER TABLEAU

"As we begin to search for an efficient way to solve our problem when the numbers grow large, we have to add one critical element to our assumptions. We must be able to buy half a bag of potatoes. That is to say, we must be able to purchase a *fractional unit* of food. If this assumption bothers anyone, we can round our numbers up to whole numbers and explore the results after we have found the fractional, exact answer.

"The particular kind of table that we must build to solve our diet problem is called in mathematics an n-simplex. The only reason the word is important is it names the set of rules that we will follow to solve our problem: the simplex method. The method is best applied to an arrangement of our table called a Tucker Tableau. So first we must arrange our data in a Tucker Tableau. Then after it has been arranged, we will apply the simplex method to it. As we apply the simplex method, we will build pieces of a BASIC program to carry out the calculations. Finally we will explore several interesting aspects of the solutions.

"Our initial problem set up in a Tucker Tableau looks like this (Fig. 8.1), where $V1, \ldots, V5$ are volumes of food; $U1$, $U2$, and $U3$ are any surplus nutrients; $X1$, $X2$, and $X3$ are the imputed cost of each nutrient; and $Y1, \ldots, Y5$ are slack in the prices. I'll explain these terms a bit later.

"After we have worked out the answers using the simplex method, our tableau will look like this" (Fig. 8.2).

"What the simplex method gives us is values for the border variables. Our most important variables are the V's, the volumes of each

	Protein x_1	Carbo x_2	Fat x_3	-1	
Milk v_1	32	48	40	58	$= y_1$
Hamburg v_2	112	0	91	139	$= y_2$
Tuna v_3	83	0	23	189	$= y_3$
Potato v_4	45	500	0	98	$= y_4$
Peanut v_5	126	95	262	159	$= y_5$
Minimum requirement -1	490	1841	392		
	u_1	u_2	u_3		

Nutrients (grms) Cost (¢)

Fig. 8-1   The Initial Tucker Tableau

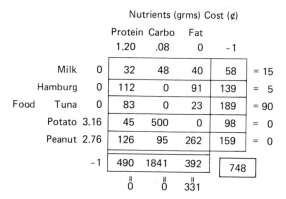

Fig. 8-2   The Final Tucker Tableau

food. In this example we buy 3.16 bags of potatoes and 2.76 jars of peanut butter and nothing else. If we do that, we will have exactly the right amount of protein (column one), exactly the right amount of carbohydrate (column two), and 331 surplus grams of fat (column three). The cost of this will be $7.48 (column four). Because we arrive at these answers using the simplex method, we are guaranteed this is the *lowest possible cost*.

"The way to verify a column is to multiply each entry by the volume, V, and add down the page. If you notice some small inaccuracies, they are due do rounding errors in the computer. These inaccuracies should warn you that computational accuracy is very important when a computer applies the simplex method.

"The question remains, 'How do we get the answers?' We get them by using the eight-step simplex method. The method manipulates the Tucker Tableau by switching rows and columns until it arrives at the answer. On each pass through the tableau the program will exchange a row and a column. This means that our border variables will move around. U's and V's will exchange places and X's and Y's will exchange places. When the program is finished, the U's and V's on the bottom, and the X's and Y's on the side will have the values found in the modified tableau. The total price appears in the lower right-hand corner of the final tableau.

"We take these answers from the final tableau and write them down in their original places in the initial tableau to see what the solution looks like."

THE EIGHT-STEP SIMPLEX METHOD

"1. Set up a Tucker Tableau. For our problem this will look like this:

	x_1	x_2	x_3	-1	
v_1	$t_{1,1}$	$t_{1,2}$	$t_{1,3}$	c_1	$= y_1$
v_2	$t_{2,1}$	$t_{2,2}$	$t_{2,3}$	c_2	$= y_2$
v_3	$t_{3,1}$	$t_{3,2}$	$t_{3,3}$	c_3	$= y_3$
v_4	$t_{4,1}$	$t_{4,2}$	$t_{4,3}$	c_4	$= y_4$
v_5	$t_{5,1}$	$t_{5,2}$	$t_{5,3}$	c_5	$= y_5$
	b_1	b_2	b_3	b_4	
	$\parallel$	$\parallel$	$\parallel$		
	u_1	u_2	u_3		

Fig. 8-3   Symbolic Tucker Tableau

"When M is the number of rows, and N is the number of columns, the setup looks like this in BASIC:

```
530     FOR I = 1 TO M
540          FOR J = 1 TO N
550               READ T(I,J)
560          NEXT J
570          READ C(I)
580     NEXT I
590     FOR J = 1 TO N
600          READ B(J)
610     NEXT J
620     DATA  32,  48,  40,   58
622     DATA 112,   0,  91,  139
624     DATA  83,   0,  23,  189
626     DATA  45, 500,   0,   98
628     DATA 126,  95, 262,  159
629 '
630     DATA 490,1841, 392
632 '
```

"The B(J)s are called the indicators. They will be important later.

"2. Find the column of the largest positive indicator and call that column P2, the pivot column. (If none of the indicators is positive, you have arrived at the solution, so stop.)

"In BASIC doing this would look like this:

```
680 REM    STEP 2. FIND PIVOT COLUMN OR STOP
690 '
700       LET M1 = 0
710       LET P2 = 0
720 '
730       FOR J = 1 TO N
740          IF B(J) > M1 THEN 750 ELSE 770
750             LET M1 = B(J)
760             LET P2 = J
770 '        IFEND
780       NEXT J
790       IF M1 < = 0 THEN 800 ELSE 810
800          GOTO 1360      'LOOP EXIT
810 '     IFEND
820 '
```

"When the program has completed step 2, we have either arrived at an answer or selected a pivot column, P2. The word pivot is used here to denote the element that will determine which row will switch with which column. This switching is called pivoting.

"3. Check the pivot column from $T(1,P2)$ to $T(M,P2)$. If all the entries are negative or zero, the problem has no solution. Find the row with the positive $T(I,P2)$ whose cost per unit $(C(I)/T(I,P2))$ is lowest and call that row P1, the pivot row.

```
830 REM    STEP 3. FIND PIVOT ROW OR STOP
835 '
840       LET M2 = 1000000
850       LET P1 = 0
860       FOR I = 1 TO M
870          LET S(I) = T(I,P2)    'STORE COPY FOR STEP 6
880          IF T(I,P2)>0 AND C(I)/T(I,P2)<=M2 THEN 900 ELSE 920
900             LET M2 = C(I)/T(I,P2)
910             LET P1 = I
920 '        IFEND
930       NEXT I
935       LET S(M+1) = B(P2)    'STORE COPY FOR STEP 6
940       IF P1 = 0 THEN 950 ELSE 970
950          PRINT "NO SOLUTION EXISTS"
960          STOP
970 '     IFEND
980 '
990       LET P = T(P1,P2)    'PIVOT ELEMENT
1000 '
```

"Now we have arrived at a pivot row, P1, and a pivot column, P2, and a pivot element, $T(P1,P2)$. We assign the value of the pivot element to the variable called P.

"4. Divide the pivot row by the pivot element.

```
1010 REM    STEP 4. DIVIDE PIVOT ROW BY PIVOT ELEMENT
1015 '
1020        FOR J = 1 TO N
1030            LET T(P1,J) = T(P1,J)/P
1040        NEXT J
1050        LET C(P1) = C(P1)/P
1060 '
```

"5. Take each other row and subtract the pivot column element, $T(I,P2)$, times the pivot row, from it.

```
1070 REM    STEP 5. READJUST ROWS TO NEW PIVOT ROW
1075 '
1080        FOR I = 1 TO M
1090            IF I < > P1 THEN 1100 ELSE  1140
1100                LET X = T(I,P2)
1110                FOR J = 1 TO N
1120                    LET T(I,J) = T(I,J) − X*T(P1,J)
1130                NEXT J
1132                LET C(I) = C(I) − X*C(P1)
1140 '          IFEND
1150        NEXT I
1160 '
1170        LET X = B(P2)
1180        FOR J = 1 TO N
1190            LET B(J) = B(J) − X*T(P1,J)
1200        NEXT J
1205        LET B(N+1) = B(N+1) − X*C(P1)
1210 '
```

"6. Substitute for each entry in the pivot column, $T(I,P2)$, the negative of the original entry over the pivot, $-T(I,P2)/P$, and for the pivot entry itself, its inverse, $1/P$.

```
1220 REM    STEP 6. RE-DO THE PIVOT COLUMN
1225 '
1230        FOR I = 1 TO M
1240            LET T(I,P2) = − S(I)/P
1250        NEXT I
1260        LET B(P2) = − S(M+1)/P
1270        LET T(P1,P2) = 1/P
1280 '
```

"In our BASIC program we saved a spare copy, $S( )$, of our pivot column so we could use it here.

"7. Interchange the markers of the horizontals and the verticals, the rows and the columns. By setting these up initially to look like this:

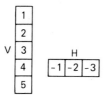

Fig. 8-4   Initial Row (Vertical) and Column (Horizontal) Markers

We are able to exchange, for example, row four and column two like this:

Fig. 8-5   Row (Vertical) and Column (Horizontal) Markers after an Exchange

```
1290 REM   STEP 7. EXCHANGE THE ANSWER INDICATORS
1295 '
1300      LET X = H(P2)
1310      LET H(P2) = V(P1)
1320      LET V(P1) = X
1330 '
```

"8. Repeat steps 2 through 8 until done. When we actually run the program on this particular problem the program goes around the cycle four times before arriving at a solution. While the method is complicated, it takes less work than our 5000-trial, brute-force method."

```
650 REM    MAIN LOOP
660 '
670        FOR L = 1 TO 10000
                 .
                 .
                 .
1340 REM    STEP 8.  REPEAT STEPS 2 THROUGH 8
1350       NEXT L
1355       PRINT "DID NOT FIND AN ANSWER"
1357       STOP
1360 '
```

THE ANSWERS

"The answers are printed by the program. It remains for us to place them correctly around the border of our initial tableau. The V's and the U's tell us most of what we want to know. The V's indicate how much of which food to buy. In this diet the answers are 3.16 bags of potatoes and 2.76 jars of peanut butter, and nothing else. The U's tell us that we will have no surplus protein, no surplus carbohydrates, and 331 grams of surplus fat.

"The X's and Y's have a small bit to add as well. The X's tell us the cost per ingredient in our low-budget diet. At our solution, the cost of the next gram of protein is \$.0119, the cost of the next gram of carbohydrate is \$.0008, and the cost of the next gram of fat is zero. The fat is free because at the solution we have a surplus of fat.

"The Y's are the slack in different food prices. The foods we use in the solution, potatoes and peanut butter, have no slack in their prices. They were priced low enough that they were used in the diet. $Y(1)$ at 15.5 indicates that a quart of milk would have to drop in price 15.5 cents to be cheap enough to be included in our diet. A pound of hamburger would have to be 5 cents cheaper; a can of tuna fish, 89 cents cheaper."

A RELATED PROBLEM

"The diet problem's tableau can be abbreviated to this (Fig. 8.6) where the problem is how much of each row to use in order to meet the minimum requirements at the lowest total cost.

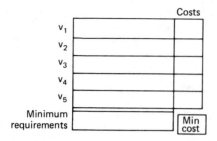

Fig. 8-6   Abbreviated Tucker Tableau for Low-Cost Problem (Diet)

"There is a sister problem to our diet problem where the tableau looks like this:

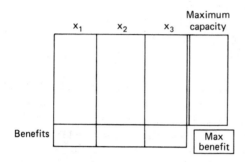

Fig. 8-7   Abbreviated Tucker Tableau for High-Benefit Problem (Dial)

"Here the problem is how much of each column to use to stay within the maximum capacities and achieve the highest total benefit."

DIAL A BENEFIT

"Imagine for a moment that we have a magical machine for creating an island agriculture. Our machine has three dials: a protein dial, a carbohydrate dial, and a fat dial. If we turn the protein dial to 1 we get:

> 32 cows
> 112 steers
> 83 fish
> 45 vegetables
> 126 nuts

and 49 units of political advantage.

"If we turn the carbohydrate dial to 1 we get:

> 48 cows
> 0 steers
> 0 fish
> 500 vegetables
> 95 nuts

and 184.1 units of political advantage.

"If we turn the fat dial to 1 we get:

> 40 cows
> 91 steers
> 23 fish
> 0 vegetables
> 262 nuts

and 39.2 units of political advantage.

"When we wish to obtain the most political advantage we turn all the dials as high as they can go. But we can't really do that because our island has limits. They are rather constraining:

> cows $<=58$
> steers $<=139$
> fish $<=189$
> vegetables $<=98$
> nuts $<=159$

"So our problem becomes how to set the dials of our machine to obtain the most political advantage within the limits of the island and the characteristics of the machine itself. We can summarize our results like this" (Fig. 8.8).

"Of course, if we know how to set the dials, we will know how much total political advantage is possible. Now how do we solve this problem?

	Dials			
	#1 x_1	#2 x_2	#3 x_3	Island capacity −1
Cows v_1	32	48	40	58	= y_1
Steers v_2	112	0	91	139	= y_2
Fish v_3	83	0	23	189	= y_3
Vegetables v_4	45	500	0	98	= y_4
Nuts v_5	126	95	262	159	= y_5
Political advantage	49	184.1	39.2		
	‖ u_1	‖ u_2	‖ u_3		

Fig. 8-8   Tucker Tableau for the Dial Problem

"There are several questions to ask here. What method can we use? Will it give us the right answer? How close is it to the method we used in the diet problem?

"The answer to these questions is really quite surprising: the simplex method will work exactly the way we used it before. In fact, given that the numbers in the new problem are similar to the numbers in the diet problem, the answers will be similar numbers with a new interpretation. We will set our dials as follows:

Protein	Carbohydrate	Fat
1.19	.08	0

The total political advantage we make is:

1.19 x 49 + .08 x 184.1 + 0 x 39.2 = 74.8

"We have just stumbled onto one of the most remarkable discoveries of the mathematics behind the simplex method. For every minimum problem (the diet problem) there is a dual maximum problem (the dial problem) and, if a solution exists, *both problems have the same solution*!

"The border variables have a new interpretation in our dial problem. The X's are where we set the dials to get the most benefit out of our island agriculture machine. The Y's are slack items at the solution. We find we have no room for any more vegetables or nuts, but we do have room for about 15 extra cows, 5 extra steers, and 90 extra fish.

"The V's are the imputed contribution rate at the solution. The vegetables contribute 3.16 units of political advantage per vegetable. The nuts contribute 2.76 units of political advantage each. The other items contribute, but at our solution they still have plenty of slack, so their imputed rate at the solution is zero.

"The U's indicate surplus advantage. Dial 1 and dial 2 have no surplus because they are used in the solution. The rates at the solution would force dial 3 to produce 33.1 units of advantage more than it can, so it is excluded from the solution. Dial 3 is set at zero."

APPLICATIONS

"Are there many places these problems apply?" one manager asked.

"Sure," said Anderson. "We mentioned a few at the beginning of the talk. Here's how some of them would fit what we have just done.

"For the diet problem: an economy must supply certain amounts of food, clothing, and shelter. Both the public and the private sector can provide a mix of all three. The public sector is more expensive than the private sector. How much of each do you use to cover the required needs for the lowest cost?

"For the dial problem: several crops require different mixes of labor and capital investment and yield different net profits. The farmer has only a certain amount of capital to invest and a limited amount of labor. How much of each crop is it best for him to plant?

"Another dial problem: three products require parts made on each of four machines. Each product has its own distinct profit. The machines are available only a certain number of hours each week. What amounts of each product maximize the total profit?"

"Thanks, those are interesting examples."

"Yes, they are. Our simple technique will solve a large variety of problems. After lunch I will show you several examples. Right now I want to show you a limitation of our present method."

EQUALITIES

"All our work so far has been with well behaved systems. What we mean by well-behaved is that the right-hand column (either costs or upper limits) has always been filled with positive numbers. The world is not so nice in practice.

"Why should we get negative numbers in that column? Consider for a moment the second limitation in our 'dial' problem. The limitation was that we could have no more than 139 steers. We can express this limitation by looking at the second row in the Tucker Tableau for the problem and pulling out the following equation:

$$112 \times X1 + 0 \times X2 + 91 \times X3 =< 139$$

That is, whatever our final dial settings for $X1$, $X2$, and $X3$, they can't be turned up any further than the island limit of 139 steers.

"But what if we wanted to have exactly 139 steers? How could we do that? The answer is by adding another restriction to our tableau. We will do this in three steps.

"The first step is the restriction itself. If we want exactly 139 steers and we have already specified the solution must not exceed 139, then we have to add a new requirement that it not fall short of 139. We can express that idea like this:

$$112 \times X1 + 0 \times X2 + 91 \times X3 >= 139$$

"To put this in our tableau, we must reverse the inequality, so the second step is to express the same thing in another way:

$$-112 \times X1 - 0 \times X2 - 91 \times X3 =< -139$$

"The third step is to include this equation in our tableau at the bottom so it looks like this" (Fig. 8.9).

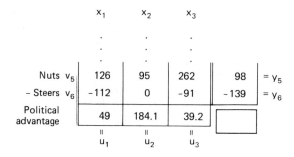

Fig. 8-9 Addition to the Tucker Tableau

"When we solve this problem we find the answer is a little different:

Protein dial	Carbohydrate dial	Fat dial
1.24	.03	0.00

We have turned up our protein dial, X1, enough to make exactly 139 steers. Our new solution still satisfies the other conditions because we turned down the carbohydrate dial.

"But now we run into the problem we mentioned initially. We have a negative number in our right-hand column. We modify our simplex method to take care of these rows first by checking for a negative number and, if we find it, choosing our pivot element from that row. After all the negative numbers are eliminated we use our method as before. Our new check looks like this in BASIC:

```
2030 REM    SUBROUTINE: CHECK TABLEAU
2040 REM      IN: B(), C(), H(), M, N, T(), V()
2050 REM    OUT: B(), C(), H(), T(), V()
2060 '
2070       LET G$ = "OKAY" 'LOOP
2080          FOR I = M TO 1 STEP −1
2090             IF C(I) < −.00001 THEN 2110 ELSE 2130
2110                GOSUB 3620      'TABLEAU REWORK
2120                LET G$ = "RETRY"
2130 '             IFEND
2140          NEXT I
2150          IF G$ = "OKAY" THEN 2170      'LOOP EXIT
2160       GOTO 2070          'LOOP
2170 '
2180 RETURN
2190 '
2200 '
```

"Our new pivot element selection looks like this:"

```
3620 REM    SUBROUTINE: TABLEAU REWORK
3630 REM      IN: B(), C(), H(), I, M, N, T(), V()
3640 REM    OUT: B(), C(), H(), T(), V()
3650 '
3660 '
3670        LET P1 = I
3680        FOR J = 1 TO N
3690            IF T(P1,J)  < −.00001 THEN 3700 ELSE 3710
3700                GOTO 3760 'OKAY EXIT
3710 '          IFEND
3720        NEXT J
3730        PRINT "MAXIMUM PROBLEM HAS NO FEASIBLE SOLUTION,"
3740        PRINT "MINIMUM PROBLEM HAS AN UNBOUNDED SOLUTION."
3750        STOP
3760 '
3770        LET P2 = J
3780 '
3790        FOR I = 1 TO M
3800            LET S(I) = T(I,P2)      'STORE FOR STEP 6
3810        NEXT I
3820        LET S(M+1) = B(P2)
3830 '
3840        LET M2 = C(P1)/T(P1,P2)
3850        FOR I = P1 TO M
3860            IF (C(I)/T(I,P2)) < = M2 THEN 3870 ELSE 3900
3870            IF T(I,P2) > = .00001 THEN 3880 ELSE 3900
3880                LET P1 = I
3890                LET M2 = C(I)/T(I,P2)
3900 '          IFEND
3910        NEXT I
3920        LET P = T(P1,P2)
3930        GOSUB 2730       'STEPS 4-7
3940 RETURN
3950 '
3960 '
```

"With these changes our program SIMPLEX will solve any tableau that has a solution. Note in passing that we don't have to worry about adding extra columns to 'diet' problems. Negative numbers on the bottom row are all right."

THE PROGRAM SIMPLEX

```
1200 REM     SIMPLEX    14 SEPTEMBER 1981   HELEN ANDERSON
1210 '
1220 REM     © COPYRIGHT 1980  BY JOHN M. NEVISON ASSOCIATES
1230 '
1240 '
1250 REM   THIS PROGRAM SOLVES A LINEAR PROGRAMMING
1260 REM   PROBLEM USING A TUCKER TABLEAU AND THE SIMPLEX
1270 REM   METHOD.
1280 '
1290 REM   REFERENCE: NEVISON, JOHN M., EXECUTIVE COMPUTING,
1300 REM              READING, MA: ADDISON-WESLEY PUBLISHING
1310 REM              COMPANY, 1981.
1320 '
1330 REM   VARIABLES:
1340 REM     B() ........ THE BENEFIT (OR REQUIREMENT) ROW
1350 REM     C() ........ THE CAPACITY (OR COST) COLUMN
1360 REM     G$.......... THE GO-AHEAD FLAG
1370 REM     H() ........ HORIZONTAL ANSWER GUIDE
1380 REM     I,J ........ LOOP INDEX VARIABLES
1390 REM     L .......... THE MAIN PROGRAM LOOP INDEX
1400 REM     M1 ........ THE MAXIMUM ELEMENT
1410 REM     M2 ........ THE MINIMUM ELEMENT
1420 REM     M........... NUMBER OF ROWS IN TABLE
1430 REM     N........... NUMBER OF COLUMNS IN TABLE
1440 REM     P .......... THE PIVOT ELEMENT VALUE
1450 REM     P1.......... THE PIVOT ROW
1460 REM     P2.......... THE PIVOT COLUMN
1470 REM     S() ........ SAVED COPY OF PIVOT COLUMN
1480 REM     T() ........ THE TUCKER TABLEAU TABLE
1490 REM     V() ........ VERTICAL ANSWER GUIDE
1500 REM     X .......... TEMPORARY VARIABLE
1510 '
1520 REM   MAIN PROGRAM
1530 '
1540       GOSUB 1610     'STEP 1
1550       GOSUB 2030     'CHECK TABLEAU
1560       GOSUB 2210     'STEPS 2-8
1570       GOSUB 3190     'PRINT THE ANSWERS
1580       STOP
1590 '
1600 '
```

```
1610 REM    SUBROUTINE: STEP 1
1620 REM      IN: --
1630 REM    OUT: B(), C(), H(), M, N, T(), V()
1640 '
1650 REM    SET UP ANSWER GUIDES AND TUCKER TABLEAU
1660 '
1670 REM    PLEASE BE SURE THAT ANY ROWS WITH NEGATIVE
1680 REM    LAST COLUMNS ARE AT THE *BOTTOM* OF THE TABLEAU.
1690 '
1700        DIM B(4), C(6), H(3), T(6,3), V(6)
1710 '
1720        LET M = 6
1730        LET N = 3
1740 '
1750        FOR I = 1 TO M
1760           LET V(I) = I
1770        NEXT I
1780        FOR J = 1 TO N
1790           LET H(J) = −J
1800        NEXT J
1810 '
1820        FOR I = 1 TO M
1830           FOR J = 1 TO N
1840              READ T(I,J)
1850           NEXT J
1860           READ C(I)
1870        NEXT I
1880        FOR J = 1 TO N
1890           READ B(J)
1900        NEXT J
1910        DATA   32,  48,  40,    58
1920        DATA  112,   0,  91,   139
1930        DATA   83,   0,  23,   189
1940        DATA   45, 500,   0,    98
1950        DATA  126,  95, 262,   159
1960        DATA −112,   0, −91,  −139
1970 '
1980        DATA 490,1841, 392
1990 '
2000 RETURN
2010 '
2020 '
```

```
2030 REM    SUBROUTINE:  CHECK TABLEAU
2040 REM      IN: B(), C(), H(), M, N, T(), V()
2050 REM    OUT: B(), C(), H(), T(), V()
2060 '
2070     LET G$ = "OKAY" 'LOOP
2080        FOR I = M TO 1 STEP −1
2090           IF C(I) < −.00001 THEN 2110 ELSE 2130
2110              GOSUB 3620        'TABLEAU REWORK
2120              LET G$ = "RETRY"
2130 '           IFEND
2140        NEXT I
2150        IF G$ = "OKAY" THEN 2170      'LOOP EXIT
2160     GOTO 2070          'LOOP
2170 '
2180 RETURN
2190 '
2200 '
2210 REM    SUBROUTINE: STEPS 2-8
2220 REM      IN: B(), C(), H(), M, N, T(), V()
2230 REM    OUT: B(), C(), H(), T(), V()
2240 '
2250     FOR L = 1 TO 10000
2260 '
2270 REM    2. FIND PIVOT COLUMN OR STOP
2280 '
2290        LET M1 = 0
2300        LET P2 = 0
2310 '
2320        FOR J = 1 TO N
2330           IF B(J) > M1 THEN 2340 ELSE 2360
2340              LET M1 = B(J)
2350              LET P2 = J
2360 '           IFEND
2370        NEXT J
2380        IF M1 <= 0 THEN 2390 ELSE 2400
2390          GOTO 2690 'LOOP EXIT
2400 '        IFEND
2410 '
```

```
2420 REM    3.  FIND PIVOT ROW OR STOP
2430 '
2440            LET M2 = 1000000
2450            LET P1 = 0
2460            FOR I = 1 TO M
2470                LET S(I) = T(I,P2)     'STORE COPY FOR STEP 6
2480                IF T(I,P2) > .00001 THEN 2490 ELSE 2520
2490                IF C(I)/T(I,P2) <= M2 THEN 2500 ELSE 2520
2500                    LET M2 = C(I)/T(I,P2)
2510                    LET P1 = I
2520 '              IFEND
2530            NEXT I
2540            LET S(M+1) = B(P2)     'STORE COPY FOR STEP 6
2550            IF P1 = 0 THEN 2560 ELSE 2580
2560              PRINT "NO SOLUTION EXISTS"
2570 '          STOP
2580 '          IFEND
2590 '
2600            LET P = T(P1,P2)     'PIVOT ELEMENT
2610 '
2620            GOSUB 2730  'STEPS 4-7
2630 '
2640 REM    8.  REPEAT 2 THROUGH 8
2650 '
2660        NEXT L
2670        PRINT "DID NOT FIND ANSWER"
2680        STOP
2690 '
2700 RETURN
2710 '
2720 '
2730 REM    SUBROUTINE:  STEPS 4-7
2740 REM      IN: B(), C(), H(), M, N, P, P1, P2, S(), T(), V()
2750 REM      OUT: B(), C(), H(), T(), V()
2760 '
2770 REM    4.  DIVIDE PIVOT ROW BY PIVOT ELEMENT
2780 '
2790        FOR J = 1 TO N
2800            LET T(P1,J) = T(P1,J)/P
2810        NEXT J
2820        LET C(P1) = C(P1)/P
2830 '
```

```
2840 REM    5. READJUST ROWS TO NEW PIVOT ROW
2850 '
2860      FOR I = 1 TO M
2870          IF I < > P1 THEN 2880 ELSE 2930
2880             LET X = T(I,P2)
2890             FOR J = 1 TO N
2900                LET T(I,J) = T(I,J) − X*T(P1,J)
2910             NEXT J
2920             LET C(I) = C(I) − X*C(P1)
2930 '          IFEND
2940      NEXT I
2950 '
2960      LET X = B(P2)
2970      FOR J = 1 TO N
2980          LET B(J) = B(J) − X*T(P1,J)
2990      NEXT J
3000      LET B(N+1) = B(N+1) − X*C(P1)
3010 '
3020 REM    6. RE-DO THE PIVOT COLUMN
3030 '
3040      FOR I = 1 TO M
3050          LET T(I,P2) = − S(I)/P
3060      NEXT I
3070      LET B(P2) = − S(M+1)/P
3080      LET T(P1,P2) = 1/P
3090 '
3100 REM    7. EXCHANGE THE ANSWER INDICATORS
3110 '
3120      LET X = H(P2)
3130      LET H(P2) = V(P1)
3140      LET V(P1) = X
3150 '
3160 RETURN
3170 '
3180 '
3190 REM    SUBROUTINE:  PRINT THE ANSWERS
3200 '
3210      PRINT "MAXIMUM BENEFIT AND MINIMUM COST IS: "; −B(N+1)
3220      PRINT
3230 '
3240      PRINT
3250      FOR J = 1 TO N
3260          IF H(J) > 0 THEN 3270 ELSE 3290
3270             PRINT "V("; H(J); ") = "; −B(J)
3280             GOTO 3310 'IFEND
3290 '          ELSE
3300             PRINT "U("; −H(J); ") = "; −B(J)
3310 '          IFEND
3320      NEXT J
3330      PRINT "ALL OTHER V'S AND U'S ARE ZERO"
3340 '
```

```
3350       PRINT
3360       PRINT
3370       FOR I = 1 TO M
3380           IF V(I) < 0 THEN 3390 ELSE 3410
3390               PRINT "X("; −V(I); ") ="; C(I)
3400               GOTO 3430 'IFEND
3410 '         ELSE
3420               PRINT "Y("; V(I); ") = "; C(I)
3430 '         IFEND
3440       NEXT I
3450       PRINT "ALL OTHER X'S AND Y'S ARE ZERO"
3460       PRINT
3470       PRINT "FINAL TABLEAU IS:"
3480       FOR I = 1 TO M
3490           FOR J = 1 TO N
3500               PRINT T(I,J),
3510           NEXT J
3520           PRINT C(I)
3530       NEXT I
3540       FOR J = 1 TO N+1
3550           PRINT B(J),
3560       NEXT J
3570       PRINT
3580 '
3590 RETURN
3600 '
3610 '
3620 REM    SUBROUTINE: TABLEAU REWORK
3630 REM       IN: B(), C(), H(), I, M, N, T(), V()
3640 REM      OUT: B(), C(), H(), T(), V()
3650 '
3660 '
3670       LET P1 = I
3680       FOR J = 1 TO N
3690           IF T(P1,J) < −.00001 THEN 3700 ELSE 3710
3700               GOTO 3760 'OKAY EXIT
3710 '         IFEND
3720       NEXT J
3730       PRINT "MAXIMUM PROBLEM HAS NO FEASIBLE SOLUTION,"
3740       PRINT "MINIMUM PROBLEM HAS AN UNBOUNDED SOLUTION."
3750       STOP
3760 '
3770       LET P2 = J
3780 '
3790       FOR I = 1 TO M
3800           LET S(I) = T(I,P2)      'STORE FOR STEP 6
3810       NEXT I
3820       LET S(M+1) = B(P2)
3830 '
```

```
3840        LET M2 = C(P1)/T(P1,P2)
3850        FOR I = P1 TO M
3860            IF T(I,P2) > .00001 THEN 3870 ELSE 3900
3870            IF (C(I)/T(I,P2)) <= M2 THEN 3880 ELSE 3900
3880                LET P1 = I
3890                LET M2 = C(I)/T(I,P2)
3900 '          IFEND
3910        NEXT I
3920        LET P = T(P1,P2)
3930        GOSUB 2730        'STEPS 4-7
3940 RETURN
3950 '
3960 '
3970        END
```

MAXIMUM BENEFIT AND MINIMUM COST IS: 658.995

$V(6) = 17.4263$
$V(5) = 19.3789$
$U(3) = 3099.49$
ALL OTHER V'S AND U'S ARE ZERO

$Y(1) = 16.9594$
$Y(2) = -4.76837\text{ E}{-7}$
$Y(3) = 85.9911$
$Y(4) = 28.336$
$X(2) = 2.76316\text{ E}{-2}$
$X(1) = 1.24107$
ALL OTHER X'S AND Y'S ARE ZERO

FINAL TABLEAU IS:

−0.282707	−0.505263	−66.6526	16.9594
1	0	0	−4.76837 E−7
0.741071	0	−44.4375	85.9911
−5.51927	−5.26316	−876.694	28.336
1.18421 E−2	1.05263 E−2	1.68026	2.76316 E−2
−8.92857 E−3	0	0.8125	1.24107
−17.4263	−19.3789	−3099.49	−658.995

The program is large enough that it has been broken into pieces called subroutines. Each subroutine is less than one page in length so that it may be read without turning pages. The subroutines in the program are organized in the following manner:

```
STEP 1
CHECK TABLEAU
    TABLEAU REWORK
        STEPS 2-7
    STEPS 2-8
        STEPS 2-7
PRINT THE ANSWERS
```

The outline shows how the subroutine STEPS 2-7 is called at different places in the program. The RETURN statement in STEPS 2-7 is smart enough to go back to the particular GOSUB that invoked the subroutine.

SIMPLEX features two loops that will repeat an indefinite number of times. The loop that drives steps 2-8, FOR L = 1 to 1000, will usually be repeated only a few times before the program finds a satisfactory solution. In the subroutine CHECK TABLEAU a loop is made using a GOTO statement. The top and bottom of the loop are marked 'LOOP. A GOTO loop needs an IF . . . THEN line to exit from the loop. In this loop the exit line is IF G\$ = "OKAY" THEN 2170 'LOOP EXIT.

Steps 2 and 3 show how to find the maximum and minimum of a set of positive numbers. The idea is one you may find handy in other programs.

Some of the IF . . . THEN . . . ELSE statements in SIMPLEX look a little unusual. Instead of simply saying:

```
IF C(I) < 0 THEN 2110 ELSE 2130
```

the program says:

```
IF C(I) < -.00001 THEN 2110 ELSE 2130
```

The second IF . . . THEN . . . ELSE asks if the value is very close to zero. By phrasing the condition in this way, we catch all the tiny numbers close to zero, both positive and negative. These tiny numbers are "computed zeros," zero with a little rounding error. The program treats anything between −.00001 and +.00001 as zero. This kind of programming is another indication that numerical accuracy is important in the simplex method.

NOTE: Before using this program on real data, verify the program by using a set of data with known answers and get professional advice on the use and limitations of the method.

_____ *Exercises* _____

1. Change the data in SIMPLEX to solve the following economic problem.

	Houses	Food	Clothes	Cost
Public sector	66	80	70	150
Private sector	50	125	100	120
Country's need	100	200	160	

What will it cost to meet the country's needs? Which sector will do the most work? What goods will exist in surplus?

2. Alter the economy described in the first problem and see how it should be managed.

3. What if three goods require the following numbers of hours of work on three machines?

	Good A	Good B	Good C	Machine Limits
Machine 1	22	33	44	100
Machine 2	30	25	50	80
Machine 3	48	42	6	160
Profits/good	20	10	30	

How much of each kind of good do we make? How much total profit? Which machines are working at their limit?

4. Make a diet problem of your own and solve it with SIMPLEX.

5. Make a dial problem of your own (or use the farming example suggested earlier) and try it out.

6. Modify any of the above "dial" programs to include one equality constraint and see if the problem still has a solution, and if so, what it is.

7. Make a problem for the manager who has just been told that the government banned one of the components in his product, be it a drug or an automobile, and he must find which of three alternatives he should substitute.

8. Make a problem for a manager who must decide on which of three methods of shipping—air freight, mail, or trucking—she should select for her four products.

TRANSPORTATION PROBLEMS

"Among the problems I mentioned this morning," said Helen Anderson as she began the afternoon's talk, "was one that has come to be known as the transportation problem. It takes many forms, but the next example will show you its fundamental features.

"Consider three warehouses and three stores. The numbers on the lines connecting them indicate the unit cost to ship from the warehouse to the store.

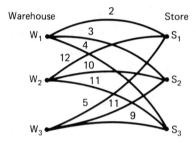

Fig. 8-10   Warehouses' Distance to Stores

"We can represent the same information in a table like this:

Warehouses	Stores S_1	S_2	S_3
120 W_1	2	3	4
60 W_2	12	10	11
200 W_3	5	11	9
	100	200	80

Fig. 8-11   Distance Table from Warehouse to Store

"The part being shipped is a screwdriver. Warehouse 1 has 120 screwdrivers, warehouse 2 has 60, and warehouse 3 has 200. Store 1 needs 100, store 2 needs 200, and store 3 needs 80.

"The problem is how to ship the parts in the cheapest way. One possible way is to use the cheapest means first. If we do that we move things from warehouse 1 to store 1 like this:

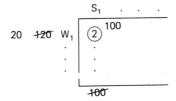

Fig. 8-12   Moving Goods from Warehouse to Store

and so on until we are done. A second way to get the answer is to notice that this problem can be thought of as a 'diet' problem when you set the Tucker Tableau up as follows:

		W_1	W_2	W_3	S_1	S_2	S_3	Cost -1
V_{11}		1	0	0	1	0	0	2
V_{12}		1	0	0	0	1	0	3
V_{13}		1	0	0	0	0	1	4
V_{21}		0	1	0	1	0	1	12
V_{22}		0	1	0	0	1	0	10
V_{23}		0	1	0	0	0	1	11
V_{31}		0	0	1	1	0	0	5
V_{32}		0	0	1	0	1	0	11
V_{33}		0	0	1	0	0	1	9
Minimum requirements	-1	120	60	200	100	200	80	

Fig. 8-13   Tucker Tableau for Transportation Problem

"When we apply our program SIMPLEX to the problem we get an answer that looks like this" (Fig. 8.14).

"The program's solution to the problem is not completely right. Why? The program would like us to ship an extra 100 units from warehouse 1 and send an extra 100 units to store 1. The program is moving goods we don't have! But look for a moment at our Tucker tableau. It is the 'diet' problem, 'give the cheapest solution that meets my minimum needs.' The program did just that.

"Actually, the answer is interesting in that it tells us that we can ship all our units plus an extra 100 cheaper than any way we can ship

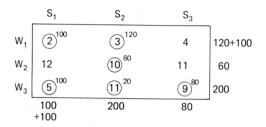

Fig. 8-14   First Solution to Transportation Problem

just our current number. We might look hard to see if we could find the extra units in warehouse 1 (and even hold back on 100 in warehouse 3).

"What we wanted, but did not write down in our Tucker Tableau, was for our solution to *exactly equal* our needs. To state this fully would require another six columns. Rather than do all that, let's try just adding one column that requires warehouse 1 be exactly used. To do this we add a column that looks like this:

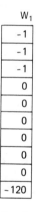

Fig. 8-15   Additional Restriction for Transportation Tableau

"When we generate our enlarged tableau, we get an answer that meets our needs. It exactly uses all of our supplies.

"Transportation problems have two interesting additional applications that you should be aware of," continued Anderson.

"Consider the following network:

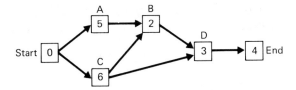

Fig. 8-16   Sample Network

"If you want to travel through it for the minimum cost, think of shipping a single item down the line. That's equivalent to a transportation table like this:

	A	B	C	D	Finish	
Start	5	–	6	–	–	1
A	0	2	–	–	–	1
B	–	0	–	3	–	1
C	–	2	0	3	–	1
D	–	–	–	0	4	1
	1	1	1	1	1	

Fig. 8-17   Distance Table of Network

"Notice that the edge values are all one. This means each node can receive and ship only one item. The start node cannot receive one. The finish node can not send one. Every other node can send to itself for zero costs. The solution will be those nodes that do not service themselves. Before solving this problem, each dash must be replaced with a large number. In this example 100 would do.

"When we solve this problem, we will see that the solution is the shortest route through this network. If we were to make all costs negative, then the solution would be the longest path (the critical path) through the network."

"Should we use this program to do the critical path?" one student asked.

"No, the program called CPM that you saw at another lecture gives a faster solution to this particular problem," answered Anderson.

"The second interesting application of transportation problems is matching people to jobs: the assignment problem. Begin with persons A, B, and C, and jobs 1, 2, and 3. One can make a table of how much it would cost to train a given person for a given job. In our example it would cost $470 to train person B for job 3. The table would look like this:

	Jobs			
	#1	#2	#3	
A	300	100	500	1
People B	280	250	470	1
C	600	500	200	1
	1	1	1	

Fig. 8-18 Table for Assignment Problem

"Again, one person will be matched to one job so the edge values are all ones.

"In closing, I would like to mention that there is another method for solving transportation problems that takes advantage of the way they appear in a table. The method is called the stepping-stone method. If any of you are curious to learn more about how it works, I'll recommend a couple of good books."

Anderson answered a few questions and closed the meeting.

_____ *Exercises* _____

1. Use SIMPLEX to solve each of the above transportation problems.

References

1. Daellenbach, Hans G., and George, John A., *Introduction to Operations Research Techniques*, Boston, MA: Allyn and Bacon, 1978.
2. Kemeny, John G., Schleifer, Arthur, Jr., Snell, J. Laurie, and Thompson, Gerald L., *Finite Mathematics with Business Applications*, Englewood Cliffs, NJ: Prentice-Hall, 1972.

The Raincoat Problem: Decision Analysis

The universe is wider than our views of it.

Henry David Thoreau

George Lee looked at the threatening sky and smiled because today he was teaching a class in decision analysis and the weather exactly illustrated the problem he wished to discuss. There was a chance it would rain and he had to decide whether or not to take his raincoat. It was late summer so the raincoat would be a nuisance if it did not rain. He would have to carry it around all day. He glanced at the sky again and he decided not to take his raincoat.

By the time the class filed into the room it was raining outside.

"The topic for this week's seminar is decision analysis," began Lee. "I am going to try to illustrate the idea today with a couple of simple examples and a computer program. As the week goes along, you may refine the programs to include new issues raised each day. Later on today I will give you a chance to begin to work on a problem of your own.

"The example we are going to use is the raincoat problem: whether or not to take your raincoat on a cloudy day. The cloudy day is important. Notice I did not say a rainy day. You don't know whether or not it will rain. As a matter of fact, the weather forecast was a 50-percent chance of rain.

"So the cloudy day represents nature's uncertain future. Here's one way of diagramming the predicament" (Fig. 9.1).

"If you were to get a dime when it rained and a dollar when the sun came out, then the expected value of the situation is the total of the reward times the chance of getting the reward; that is:

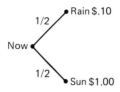

Fig. 9-1   Nature's Game

Expected value = (1/2) * 10 + (1/2) * 100
                       = 55

"If the weather forecast is only a one-third chance of rain the odds in this problem would change and the expected value would change as well:

Expected value = (1/3) * 10 + (2/3) * 100
                       = 70

"We see that as the odds shift toward a favorable outcome the expected value of the forecast goes up. This is only common sense.

"The reason this game of nature is important is that it will influence our decision. Suppose for a moment that having a raincoat when it rains pleased you 10 points, having to carry your raincoat around in the sun displeased you −20 points, not having a raincoat when it rains displeased you −50 points, and not having your raincoat on a sunny day pleased you 80 points.

"With values for the possible outcomes you are ready to make your decision in the face of the weather's uncertainty. You could diagram your situation like this" (Fig. 9.2).

"We have added our individual decision before two plays of nature's game. The reason for the two plays is that the outcomes have different values:

Raincoat game   = (1/2) * 10 + (1/2) * −20
                        = −5

No raincoat game = (1/2) * −50 + (1/2) * 80
                        = 15

"Fifteen points is better than −5 points, so we chose not to take a raincoat when the forecast is only a 50 percent chance of rain."

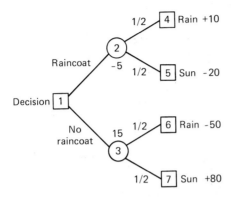

Fig. 9-2   Raincoat Decision Tree

A COMPUTER PROGRAM

"Now let's look at our raincoat problem again with an eye to writing a computer program to handle it. Notice that each of the nodes in the decision tree is numbered.

"One of the first observations we can make about the tree is that there are three kinds of nodes: decision nodes (#1), nature's game nodes (#2, #3), and end nodes (#4, #5, #6, #7). The task for the program is to evaluate each node. If the node is an end node the value is one number. If the node is a game node then we must evaluate the game just as we have done before. If the node is a decision node we must choose the best (biggest) alternative.

"In order to evaluate the nodes we work backwards from the end to the beginning. In order to have a computer help us with our work the nodes must be numbered. We can read the initial variables like this:

```
205 REM    READ IN THE DATA
210 '
215        LET N9 = 7        'NUMBER OF NODES IN TREE
220 '
225 REM    FOR 'DEC' DECISION NODES, READ THE NUMBER OF
227 REM    SUB-NODES AND THE NODE NUMBER OF EACH SUB-NODE.
230 REM    FOR 'NAT' NATURE'S GAME, THE NUMBER OF SUB-NODES
235 REM    AND THE PROBABILITY AND NODE NUMBER
240 REM    OF EACH SUBORDINATE NODE.  FOR 'END' NODES, READ
245 REM    THE VALUE OF THE NODE.
250 '
```

```
255        FOR I = 1 TO N9
260            READ X, N$(I)
265            IF N$(I) = "DEC" THEN 270 ELSE 295
270                READ N(I,0)    'NUMBER OF SUB-NODES
275                FOR J = 1 TO N(I,0)
280                    READ N(I,J)
285                NEXT J
290                GOTO 365    'LOOP BOTTOM
295 '          IFEND
299 '
300            IF N$(I) = "NAT" THEN 305 ELSE 330
305                READ N(I,0)    'NUMBER OF SUB-NODES
310                FOR J = 1 TO N(I,0)
315                    READ P(I,J), N(I,J)
320                NEXT J
325                GOTO 365    'LOOP BOTTOM
330 '          IFEND
331 '
335            IF N$(I) = "END" THEN 340 ELSE 345
340                READ V(I)
345                GOTO 365    'LOOP BOTTOM
350 '          IFEND
355            PRINT "ERROR IN DATA READ"
360            STOP
365 '
370        NEXT I
375 '
380        DATA 1, DEC, 2, 2,3
385        DATA 2, NAT, 2, .5, 4, .5, 5
390        DATA 3, NAT, 2, .5, 6, .5, 7
395        DATA 4, END, 10
400        DATA 5, END, −20
405        DATA 6, END, −50
410        DATA 7, END, 80
```

"The program labels each node either DEC or NAT or END. Following the label is the appropriate information: for a decision node, how many nodes are attached and the node number of each; for nature's game nodes, how many nodes are attached, and the probability and node number of each; for the end nodes, the value at that point.

"Our program will have three parts in the section that reads in the data and three corresponding parts in the section that evaluates the tree. The value for the end nodes was read in as data, so we skip the end node when we evaluate the tree:

```
450        IF N$(I) = "END" THEN 455 ELSE 460
455            GOTO 605        'LOOP BOTTOM
460 '      IFEND
465 '
```

"The code for nature's game node sums up the values of all the subordinate nodes that come into it:

```
470      IF N$(I) = "NAT" THEN 475 ELSE 510
475        LET S = 0
480        FOR J = 1 TO N(I,0)
485          LET V = P(I,J) * V(N(I,J))
490          LET S = S + V
495        NEXT J
500        LET V(I) = S
505        GOTO 605        'LOOP BOTTOM
510 '    IFEND
515 '
```

"Finally, the code for a decision looks like this:

```
520      IF N$(I) = "DEC" THEN 525 ELSE 590
525        LET M = −1E36
530        FOR J = 1 TO N(I,0)
535          LET V = V(N(I,J))
540          IF V > M THEN 545 ELSE 555
545            LET M = V
550            LET N1 = N(I,J)
555 '        IFEND
565        NEXT J
570        LET V(I) = M
575        PRINT "DECISION AT NODE "; I; " IS NODE "; N1
580        PRINT "VALUE OF DECISION IS "; V(I)
582        PRINT
585        GOTO 605        'LOOP BOTTOM
590 '    IFEND
592 '
```

"We remember what we said earlier that in order to evaluate our diagram we must work back from the end. We place our three routines inside a large loop that walks the nodes backwards:

```
FOR I = N9 TO 1 STEP -1
   .
   .
   .
NEXT I
```

"Each time we pass a decision node we announce the result, and when we are done we will see what the correct decision will be. These comments will give us a narrative history of our program as it works backwards toward the first and final decision in the tree.

```
575        PRINT "DECISION AT NODE "; I; " IS NODE "; N1
580        PRINT "VALUE OF DECISION IS "; V(I)
582        PRINT
```

"When we assemble the pieces the program does the following:

```
DECISION AT NODE  1  IS NODE  3
VALUE OF DECISION IS  15

NODE VALUES
1   15        2 –5        3   15        4   10        5 –20
6 –50        7   80
```

"The answer agrees with our hand evaluation of a few minutes ago."

THE PROGRAM DECIDE

```
100 REM    DECIDE      15 DECEMBER 1981    GEORGE LEE
105 '
110 REM    © COPYRIGHT 1980 JOHN M. NEVISON ASSOCIATES
115 '
120 REM    EVALUATE A DECISION TREE TO FIND THE BEST DECISION.
125 '
130 REM    REFERENCE: NEVISON, JOHN M., EXECUTIVE COMPUTING,
135 REM                READING, MA: ADDISON-WESLEY PUBLISHING
140 REM                COMPANY, 1981.
145 '
150 REM    VARIABLES:
155 REM        I,J . . . . . . . . . . . INDEX VARIABLES
160 REM        M . . . . . . . . . . . MAXIMUM VARIABLE
165 REM        N$() . . . . . . . . . NODE TYPE
170 REM        N1 . . . . . . . . . . CHOSEN NODE'S NUMBER
175 REM        N(I,0) . . . . . . . NUMBER OF NODES ATTACHED TO I
180 REM        N(I,J) . . . . . . . . NODE NUMBERS OF ATTACHED NODES
182 REM        P() . . . . . . . . . . PROBABILITY OF NODE OCCURRING
185 REM        S . . . . . . . . . . . SUM VARIABLE
190 REM        V . . . . . . . . . . . TEMPORARY VALUE VARIABLE
195 REM        V() . . . . . . . . . . THE VALUE OF A NODE
196 REM        X . . . . . . . . . . . TEMPORARY VARIABLE
197 '
198        DIM N$(24),N(24,10),P(24,10),V(24)
199 '
```

```
205 REM    READ IN THE DATA
210 '
215        LET N9 = 7          'NUMBER OF NODES IN TREE
220 '
225 REM    FOR 'DEC' DECISION NODES, READ THE NUMBER OF
227 REM    SUB-NODES AND THE NODE NUMBER OF EACH SUB-NODE.
230 REM    FOR 'NAT' NATURE'S GAME, THE NUMBER OF SUB-NODES
235 REM    AND THE PROBABILITY AND NODE NUMBER
240 REM    OF EACH SUBORDINATE NODE.  FOR 'END' NODES, READ
245 REM    THE VALUE OF THE NODE.
250 '
255        FOR I = 1 TO N9
260           READ X, N$(I)
265           IF N$(I) = "DEC" THEN 270 ELSE 295
270             READ N(I,0)    'NUMBER OF SUB-NODES
275             FOR J = 1 TO N(I,0)
280                 READ N(I,J)
285             NEXT J
290             GOTO 365    'LOOP BOTTOM
295 '         IFEND
299 '
300           IF N$(I) = "NAT" THEN 305 ELSE 330
305             READ N(I,0)   'NUMBER OF SUB-NODES
310             FOR J = 1 TO N(I,0)
315                 READ P(I,J), N(I,J)
320             NEXT J
325             GOTO 365     'LOOP BOTTOM
330 '         IFEND
331 '
335           IF N$(I) = "END" THEN 340 ELSE 345
340             READ V(I)
345             GOTO 365     'LOOP BOTTOM
350 '         IFEND
355           PRINT "ERROR IN DATA READ"
360           STOP
365 '
370        NEXT I
375 '
380        DATA 1, DEC, 2, 2,3
385        DATA 2, NAT, 2,   .5, 4,  .5, 5
390        DATA 3, NAT, 2,   .5, 6,  .5, 7
395        DATA 4, END, 10
400        DATA 5, END, −20
405        DATA 6, END, −50
410        DATA 7, END, 80
417 '
```

```
420 REM    EVALUATE THE TREE
425 '
430 REM    FIND THE TOTAL VALUE OF A 'NAT' NODE, THE BEST
435 REM    CHOICE OF A 'DEC' NODE, AND SKIP THE END NODES.
440 '
445        FOR I = N9 TO 1 STEP −1
450            IF N$(I) = "END" THEN 455 ELSE 460
455              GOTO 605     'LOOP BOTTOM
460 '          IFEND
465 '
470            IF N$(I) = "NAT" THEN 475 ELSE 510
475              LET S = 0
480              FOR J = 1 TO N(I,0)
485                  LET V = P(I,J) * V(N(I,J))
490                  LET S = S + V
495              NEXT J
500              LET V(I) = S
505              GOTO 605     'LOOP BOTTOM
510 '          IFEND
515 '
520            IF N$(I) = "DEC" THEN 525 ELSE 590
525              LET M = −1E36
530              FOR J = 1 TO N(I,0)
535                  LET V = V(N(I,J))
540                  IF V > M THEN 545 ELSE 555
545                    LET M = V
550                    LET N1 = N(I,J)
555 '                IFEND
565              NEXT J
570              LET V(I) = M
575              PRINT "DECISION AT NODE "; I; " IS NODE "; N1
580              PRINT "VALUE OF DECISION IS "; V(I)
582              PRINT
585              GOTO 605     'LOOP BOTTOM
590 '          IFEND
592 '
595            PRINT "ERROR IN TREE EVALUATION"
600            PRINT
605 '
610        NEXT I
615 '
620        PRINT "NODE VALUES"
625        FOR I = 1 TO N9
630            PRINT I;V(I),
635        NEXT I
640 '
645        END
```

The program uses the string variable N$(I) to decide which kind of node the program is working with. String variables have a couple of advantages over numeric variables in a case like this. They help document the DATA lines and they allow the IF . . . THEN . . . ELSE lines to be written in a way that helps explain what the program is doing.

The program depends completely on the numbering of the nodes as it works backwards toward the answer. All of a node's subordinates must be evaluated before the node itself can be evaluated.

Notice how both the "read the data" loop and the "evaluate the tree" loop have error traps to catch any nodes that are not legal. Such traps in the program are safety features that assure us the program will stop if it gets into this kind of trouble.

The decision node seeks to find the maximum value, M, of the choices available. The variable M begins each time as −1E36, minus ten to the 36th power, a number smaller than any we expect to see. So M will be reassigned to the value of the first choice and then of any subsequent choice that is larger.

_____ *Exercises* _____

1. Change the likelihood of rain to .33 (and sun to .67). Rerun DECIDE and look closely at the answer. How do nature's probabilities affect your decisions? Is there a point at which you do not have a best decision?

2. Modify DECIDE to catch mistakes in the node order. First initialize all the V's to −.11111 at the beginning of the program. In the loop where the tree is evaluated, insert a check that begins IF V(I) = −.11111 . . . When a mistake occurs, print out an appropriate error message and stop.

3. Compare DECIDE with the program RISKY in Chapter 4. When would you use each?

A MARKETING DECISION

"Our next example should make our computer program do a little more work as well as illustrate more of the power of decision analysis," said Lee.

"A marketing manager has a choice of releasing a new breakfast cereal or continuing with the current line. He has researched his alternatives and arrived at a decision tree that looks like this" (Fig. 9.3).

"The cost of the new product release is $50,000. The expected final payoff if the market likes it is $80,000. The current mix earns a cool $200,000. The manager's estimate of the new product's chance of success is three in four, 75 percent.

"We could analyze the problem with our program, but we have not yet completely described our manager's options. He could take a survey sample of the market and afterwards he would be 90 percent certain whether the market would or would not buy the product. His choices now look like this" (Fig. 9.4).

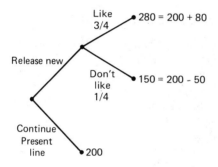

Fig. 9-3 New Product Decision Tree

"When the diagram is entered as data it looks like this:

```
380       DATA 1, DEC, 2, 2, 3
382       DATA 2, DEC, 2, 4, 5
384       DATA 3, NAT, 2,  .75, 6,  .25, 7
386       DATA 4, NAT, 2,  .75, 8,  .25, 9
388       DATA 5, END, 200
390       DATA 6, DEC, 2, 10, 11
392       DATA 7, DEC, 2,  12, 13
394       DATA 8, END, 280
396       DATA 9, END, 150
402       DATA 10, NAT, 2, .9, 14, .1, 15
404       DATA 11, END, 200
405       DATA 12, NAT, 2, .1, 16, .9, 17
406       DATA 13, END, 200
407       DATA 14, END, 280
408       DATA 15, END, 150
412       DATA 16, END, 280
413       DATA 17, END, 150
417 '
```

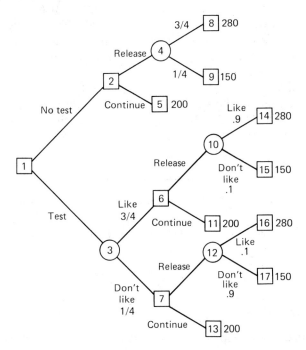

Fig. 9-4   Decision Tree for New Product with Market Research

"A run of the program yields the following decisions:

DECISION AT NODE 7 IS NODE 13
VALUE OF DECISION IS 200

DECISION AT NODE 6 IS NODE 10
VALUE OF DECISION IS 267

DECISION AT NODE 2 IS NODE 4
VALUE OF DECISION IS 247.5

DECISION AT NODE 1 IS NODE 3
VALUE OF DECISION IS 250.25

NODE VALUES

1 250.25	2 247.5	3 250.25	4 247.5	5 200
6 267	7 200	8 280	9 150	10 267
11 200	12 163	13 200	14 280	15 150
16 280	17 150			

"So our manager decides that doing a test might be a good idea. The market research group says the test will cost $1000. The marketing manager reexamines his results. His decision without the test is worth $247,500; his decision with the test is worth $250,250. The test is worth $2750 to him, so he does the test."

"Does this example give me a way to tell what additional information is worth?" asked one of the students. "It seems as though it does."

"Yes, you're right, it does. As a matter of fact, this example is dear to the heart of market research analysts."

_____ *Exercises* _____

1. If research costs $3000 what level of certainty do you need to make it worthwhile?
2. At the higher research costs, what changes in the outcomes would make it worthwhile?

THE END GAME

"In our raincoat problem we did not really have very pleasing numeric values for the various outcomes of the decisions. The question arises how to assign better values to these outcomes.

"One better way would be to assign a zero to the worst outcome and a one to the best outcome. We could then assign a fraction to everything in between. In our example 'no raincoat and rain' is the worst, so we give it a zero. 'No raincoat and sun' is the best, so we give it a one. The problem gets trickier when we look at 'raincoat and rain' and 'raincoat and sun.'

"Here we must play a little game at our END nodes. To get the 'raincoat and rain' value we ask what kind of a chance at the best outcome would we need to exchange our present outcome for a best-worst lottery. Well, having a raincoat in the rain is certainly much better than 'no raincoat and rain,' but it's not as good as 'no raincoat and sun.' We decide if we had a 65 percent chance at the best outcome we might exchange our situation for a try at the best-worst game.

"Having a raincoat in the sun is no fun, so we would need only a 25 percent chance at the best outcome to exchange our situation for a try at the best-worst game.

"In a larger problem we would repeat this 'end game' exercise for every other outcome between the best and the worst. When we finish this exercise we have a value that is the called the 'utility' of the outcome. One interesting by-product of this utility is that it incorporates estimates of risk about each outcome. We then need only to chose the greatest utility in making our decision. The risk has already been accounted for.

"The utilities for our raincoat problem are:"

- Raincoat and rain   .65
- Raincoat and sun   .25
- No raincoat and rain   0.00
- No raincoat and sun   1.00

After class that evening, George Lee was soaked to the skin as he walked to the station to catch the train home.

_____ *Exercises* _____

1. Redo the raincoat problem using utilities. Does the decision change?
2. Redo the marketing problem using utilities. Assign them strictly according to the dollar value of the outcome.
3. Assume you may be fired if you lose more than $60,000 in your marketing decision. Reestimate your utilities in the light of this information. Did your new values change your decision?

References

1. Kemeny, John G., Schleifer, Arthur, Jr., Snell, J. Laurie, and Thompson, Gerald L., *Finite Mathematics with Business Applications*, Englewood Cliffs, NJ: Prentice-Hall, 1972.

2. Raiffa, Howard, *Decision Analysis*, Reading, MA: Addison-Wesley, 1978.

3. Schlaifer, Robert, *Analysis of Decisions Under Uncertainty*, New York: McGraw-Hill, 1969.

10

Looking Ahead:
Next Month's Sales,
Next Week's Meetings

Read your fate, see what is before you, and walk on into futurity.

Henry David Thoreau

Peter Bates sighed. After wrestling with a statistics text for half an hour he had what he needed: the equation of the best-fitting line through a set of points. The equation had two parts, M, the slope of the line, and B, the point where the line crossed the Y axis. The slope of the line was calculated:

$$M = \frac{\sum_{i=1}^{n}(Y_i - \bar{Y})(X_i - \bar{X})}{\sum_{i=1}^{n}(X_i - \bar{X})^2}$$

where X_i, Y_i were the coordinates of the i points and where $\bar{X}$ was the average of the X_i's and $\bar{Y}$ was the average of the Y_i's.

The Y intercept of the line, B, had an even easier formula:

$$B = \bar{Y} - M * \bar{X}$$

The equation of the line that best fits the i points was:

$$Y = M * X + B$$

With this equation, Bates could put in new X values, such as the number of the next month, and get the Y value which would be the best-fitting line's projection of sales in the next month.

For example, the first eight months' sales figures were 27, 24, 21, 25, 30, 37, 35, 32. The best-fitting line's equation was $Y = 2.1 X + 18.7$ where X was the month number. To find out what might happen in month 9, Bates plugged a 9 into his equation and calculated 37.8.

As he looked at the answer he decided that with data like this he would almost always want the projections for the next few periods. In addition, most of the time he would like the answers to be plotted. So he wrote a short program to make what he wanted. He realized that his straight line was an assumption that grew weaker and weaker the farther out he extended the projection, but for the next period or two it was okay.

When he was finished, the results looked like the facing page.

THE PROGRAM LINEFIT

```
100 REM    LINEFIT      20 DECEMBER 1981    PETER BATES
102 '
104 REM    © COPYRIGHT 1980 JOHN M. NEVISON ASSOCIATES
110 '
120 REM    FIND THE BEST LINE THROUGH A SET OF POINTS.
130 REM    IN THIS EXAMPLE THE POINTS ARE  IN A TIME
140 REM    SERIES.
150 '
160 REM    BY *READING* BOTH X(I) AND Y(I) ANY
170 REM    SET OF POINTS CAN BE FIT WITH A LINE.
180 '
190 REM    ***NOTE*** FOR DIFFERENT POINTS THE GRAPH MAY HAVE
200 REM    TO BE CHANGED.
210 '
220 REM    VARIABLES:
230 REM       B . . . . . . . . . . . . THE Y INTERCEPT OF THE BEST FIT LINE
240 REM       G$() . . . . . . . . THE STRING OF CHARACTERS THAT MAKE A
250 REM                          LINE OF THE GRAPH
260 REM       I,J . . . . . . . . . . INDEX VARIABLES
270 REM       L . . . . . . . . . . . . THE LOCATION OF THE LINE ON THE GRAPH
280 REM       M . . . . . . . . . . . THE SLOPE OF THE BEST FIT LINE
290 REM       N . . . . . . . . . . . THE NUMBER OF POINTS
300 REM       S1,S2,S3,S4 . . VARIOUS SUM VARIABLES
310 REM       X(),Y() . . . . . . . THE COORDINATES OF THE POINTS
320 REM       X . . . . . . . . . . . THE AVERAGE OF THE X() COORDINATES
330 REM       Y . . . . . . . . . . . THE AVERAGE OF THE Y() COORDINATES
340 '
```

BEST FIT LINE IS Y = 2.11905 X + 18.7143

X AXIS GOES DOWN THE PAGE; Y AXIS GOES ACROSS

```
0            10          20          30         40 POINTS
+----------+----------+----------+----------+Y X(I),    Y(I)
I
I
+                     +   *                       1       22
I
I
+                       +   *                     2       24
I
I
+                   *       +                     3       21
I
I
+                         *   +                   4       25
I
I
+                           + *                   5       30
I                         .
+                             +       *           6       37
I
I
+                               +   *             7       35
I
I
+                             *     +             8       32
I
I
+                                       +         37.7857
I
I
+                                         +       39.9048
I
I
+                                                 42.0238
I
I
+                                                 44.1429
X
```

*--POINT
+--FIT LINE

```
345 REM   DIMENSIONS:
350       DIM G$(50), X(12), Y(12)
352 '
355 REM   INITIAL VALUES AND DATA
360       FOR I = 1 TO 40
370           LET G$(I) = " "
380       NEXT I
390 '
400       LET N = 8
410       DATA 22, 24, 21, 25, 30, 37, 35, 32
420 '
425 REM   FIND BEST FITTING LINE
430       LET S1 = 0
440       LET S2 = 0
450       FOR I = 1 TO N
460           LET X(I) = I
470           READ Y(I)
480           LET S1 = S1 + X(I)
490           LET S2 = S2 + Y(I)
500       NEXT I
510 '
520       LET X = S1/N
530       LET Y = S2/N
540 '
550       LET S3 = 0
560       LET S4 = 0
570       FOR I = 1 TO N
580           LET S3 = S3 + (Y(I) − Y) * (X(I) − X)
590           LET S4 = S4 + (X(I)−X) * (X(I)−X)
600       NEXT I
610 '
620       LET M = S3/S4
630       LET B = Y − M * X
640 '
```

```
650      PRINT "BEST FIT LINE IS  Y ="; M; " X +";B
660      PRINT
662 '
664 REM    PLOT BEST LINE (+), AND POINTS (*)
666 REM    PROJECT LINE BEYOND POINTS.
668 '
670      PRINT "X AXIS GOES DOWN THE PAGE; Y AXIS GOES ACROSS"
680      PRINT
690 '
700      PRINT "0              10        20        30";
710      PRINT "          40 POINTS"
720      PRINT "+---------+---------+---------+";
725      PRINT "---------+Y";
730      PRINT "  X(I), Y(I)"
740      FOR I = 1 TO N+4
744         LET X(I) = I
750         LET L = M * X(I) + B
760         LET G$(L) = "+"
765         IF I <= N THEN 770 ELSE 775
770           LET G$(Y(I)) = "*"
775 '         IFEND
780         PRINT "I"
790         PRINT "I"
800         PRINT "+";
810         FOR J = 1 TO 40
820            PRINT G$(J);
830            LET G$(J) = " "
840         NEXT J
845         IF I <= N THEN 850 ELSE 855
850           PRINT TAB(40); X(I); Y(I)
852           GOTO 859     'IFEND
855 '         ELSE
856           PRINT TAB(40); L
859 '         IFEND
860      NEXT I
870      PRINT"X"
872      PRINT
874      PRINT "*--POINT"
876      PRINT "+--FIT LINE"
880      END
```

The program finds the best-fitting line by using the formula Bates found in the statistics book. The complicated expression:

$$M = \frac{\sum\limits_{i=1}^{n} (Y_i - \bar{Y})(X_i - \bar{X})}{\sum\limits_{i=1}^{n} (X_i - \bar{X})^2}$$

becomes eight simple lines of BASIC:

```
550     LET S3 = 0
560     LET S4 = 0
570     FOR I = 1 TO N
580         LET S3 = S3 + (Y(I) − Y) * (X(I) − X)
590         LET S4 = S4 + (X(I)−X) * (X(I)−X)
600     NEXT I
610 '
620     LET M = S3/S4
```

The plotting routine plots both the points and the line. After the points run out, the values of the extended line are printed.

The program loads up a 40-character line by using the subscripted string variable G$(). After the correct characters are inserted into the right locations in G$(), the whole line is printed out, erased, and the process repeated.

Fitting a line to a set of points is also called linear regression. The method used in LINEFIT is called a "least-squares linear regression."

____ *Exercises* _____

1. Use LINEFIT to do a set of your own data.
2. Modify LINEFIT to read X(I), Y(I), and run it with a different set of points. Modify the plot section to produce what you want.

_____

NEXT MONTH'S FORECAST

When he needed detailed forecasts of a product line's sales, Bates always used an econometric modeling service. The model did what the simple program LINEFIT did, but in higher dimensions. It would fit a flat plane through a set of points with several independent variables (several kinds of X's), to arrive at the forecast of Y.

Bates knew it took time and money to get a projection from the econometric model. He thought it would be easy enough to take a quick look at the data itself and see if he needed to double-check with the econometric model.

What he really wanted to know was the next month's sales. When he fit a line to the last twelve months' sales, his line looked like a slow uphill climb. The line did not catch all the action. As he shortened the line to nine and then six months, he found sharper and sharper short-term predictions that ignored the long-term trend.

If on the one hand, the forecasts changed rapidly as the projection base diminished from 12 to 2, then Bates knew something important was occurring and he should consult a larger model. If, on the other hand, his values for the projected month closed in on a central value as the projection base diminished from 12 to 2, then he could bet that his projection was okay by itself.

The program to do these projections was a modification that used the central part of LINEFIT over and over to get an animated series of projections from the 12-month line, right down to the 2-month line.

He modified his old program to fit the base number of months and predict the next month. He added the last four months of the last year to his data: 30, 27, 20, 24. He set up the forecast base as a variable called F and ran the loop FOR F = 12 TO 2 STEP −1. The results looked like the next two pages. The results seemed to be dropping toward a shade less than 29. However, the sharp turn made the last predictions a little tricky, so Bates decided to get a full projection from the modeling service to back up his own idea of what was going to happen. The service predicted next month's sales would be 28.8 and confirmed Bates's projection.

Bates took the value and fed it into his materials requirements plan (MRP) to generate appropriate inventories for the next month. (See the discussion of demand in Chapter 7.) The MRP would in turn generate an estimate for the financial model of the next month's cash flow.

WITH A FORECAST BASIS OF 12 MONTHS, THE
BEST FIT LINE IS Y = 0.870629 X + 21.5909

X AXIS GOES DOWN THE PAGE; Y AXIS GOES ACROSS

```
0              10           20           30           40 POINTS
+----------+----------+----------+----------+Y X(I),        Y(I)
I
I
+                             +           *                1         30
I
I
+                               +       *                  2         27
I
I
+                         *       +                        3         20
I
I
+                               *+                         4         24
I
I
+                         *         +                      5         22
I
I
+                             *       +                    6         24
I
I
+                       *             +                    7         21
I
I
+                           *         +                    8         25
I
I
+                                   +*                     9         30
I
I
+                                 +       *               10         37
I
I
+                                     +     *             11         35
I
I
+                                       *                12         32
I
I
I
+                             23    A  40956  <FORECASTS
X
```

*--POINT
+-- 12 MTH LINE

BASIS (MTHS)	FORECAST	PLOT CHARACTER
12	32.9091	A
11	34.6909	1
10	36.4	0
9	36.6111	9
8	37.7857	8
7	38.2857	7
6	39.2	6
5	37.5	5
4	34.5	4
3	29.6667	3
2	29	2

SOME POINTS MAY BE PLOTTED OVER OTHER POINTS ON THE GRAPH

THE PROGRAM NEXTMNTH

```
100 REM    NEXTMNTH    28 DECEMBER 1981   PETER BATES
105 '
110 REM    © COPYRIGHT 1980 JOHN M. NEVISON ASSOCIATES
115 '
120 '
125 REM    FIND THE NEXT MONTH'S FORECAST FROM
130 REM    LINES THAT FIT THROUGH THE LAST 12 MONTHS,
135 REM    THE LAST 11 MONTHS, THE LAST 10 MONTHS,
140 REM    AND SO ON DOWN TO THE LAST 2 MONTHS.
145 '
150 REM    IN THIS EXAMPLE THE POINTS ARE  IN A TIME
155 REM    SERIES, BUT BY READING BOTH X(I) AND Y(I) ANY
160 REM    SET OF POINTS CAN BE FIT WITH A LINE.
165 '
170 REM    ***NOTE*** FOR DIFFERENT POINTS THE GRAPH MAY HAVE
175 REM    TO BE CHANGED.
180 '
```

```
185 REM    VARIABLES:
190 REM        B() . . . . . . . . . THE Y INTERCEPTS OF THE BEST FIT LINES
195 REM        F . . . . . . . . . . . THE FORECAST BASE IN MONTHS
200 REM        F9 . . . . . . . . . . THE FORECAST BASE THAT IS PLOTTED
205 REM        G$() . . . . . . . . THE STRING OF CHARACTERS THAT MAKE A
210 REM            LINE OF THE GRAPH
215 REM        I,J . . . . . . . . . . INDEX VARIABLES
220 REM        L . . . . . . . . . . . THE LOCATION OF THE LINE ON THE GRAPH
225 REM        M() . . . . . . . . . THE SLOPES OF THE BEST FIT LINES
230 REM        N . . . . . . . . . . . THE NUMBER OF POINTS
235 REM        P(). . . . . . . . . . THE POINTS FORECAST FOR THE NEXT
237 REM                 MONTH
240 REM        P$() . . . . . . . . THE CHARACTERS FOR THE FORECAST
242 REM                  POINTS
245 REM        S1,S2,S3,S4 . . VARIOUS SUM VARIABLES
250 REM        X(),Y() . . . . . . . THE COORDINATES OF THE POINTS
255 REM        X . . . . . . . . . . . THE AVERAGE OF THE X() COORDINATES
260 REM        Y . . . . . . . . . . . THE AVERAGE OF THE Y() COORDINATES
265 '
270 REM    DIMENSIONS:
275        DIM B(25), G$(50), M(25), P$(12), P(12), X(25), Y(25)
280 '
285 REM    INITIAL VALUES AND DATA
290 '
295        LET F9 = 12
300        FOR I = 1 TO 40
305            LET G$(I) = " "
310        NEXT I
315        FOR I = 2 TO 12
320            READ P$(I)
325        NEXT I
330        DATA "2", "3", "4", "5", "6", "7", "8", "9", "0", "1", "A"
335 '
340        LET N = 12
345        FOR I = 1 TO N
350            LET X(I) = I
355            READ Y(I)
360        NEXT I
365        LET X(N+1) = N+1
370        DATA 30, 27, 20, 24
375        DATA 22, 24, 21, 25, 30, 37, 35, 32
380 '
385 REM    FIND BEST FITTING LINES
390        FOR F = 12 TO 2 STEP −1
395            LET S1 = 0
400            LET S2 = 0
405            FOR I = (N−F+1) TO N
410                LET S1 = S1 + X(I)
415                LET S2 = S2 + Y(I)
420            NEXT I
425 '
```

```
430          LET X = S1/F
435          LET Y = S2/F
440 '
445          LET S3 = 0
450          LET S4 = 0
455          FOR I = (N−F+1) TO N
460              LET S3 = S3 + (Y(I) − Y) * (X(I) − X)
465              LET S4 = S4 + (X(I)−X) * (X(I)−X)
470          NEXT I
475 '
480          LET M(F) = S3/S4
485          LET B(F) = Y − M(F) * X
490          LET P(F) = M(F) * X(N+1) + B(F)
495      NEXT F
500      PRINT
505 '
510 REM    PLOT PREFERRED GRAPH (SEE F9)
515 '
520      PRINT "WITH A FORECAST BASIS OF "; F9; "MONTHS, THE "
525      PRINT "BEST FIT LINE IS  Y ="; M(F9); " X +";B(F9)
530      PRINT
535 '
540 REM    PLOT BEST LINE (+), AND POINTS (*)
545 REM    PROJECT LINE BEYOND POINTS.
550 '
555      PRINT "X AXIS GOES DOWN THE PAGE; Y AXIS GOES ACROSS"
560      PRINT
565 '
570      PRINT "0                10              20              30";
575      PRINT "            40 POINTS"
580      PRINT "+---------+---------+---------+";
585      PRINT "---------+Y";
585      PRINT "  X(I), Y(I)"
590      FOR I = (N−F9+1) TO N
595          LET X(I) = I
600          LET L = M(F9) * X(I) + B(F9)
605          LET L = INT(L+.5)
610          LET G$(L) = "+"
615          LET G$(INT(Y(I)+.5)) = "*"
620 '
625          PRINT "I"
630          PRINT "I"
635          PRINT "+";
640          FOR J = 1 TO 40
645              PRINT G$(J);
650              LET G$(J) = " "
655          NEXT J
660          PRINT TAB(40); X(I); Y(I)
665      NEXT I
670 '
```

```
675 REM    LOOK AT THE LAST TWELVE PREDICTIONS
680 '
685        FOR F = F9 TO 2 STEP −1
690            LET L = INT(P(F)+.5)
695            LET G$(L) = P$(F)
700        NEXT F
705        PRINT "I"
710        PRINT "I"
715        PRINT "+";
720        FOR J = 1 TO 40
725            PRINT G$(J);
730            LET G$(J) = " "
735        NEXT J
740        PRINT TAB(4); "<FORECASTS "
745 '
750        PRINT "X"
755        PRINT
757        PRINT "*--POINT"
758        PRINT "+--"; F9; " MTH LINE"
759        PRINT
760 '
765        PRINT "BASIS (MTHS) FORECAST    PLOT CHARACTER"
770        FOR F = 12 TO 2 STEP −1
775            PRINT F; TAB(15); P(F); TAB(25); P$(F)
780        NEXT F
785        PRINT "SOME POINTS MAY BE PLOTTED OVER OTHER POINTS";
787        PRINT " ON THE GRAPH"
790 '
795        END
READY
```

NEXTMNTH is a modification of LINEFIT. Instead of asterisks and plus signs it prints numbers as the plot characters for the forecasts. The results show that the forecasts are clustered between 29 and 39. However, the most recent predictions (plotted as 4, 3, and 2) are heading down. You can infer from the movement that next month is likely to be less than 29.

The plotting section of the program is set up to allow the user to look at the line for any particular basis, F9. The table of values shows the predictions of all twelve best-fitting lines. The plot and the table together provide an animated series of forecasts that allow you to get a feel for what the next likely value will be.

_____ *Exercises* _____

1. Try out NEXTMNTH on your own data. Be sure to provide a full year's worth. Adjust the plot routine if you need to.

NEXT WEEK'S MEETINGS

"If this computer were really going to revolutionize the office," said Carolyn Grimes, Steven Cauldwell's secretary, "it would figure out a way for me to keep track of you and your four divisional managers. Right now, I'm spending far too much time just trying to find out when everybody's free, so I can schedule a meeting."

Cauldwell raised his eyebrows. "You mean you want a way to find out when everyone's free?"

"Yes," Grimes said, "or for that matter, when two or three are free if it's a smaller meeting."

"How long would it take to get their schedules from their secretaries?" Cauldwell asked.

"Ten or fifteen minutes on the phone, I guess," answered Grimes, "Why?"

"If you can get their schedules for the week, I can get you a way to do meetings in a hurry," said Cauldwell.

"Deal," said Grimes. "I'll have the schedules before you leave today."

Steven Cauldwell owed his secretary more than one favor. He had had neither the time nor the excuse to use his computer for several months. That evening he wrote a program called FINDTIME and brought it with him to the office the next day.

"Give this a try," he said as he showed Grimes to a chair by the computer in his office. "Just follow the instructions."

Grimes was suspicious, but sat down and typed in a YES to say she wanted to schedule a meeting, a 1, 3, and 5 to indicate who was to be at the meeting, and a 0 to indicate that she was through. The computer printed out the following list:

DO YOU WANT A FULL SCHEDULE (YES OR NO)? NO

DO YOU WANT TO SCHEDULE A MEETING? YES

PEOPLE:
 1. STEVE CAULDWELL
 2. FRANK BRADSHAW
 3. EILEEN RANDALL
 4. ROSE THOMPSON
 5. TOM DELLER

PLEASE TYPE A NUMBER FROM 1 TO 5
FOR EACH PERSON IN THE MEETING.
WHEN DONE, PLEASE TYPE A 0(ZERO).
 ? 1

 ? 3

 ? 5

 ? 0

MON 5:00
MON 5:30

WED 11:30

WED 5:30

FRI 3:30
FRI 4:00
FRI 4:30
FRI 5:00
FRI 5:30

Grimes was impressed but still suspicious. "How did the computer do that?" she asked.

"Well the program looked over the schedule to find out what times were free. Here's what the schedule you gave me looks like:

DO YOU WANT A FULL SCHEDULE (YES OR NO)? YES

	STEVE	FRANK	EILEEN	ROSE	TOM
MON 8:00	*	*	*		
MON 8:30	*	*	*		
MON 9:00	*	*	*	*	
MON 9:30	*	*	*	*	
MON 10:00			*		*
MON 10:30			*		*
MON 11:00					*
MON 11:30					*
MON 12:00					*
MON 12:30					*
MON 1:00					*
MON 1:30					*
MON 2:00	*	*	*		
MON 2:30	*	*	*		
MON 3:00	*		*		
MON 3:30	*		*		
MON 4:00			*		
MON 4:30			*		
MON 5:00				*	
MON 5:30				*	
TUE 8:00	*	*	*	*	*
TUE 8:30	*	*	*	*	*
TUE 9:00	*	*		*	*
TUE 9:30	*	*		*	*
TUE 10:00	*	*	*	*	
TUE 10:30	*	*	*	*	
TUE 11:00	*	*	*	*	
TUE 11:30	*	*	*	*	
TUE 12:00	*	*		*	
TUE 12:30	*	*		*	
TUE 1:00	*	*		*	
TUE 1:30	*	*		*	
TUE 2:00	*	*	*	*	*
TUE 2:30	*	*	*	*	*
TUE 3:00	*	*	*	*	*
TUE 3:30	*	*	*	*	*
TUE 4:00	*	*		*	*
TUE 4:30	*	*		*	*
TUE 5:00	*	*		*	
TUE 5:30	*	*		*	

WED 8:00		*	*	*	
WED 8:30		*	*	*	
WED 9:00	*	*		*	*
WED 9:30	*	*		*	*
WED 10:00	*	*	*	*	*
WED 10:30	*	*	*	*	*
WED 11:00		*	*	*	
WED 11:30		*		*	
WED 12:00	*	*	*	*	*
WED 12:30	*	*	*	*	*
WED 1:00	*	*	*	*	*
WED 1:30		*	*	*	
WED 2:00		*		*	*
WED 2:30		*		*	*
WED 3:00		*	*	*	
WED 3:30		*	*	*	
WED 4:00	*	*	*	*	
WED 4:30	*	*	*	*	
WED 5:00		*	*	*	
WED 5:30		*		*	
THR 8:00	*		*	*	
THR 8:30	*		*	*	
THR 9:00	*		*	*	*
THR 9:30	*		*	*	
THR 10:00	*			*	
THR 10:30	*			*	
THR 11:00	*			*	
THR 11:30	*			*	
THR 12:00	*			*	
THR 12:30	*			*	
THR 1:00	*			*	
THR 1:30	*			*	
THR 2:00	*			*	*
THR 2:30	*			*	
THR 3:00	*			*	
THR 3:30	*			*	
THR 4:00	*		*	*	
THR 4:30	*		*	*	
THR 5:00	*		*	*	
THR 5:30	*		*	*	

```
FRI 8:00        *                                           *
FRI 8:30        *
FRI 9:00        *                              *
FRI 9:30        *                              *
FRI 10:00       *                 *            *
FRI 10:30       *                 *            *
FRI 11:00       *                 *                          *
FRI 11:30       *                 *
FRI 12:00       *                 *                          *
FRI 12:30       *                 *                          *
FRI 1:00        *                 *                          *
FRI 1:30        *                 *                          *
FRI 2:00              *           *            *
FRI 2:30              *           *            *
FRI 3:00              *           *            *
FRI 3:30                                       *
FRI 4:00
FRI 4:30
FRI 5:00
FRI 5:30
```

DO YOU WANT TO SCHEDULE A MEETING? NO

"How does the computer know this is the schedule?" asked
Grimes.

"I typed in the information you gave me yesterday. It looks like
this in the program:"

```
1992 REM    PRSN #, DAY, MEETING TIMES, 7,7
2000        DATA 1, MON,  8,10,  2,4,  7,7
2010        DATA 1, TUE,  8,6,  7,7
2020        DATA 1, WED,  9,11,  12,1.5,  4,5,  7,7
2030        DATA 1, THR,  8,6,  7,7
2040        DATA 1, FRI,  8,2,  7,7
2050        DATA 2, MON,  8,10,  2,3,  7,7
2060        DATA 2, TUE,  8,6,  7,7
2070        DATA 2, WED,  8,6,  7,7
2080        DATA 2, FRI,  2,3.5,  7,7
2090        DATA 3, MON,  8,11,  2,5,  7,7
2100        DATA 3, TUE,  8,9,  10,12,  2,4,  7,7
2110        DATA 3, WED,  8,9,  10,11.5,  12,2,  3,5.5,  7,7
2120        DATA 3, THR,  8,10,  4,6,  7,7
2130        DATA 3, FRI,  10,3.5,  7,7
2140        DATA 4, MON,  9,10,  5,6,  7,7
2150        DATA 4, TUE,  8,6,  7,7
2160        DATA 4, WED,  8,6,  7,7
2170        DATA 4, THR,  8,6,  7,7
2180        DATA 4, FRI,  9,11,  2,4,  7,7
```

```
2190      DATA 5, MON,  10,2,  7,7
2200      DATA 5, TUE,  8,10,  2,5.5,  7,7
2210      DATA 5, WED,  9,11,  12,1.5,  2,3.3,  7,7
2220      DATA 5, THR,  9,9.5,  2,2.5,  7,7
2230      DATA 5, FRI,  8,8.5,  11,11.5,  12,2,  7,7
2240      DATA 77            'LAST DATA ITEM
2242 '
```

"What's the 10.5 mean?" asked Grimes.

"Ten-thirty. I made the schedule accurate to the half hour."

Grimes nodded and looked at the data again. "How about that 7,7 at the end of each line? What does that do?"

"It tells the program that it is finished with the line," answered Cauldwell.

"That must mean that the 77 at the bottom signals the end of the data?"

"Yes, that's right," said Cauldwell.

"What if a new meeting gets added to the schedule?" asked Grimes.

"Just slip in a new line of DATA anywhere in that section," said Cauldwell.

"But what if somebody's schedule changes," persisted Grimes.

"Simply retype the day with the change," said Cauldwell.

Grimes nodded. "It might work. After any corrections, I assume that I can get a new copy of the schedule."

"Absolutely," said Cauldwell. "You can always get a fresh copy. To make this idea work, you will need everybody's schedule at the beginning of the week and everyone's commitment to keep you informed of any changes. You might be able to secure the commitment by sending them copies of the schedule."

"Sounds fair enough," said Grimes. "We spend half our lives on the phone arranging meetings. This program might let us get back to our other work. Thanks very much."

Six weeks later Grimes volunteered to Cauldwell that she was being treated to lunch by two of the divisional managers' secretaries.

"What's the occasion?" asked Cauldwell.

"FINDTIME's improvement in scheduling meetings. We've all saved hours thanks to that program."

Cauldwell smiled. "Good. Then it would be fair to say that you believe computers can be of some help in the office, even it they won't revolutionize it?"

Grimes smiled, "It would be fair to say that, yes."

That was how change really occurred, thought Cauldwell. One small victory at a time. The company had changed during the year. People were becoming computer-literate. He saw it in meetings, in conversations in the hall, in his managers' refined approach to decision-making. The little computers were changing things one small step at a time.

THE PROGRAM FINDTIME

```
1000 REM   FINDTIME      1 JANUARY 1982   STEVEN CAULDWELL
1010 '
1020 REM   © COPYRIGHT 1980 JOHN M. NEVISON ASSOCIATES
1030 '
1040 REM   SCHEDULE FIVE PEOPLE FOR THEIR WEEKLY
1050 REM   MEETINGS.  PRINT THE SCHEDULE ON REQUEST.
1060 '
1070 REM   PRINT A LIST OF AVAILABLE HOURS FOR A NEW
1080 REM   MEETING AMONG ANY OF THE PEOPLE.
1090 '
1100 REM   TO USE THIS PROGRAM, THE USER MUST ENTER THE
1110 REM   APPROPRIATE SCHEDULE IN THE SUBROUTINE 'ENTER THE
1120 REM   SCHEDULE.'
1130 '
1140 REM   VARIABLES:
1150 REM       D$.........CURRENT DAY
1160 REM       D$() ........DAY NAMES
1170 REM       D() ........DAY NUMBERS (1-5)
1180 REM       I,J,K .......LOOP INDEX VARIABLES
1182 REM       I1 .........PREVIOUS VALUE OF I
1184 REM       N() ........INPUT PERSONS' NUMBERS
1186 REM       P1.........NUMBER OF INPUT PERSONS
1190 REM       P..........PERSON NUMBER
1200 REM       S$() .......SCHEDULE TABLE
1210 REM       T1.........CURRENT BEGINNING TIME
1220 REM       T2.........CURRENT ENDING TIME
1230 REM       T3.........TEMPORARY TIME VARIABLE
1240 REM       T$() .......HALF HOUR TIME NAMES
1250 REM       T() ........HALF HOUR TIME NUMBERS (1-21)
1260 REM       X..........TEMPORARY VARIABLE
1270 '
1280 REM   CONSTANTS:
1290       LET P9 = 5        'NUMBER OF PEOPLE ON SCHEDULE
1300 '
1310 REM   DIMENSIONS:
1320       DIM D(100), S$(100,5), T(100), T$(21)
1322 '
```

```
1323 REM    MAIN ROUTINE
1324 '
1325 REM    ERASE THE TABLE
1330        FOR I = 1 TO 100
1340           FOR J = 1 TO P9
1350              LET S$(I,J) = " "
1360           NEXT J
1370        NEXT I
1390 '
1400        GOSUB 1560      'NUMBER TO DAY
1410        GOSUB 1860      'ENTER THE SCHEDULE
1415 '
1420        PRINT "DO YOU WANT A FULL SCHEDULE (YES OR NO)";
1430        INPUT A$
1440        IF A$ = "YES" THEN 1450 ELSE 1460
1450           GOSUB 2920    'PRINT THE SCHEDULE
1460 '      IFEND
1465 '
1470        PRINT
1480        PRINT "DO YOU WANT TO SCHEDULE A MEETING";
1490        INPUT A$
1500        IF A$ = "YES" THEN 1510 ELSE 1520
1510           GOSUB 3130    'FIND A MEETING TIME
1520 '      IFEND
1525 '
1530        STOP
1540 '
1550 '
1560 REM    SUBROUTINE: NUMBER TO DAY
1570 REM       IN: --
1580 REM    OUT: D$(), D(), T$(), T()
1590 '
1600 REM    COMPUTE HOW 1-100 HALF HOUR INTERVALS
1610 REM    CONVERT TO 1-5 DAYS, D(), AND 1-20 HALF HOURS, T().
1620 '
1630 REM    READ THE NAMES FOR THE DAYS, D$(),
1640 REM    AND HALF HOURS, T$().
1650 '
1660        FOR I = 1 TO 100
1670           LET T(I) = (I-1) - INT((I-1)/20)*20 + 1
1680           LET D(I) = INT((I-1)/20) + 1
1690        NEXT I
1700        FOR I = 1 TO 5
1710           READ D$(I)
1720        NEXT I
1730        DATA MON, TUE, WED, THR, FRI
```

```
1740      FOR I = 1 TO 21
1750          READ T$(I)
1760      NEXT I
1770      DATA "8:00", "8:30", "9:00", "9:30", "10:00"
1780      DATA "10:30", "11:00", "11:30", "12:00","12:30"
1790      DATA "1:00", "1:30", "2:00", "2:30", "3:00"
1800      DATA "3:30", "4:00", "4:30", "5:00", "5:30"
1810      DATA "6:00"
1820 '
1830 RETURN
1840 '
1850 '
1860 REM    SUBROUTINE: ENTER THE SCHEDULE
1870 REM      IN: --
1880 REM    OUT: S$()
1890 '
1900 REM    ENTER THE WEEKS SCHEDULE INTO THE TABLE S$().
1910 REM    DIRECTIONS:
1920 REM      1.  IF A PERSON IS FREE ALL DAY ENTER
1930 REM          NOTHING.
1940 REM      2.  IF A PERSON IS AWAY ALL DAY ENTER
1950 REM          AN ALL DAY MEETING, (8,6).
1960 REM      3.  OTHERWISE, ENTER DATA SIMILAR TO THE
1970 REM          SAMPLE INCLUDED BELOW.
1980 REM      4.  A 7,7 ENDS A LINE AND A 77 ENDS THE DATA.
1990 '
1992 REM    PRSN #, DAY, MEETING TIMES, 7,7
2000      DATA 1, MON,  8,10,  2,4,  7,7
2010      DATA 1, TUE,  8,6,  7,7
2020      DATA 1, WED,  9,11,  12,1.5,  4,5,  7,7
2030      DATA 1, THR,  8,6,  7,7
2040      DATA 1, FRI,  8,2,  7,7
2050      DATA 2, MON,  8,10,  2,3,  7,7
2060      DATA 2, TUE,  8,6,  7,7
2070      DATA 2, WED,  8,6,  7,7
2080      DATA 2, FRI,  2,3.5,  7,7
2090      DATA 3, MON,  8,11,  2,5,  7,7
2100      DATA 3, TUE,  8,9,  10,12,  2,4,  7,7
2110      DATA 3, WED,  8,9,  10,11.5,  12,2,  3,5.5,  7,7
2120      DATA 3, THR,  8,10,  4,6,  7,7
2130      DATA 3, FRI,  10,3.5,  7,7
2140      DATA 4, MON,  9,10,  5,6,  7,7
2150      DATA 4, TUE,  8,6,  7,7
2160      DATA 4, WED,  8,6,  7,7
2170      DATA 4, THR,  8,6,  7,7
2180      DATA 4, FRI,  9,11,  2,4,  7,7
```

```
2190        DATA 5, MON,  10,2,  7,7
2200        DATA 5, TUE,  8,10,  2,5.5,  7,7
2210        DATA 5, WED,  9,11,  12,1.5,  2,3.3,  7,7
2220        DATA 5, THR,  9,9.5,  2,2.5,  7,7
2230        DATA 5, FRI,  8,8.5,  11,11.5,  12,2,  7,7
2240        DATA 77              'LAST DATA ITEM
2242 '
2250        FOR I = 1 TO 150
2260           READ P
2270           IF P = 77 THEN 2640  'LOOP EXIT
2280           READ D$
2290           FOR J = 1 TO 15
2300              READ T1,T2
2310              IF T1 > 13 THEN 2320 ELSE 2340
2320                 PRINT T1; "IS TOO BIG. PERSON #"; P; "ON "; D$
2330                 STOP
2340 '               IFEND
2350              IF T2 > 13 THEN 2360 ELSE 2380
2360                 PRINT T2; "IS TOO BIG. PERSON #"; P; "ON "; D$
2370                 STOP
2380 '               IFEND
2390              IF T1 = 7 THEN 2540  'LOOP EXIT
2400              LET X = T1
2410              GOSUB 2680     'DAY TO NUMBER
2420              LET T1 = X
2430              LET X = T2-.5
2440              GOSUB 2680     'DAY TO NUMBER
2450              LET T2 = X
2460              FOR K = T1 TO T2
2470                 LET S$(K,P) = "*"
2480              NEXT K
2490           NEXT J
2500           PRINT "MORE THAN 15 MEETINGS ON "
2510           PRINT D$; " FOR PERSON # "; P; "."
2520           PRINT "PLEASE CHECK DATA."
2530           STOP
2540 '
2550              IF T2 = 7 THEN 2590
2560                 PRINT "TIMES ARE NOT PAIRED FOR PERSON #";
2570                 PRINT P; "ON "; D$
2580                 STOP
2590 '               IFEND
2600           NEXT I
2610        PRINT "MORE THAN 150 LINES OF SCHEDULE"
2620        PRINT "PLEASE CHECK DATA."
2630        STOP
2640 '
2650 RETURN
2660 '
2670 '
```

```
2680 REM    SUBROUTINE: DAY TO NUMBER
2690 REM       IN: D$, X
2700 REM    OUT: X
2710 '
2720 REM    CONVERT THE DAY AND THE TIME (8-6) TO A
2730 REM    NUMBER BETWEEN 1 AND 100.
2740 '
2750       LET T3 = X
2760       FOR K = 1 TO 5
2770          IF D$(K) = D$ THEN 2820   'LOOP EXIT
2780       NEXT K
2790       PRINT D$; " IS NOT A LEGAL DAY."
2800       PRINT "PLEASE CHECK DATA."
2810       STOP
2820 '
2830       LET X = (K-1) * 20
2840       IF T3 < 7 THEN 2850 ELSE 2860
2850         LET T3 = T3 + 12
2860 '     IFEND
2870       LET X = X + ((T3-8)*2 + 1)
2880 '
2890 RETURN
2900 '
2910 '
2920 REM    SUBROUTINE: PRINT THE SCHEDULE
2930 REM       IN: D$(), D(), S$(), T$(), T()
2940 REM    OUT: --
2950 '
2952       PRINT
2954       PRINT
2960       PRINT TAB(10);"STEVE FRANK EILEEN   ROSE   TOM"
2970       PRINT TAB(10);" -----------------------"
2980 '
2990       FOR I = 1 TO 100
3000          PRINT D$(D(I));" "; T$(T(I));TAB(10);
3010          FOR J = 1 TO P9
3020             PRINT TAB(10+(J-1)*8);S$(I,J);
3030          NEXT J
3040          PRINT
3050          IF INT(I/20) = I/20 THEN 3060 ELSE 3070
3060            PRINT
3070 '        IFEND
3080       NEXT I
3090 '
3100 RETURN
3110 '
3120 '
```

```
3130 REM    SUBROUTINE: FIND TIME
3140 REM      IN: D$(), D(), S$(), T$(), T()
3150 REM    OUT: --
3160 '
3170      PRINT
3180      PRINT "PEOPLE:"
3190      PRINT " 1. STEVE CAULDWELL"
3200      PRINT " 2. FRANK BRADSHAW"
3210      PRINT " 3. EILEEN RANDALL"
3220      PRINT " 4. ROSE THOMPSON"
3230      PRINT " 5. TOM DELLER"
3240      PRINT
3250      PRINT "PLEASE TYPE A NUMBER FROM 1 TO 5 "
3260      PRINT "FOR EACH PERSON IN THE MEETING."
3270      PRINT "WHEN DONE, PLEASE TYPE A 0(ZERO)."
3275 '
3280      FOR I = 1  TO P9+1
3282          INPUT N(I)
3284          IF N(I) = 0 THEN 3340  'LOOP EXIT
3290          IF N(I)<0 OR N(I)>5 THEN 3294 ELSE 3298
3294            PRINT "NUMBER MUST BE BETWEEN 0-5"
3295            PRINT "PLEASE RETYPE IT."
3296            LET I = I − 1
3298 '          IFEND
3310      NEXT I
3320      PRINT "NO MORE THAN "; P9; "ENTRIES."
3330      STOP
3340 '
3350      LET P1 = I − 1
3360      LET I1 = 0
3370      FOR I = 1 TO 100
3380          FOR J = 1 TO P1
3390              IF S$(I,N(J)) = "*" THEN 3460   'LOOP EXIT
3400          NEXT J
3410          IF I−1 < > I1 THEN 3420 ELSE 3430
3420            PRINT
3430 '          IFEND
3440          PRINT D$(D(I)); " "; T$(T(I))
3450          LET I1 = I
3460 '
3470      NEXT I
3480 '
3490 RETURN
3500      END
```

FINDTIME is a program broken into subroutines. Each subroutine performs a specific function and passes results back to the line of the program that invoked it. The program's organization is:

MAIN ROUTINE
    NUMBER TO DAY
    ENTER THE SCHEDULE
      DAY TO NUMBER
    PRINT THE SCHEDULE
    FIND TIME

The program uses the INPUT statement to allow the user to direct what the program will do. Cauldwell wrote this program for his secretary and he knew the kinds of things she would want to do with the program, so he made it as convenient as possible to use.

Another feature that helps the user is the series of IF ... THEN ... ELSE statements that try to trap bad data in the subroutine ENTER THE SCHEDULE. The program knows that a person can make a mistake typing in the DATA lines and it tries to catch some of these mistakes. Programs that behave in this fashion are hard to write but easy to use.

DAY TO NUMBER converts raw data into a 1–100 number and NUMBER TO DAY converts a 1–100 number into the appropriate day and time. The second conversion is held as a table in the D() and T() variables so that FIND TIME and PRINT THE SCHEDULE can proceed quickly.

_____ *Exercises* _____

1. Use FINDTIME to schedule some meetings in your office.
2. Improve the ENTER THE SCHEDULE subroutine by checking to be sure P is a legal person number and D$ is a legal day name.
3. (Difficult.) Change the program to work from 9 to 5 on whole hours.

_____

References

1. Brown, Robert Goodell, *Smoothing, Forecasting and Prediction of Discrete Time Series*, Englewood Cliffs, NJ: Prentice-Hall, 1963.
2. Fraser, D.A.S., *Statistics: An Introduction*, New York: Wiley, 1967.
3. Makridakis, Spyros, and Wheelwright, Steven C., *Forecasting Methods for Management*, New York: Wiley 1977.
4. Makridakis, Spyros, and Wheelwright, Steven C., *Interactive Forecasting; Univariate and Multivariate Methods*, Second Edition, San Francisco, CA: Holden-Day, 1978.
5. Mosteller, Frederick, and Tukey, John W., *Data Analysis and Regression: A Second Course in Statistics*, Reading, MA: Addison-Wesley, 1977.
6. Tukey, John W., *Exploratory Data Analysis*, Reading, MA: Addison-Wesley, 1977.

APPENDIXES

A

Introduction to BASIC
and Program Structure

What of architectural beauty I now see, I know has gradually grown from within outward.

Henry David Thoreau

This appendix has four parts. The novice will want to read all four. The advanced reader can skip the first part, but should read the remaining three. The four sections are: "BASIC in Action," "Style and Structure," "Program Paragraphs," and "The Larger Program."

"BASIC in Action" introduces the language BASIC and several of the language's features. "Style and Structure" discusses the fundamental ideas of program composition. "Program Paragraphs" reveals several useful programming tricks in BASIC. "The Larger Program" explains how to assemble several little programs into one big one.

BASIC IN ACTION

The programs that follow are intended to be self-explanatory. The LIST of the program together with its RUN will show you not only how the program looks in BASIC, but how it is performed by the computer. As you read these programs, you should learn what PRINT, END, LET, REM, FOR and NEXT, READ and DATA, INPUT, and IF ... THEN mean in BASIC. If you have a question about any of the programs, try it on a computer and see how it works. If you don't have a computer available, consult one of the references at the end of the appendix.

LIST

PROG1   13 SEP 80 20:16

10 PRINT "YOU CAN PRINT ANYTHING IN QUOTES"
20 END

RUN

PROG1   13 SEP 80 20:16

YOU CAN PRINT ANYTHING IN QUOTES

PROG2   13 SEP 80 20:21

10 PRINT "BY USING SEVERAL LINES, YOU CAN"
20 PRINT "PRINT QUITE ";
30 PRINT "AN EXTENDED MESSAGE. NOTICE THAT"
40 PRINT "BY USING THE SEMICOLON(;), ";
50 PRINT "YOU CAN"
60 PRINT "CONTROL HOW THE LINES LOOK WHEN THEY ARE PRINTED."
70 END

RUN

PROG2   13 SEP 80 20:21

BY USING SEVERAL LINES, YOU CAN
PRINT QUITE AN EXTENDED MESSAGE. NOTICE THAT
BY USING THE SEMICOLON(;), YOU CAN
CONTROL HOW THE LINES LOOK WHEN THEY ARE PRINTED.

LIST

PROG3   13 SEP 80 20:24

10 PRINT "1234567891123456789212345678931234567894"
20 PRINT TAB(13); "YOU CAN PRINT WHERE YOU WISH."
30 END

RUN

PROG3   13 SEP 80 20:25

1234567891123456789212345678931234567894
            YOU CAN PRINT WHERE YOU WISH.

LIST

PROG4   13 SEP 80 20:29

10 PRINT "12345678911234567892123456789312345678941234567895"
20 PRINT TAB(5); "YOU"; TAB(10); "CAN";
30 PRINT TAB(15); "PRINT"; TAB(22);
40 PRINT "WHEREVER"; TAB (40); "YOU WISH"
50 PRINT "WITH TABS."
60 END

RUN

PROG4   13 SEP 80 20:29

12345678911234567892123456789312345678941234567895
     YOU CAN PRINT   WHEREVER   YOU WISH
WITH TABS.

LIST

PROG5   13 SEP 80 20:32

10 PRINT "YOU CAN ALSO PRINT NUMBERS"
20 PRINT 3333, 1.68243, 38.2, 54321
30 END

RUN

PROG5   13 SEP 80 20:33

YOU CAN ALSO PRINT NUMBERS
 3333   1.68243   38.2   54321

```
LIST

PROG6     13 SEP 80  20:36

10 PRINT "YOU CAN PRINT OUT THE RESULTS OF A CALCULATION"
20 PRINT 666/3, 4+18, (3*4)/6, 2-4
30 END

RUN

PROG6     13 SEP 80  20:36

YOU CAN PRINT OUT THE RESULTS OF A CALCULATION
  222            22             2            -2



LIST

PROG7     13 SEP 80  20:40

10 PRINT "YOU CAN PRINT BOTH MESSAGES "
20 PRINT "AND A CALCULATION ", 33+44
30 END

RUN

PROG7     13 SEP 80  20:40

YOU CAN PRINT BOTH MESSAGES
AND A CALCULATION           77



LIST

PROG8     13 SEP 80  20:42

10 PRINT "THE REVENUE IS "; 275
20 PRINT "THE COSTS ARE "; 216
30 PRINT "THE PROFIT IS "; 275-216
40 END

RUN

PROG8     13 SEP 80  20:42

THE REVENUE IS   275
THE COSTS ARE   216
THE PROFIT IS   59
```

LIST

PROG9   13 SEP 80 20:45

10 PRINT "YOU CAN PRINT A BLANK LINE WITH "
20 PRINT
30 PRINT "AN EMPTY PRINT STATEMENT."
40 END

RUN

PROG9   13 SEP 80 20:45

YOU CAN PRINT A BLANK LINE WITH

AN EMPTY PRINT STATEMENT.

LIST

PROG10   13 SEP 80 20:48

10 PRINT "YOU CAN PRINT THE VALUE OF A VARIABLE"
20 LET V = 1776
30 PRINT "V HAS THE VALUE", V
40 END

RUN

PROG10   13 SEP 80 20:48

YOU CAN PRINT THE VALUE OF A VARIABLE
V HAS THE VALUE   1776

```
LIST

PROG11    13 SEP 80  20:51

10 PRINT "YOU CAN PRINT THE RESULT OF A COMPUTATION "
20 PRINT "THAT IS ASSIGNED TO A VARIABLE."
30 LET V = (17 * 3) / 6
40 PRINT V
50 END

RUN

PROG11    13 SEP 80  20:51

YOU CAN PRINT THE RESULT OF A COMPUTATION
THAT IS ASSIGNED TO A VARIABLE.
  8.5
```

```
LIST

PROG12    13 SEP 80  20:56

10 PRINT "YOU CAN PRINT QUITE A NUMBER OF VARIABLES."
15 PRINT
20 LET R = 2.6
30 LET D = 2 * R
40 LET C = 3.14159 * D
50 LET A = 3.14159 * R * R
60 PRINT "FOR A CIRCLE WITH A RADIUS OF ";R
70 PRINT "THE DIAMETER IS "; D
80 PRINT "THE CIRCUMFERENCE IS "; C
90 PRINT "THE AREA IS "; A
99 END

RUN

PROG12    13 SEP 80  20:56

YOU CAN PRINT QUITE A NUMBER OF VARIABLES.

FOR A CIRCLE WITH A RADIUS OF   2.6
THE DIAMETER IS   5.2
THE CIRCUMFERENCE IS   16.3363
THE AREA IS   21.2371
```

LIST

PROG13   13 SEP 80 21:03

```
10 PRINT "YOU CAN GO FROM THE OLD VALUE OF A "
20 PRINT "VARIABLE TO THE NEW VALUE."
30 LET S = 100
40 PRINT "AT LINE 40, S IS "; S
50 LET S = 1.15 * S
60 PRINT "AT LINE 60, S IS "; S
70 END
```

RUN

PROG13   13 SEP 80 21:03

```
YOU CAN GO FROM THE OLD VALUE OF A
VARIABLE TO THE NEW VALUE.
AT LINE 40, S IS   100
AT LINE 60, S IS   115.
```

LIST

PROG14   13 SEP 80 21:07

```
10 PRINT "YOU CAN MODIFY A VARIABLE SEVERAL TIMES."
20 PRINT "YOU MAY THINK OF S AS A SUM THAT "
30 PRINT "IS BEING COMPOUNDED AT 15% A YEAR."
40 LET S = 100
45 PRINT S
50 LET S = 1.15 * S
55 PRINT S
60 LET S = 1.15 * S
65 PRINT S
70 LET S = 1.15 * S
75 PRINT S
80 END
```

RUN

PROG14   13 SEP 80 21:08

```
YOU CAN MODIFY A VARIABLE SEVERAL TIMES.
YOU MAY THINK OF S AS A SUM THAT
IS BEING COMPOUNDED AT 15% A YEAR.
 100
 115.
 132.25
 152.088
```

LIST

PROG15   13 SEP 80 21:09

```
10 REM    MEANS REMARK. REMARKS ARE NEVER PRINTED.
20        PRINT "THIS IS THE ONLY LINE THAT IS PRINTED."
30        END
```

RUN

PROG15   13 SEP 80 21:10

THIS IS THE ONLY LINE THAT IS PRINTED.

LIST

PROG16   13 SEP 80 21:14

```
100 REM    YOU MAY REPEAT A PIECE OF CODE BY USING
110 REM    THE "FOR ... NEXT" PAIR OF STATEMENTS.
120 REM
130        LET S = 100
150        FOR Y = 1 TO 4
160            LET S = 1.15 * S
170            PRINT Y, S
180        NEXT Y
200        PRINT "AFTER FOUR YEARS, THE SUM IS "; S
210        END
```

RUN

PROG16   13 SEP 80 21:14

```
    1            115.
    2            132.25
    3            152.088
    4            174.901
AFTER FOUR YEARS, THE SUM IS   174.901
```

LIST

PROG17   13 SEP 80 21:17

```
110 REM   YOU MAY READ DATA USING THE
120 REM   "READ" AND "DATA" STATEMENTS.
130 REM
140       DATA 275, 216
150       READ R, C
160       LET P = R − C
170       PRINT "REVENUE", "COST", "PROFIT"
180       PRINT   R,  C,  P
190       END
```

RUN

PROG17   13 SEP 80 21:17

REVENUE	COST	PROFIT
275	216	59

LIST

PROG18   13 SEP 80 21:26

```
100 REM   YOU MAY CALCULATE SEVERAL DIVISIONS' DATA
110 REM   WITH THE HELP OF A LOOP AND SEVERAL LINES OF
120 REM   DATA.
130 REM
140       DATA 33, 22
142       DATA 600, 423
144       DATA 500, 275
146       DATA 208, 106
148 REM
150       PRINT "DIVISION", "REVENUE", "COST", "PROFIT"
160       FOR D = 1 TO 4
170          READ R,C
180          LET P = R − C
190          PRINT D, R, C, P
200       NEXT D
210       END
```

RUN

PROG18   13 SEP 80 21:26

DIVISION	REVENUE	COST	PROFIT
1	33	22	11
2	600	423	177
3	500	275	225
4	208	106	102

LIST

PROG19   13 SEP 80 21:32

```
10 REM    THIS PROGRAM WILL ONLY WORK IN 1981.
15        PRINT "YOU CAN ENTER DATA IN THE MIDDLE "
20        PRINT "OF A PROGRAM WITH AN 'INPUT' STATEMENT."
30        PRINT
40        PRINT "HOW OLD ARE YOU ON YOUR BIRTHDAY THIS YEAR"
50        INPUT A
60        LET Y = 1981 − A
70        PRINT
80        PRINT "THAT MEANS YOU WERE BORN IN "; Y
90        END
```

RUN

PROG19   13 SEP 80 21:32

YOU CAN ENTER DATA IN THE MIDDLE
OF A PROGRAM WITH AN 'INPUT' STATEMENT.

HOW OLD ARE YOU ON YOUR BIRTHDAY THIS YEAR
? 38

THAT MEANS YOU WERE BORN IN   1943

```
LIST

PROG20   13 SEP 80  21:38

100 REM   YOU CAN EXPLORE ALTERNATIVES WITH
110 REM   THE "IF ... THEN" STATEMENT.
120 REM
130       PRINT "HOW OLD ARE YOU NOW";
140       INPUT A
150       PRINT
160       IF A <= 30 THEN 170 ELSE 190
170         PRINT "YOU ARE A YOUNG WHIPPER-SNAPPER."
180         GOTO 210          'IFEND
190 '     ELSE
200         PRINT "YOU ARE AN OLD FUDDY-DUDDY."
210 '     IFEND
220       END

RUN

PROG20   13 SEP 80  21:39

HOW OLD ARE YOU NOW? 44


YOU ARE AN OLD FUDDY-DUDDY.


RUN

PROG20   13 SEP 80  21:39

HOW OLD ARE YOU NOW? 22


YOU ARE A YOUNG WHIPPER-SNAPPER.
```

STYLE AND STRUCTURE

Every program has three essential features: input, process, and output. Input uses a LET statement, an INPUT statement, or a READ statement. Process works with an appropriate LET statement. Output comes from the PRINT statement. As the program gets data, processes it, and prints out answers, its work flow should be controlled in three ways:

1. Sequence (line numbers),
2. Decision (IF ... THEN ... ELSE statement),
3. Repetition (FOR-NEXT statement pair).

By using these three structures to control your program's flow you can write a program that is more likely to be correct. By adopting stylistic conventions for indentation and for blank lines you can write a program that will be easier to read (and easier to revise when it is incorrect).

Sequence

Simple sequence is the flow the computer follows unless it is interrupted by a decision or a loop.

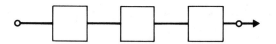

Fig. A-1   Flow Diagram for Sequence

Example

```
100     LET R = 5
200     LET D= 2 * R
300     LET C= 3.14159 * D
400     LET A= 3.14159 * R * R
```

Decision

Logical decisions are made with the IF ... THEN ... ELSE statement. Most of the time, a decision is confined to two alternatives.

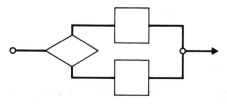

Fig. A-2   Flow Diagram for Decision

Example (TRS-80 Level II BASIC)

```
100      IF X > 6 THEN 110 ELSE 150
110         PRINT "X IS BIGGER THAN SIX"
120         GOTO 190          'IFEND
150 '    ELSE
160         PRINT "X IS LESS THAN OR EQUAL TO SIX"
190 '    IFEND
```

This example is the preferred way to handle the IF ... THEN ... ELSE statement in TRS-80 Level II BASIC. If your BASIC has the logical operators NOT, AND, and OR, but does not have the ELSE part of the IF ... THEN statement, then write your decisions this way.

Example (with NOT but without ELSE)

```
100      IF NOT (X > 6) THEN 150
110         PRINT "X IS BIGGER THAN SIX"
120         GOTO 190          'IFEND
150 '    ELSE
160         PRINT "X IS LESS THAN OR EQUAL TO SIX"
190 '    IFEND
```

If your BASIC is only ANSI Minimal BASIC and does not have the logical operators NOT, AND, and OR, then write your decisions this way.

Example (ANSI Minimal BASIC)

```
100      IF X <= 6 THEN 150
110         PRINT "X IS BIGGER THAN SIX"
120         GOTO 190            'IFEND
150 '    ELSE
160         PRINT "X IS LESS THAN OR EQUAL TO SIX"
190 '    IFEND
```

Your IF ... THEN ... ELSE structure should always have at least six lines. Of course it can have many more. In the above example, each of the PRINT lines could be replaced with several lines of program.

The IF ... THEN ... ELSE statement has a reduced version called IF ... THEN.

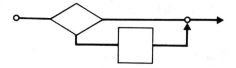

Fig. A-3   Flow Diagram for Reduced Decision

Example (TRS-80 Level II BASIC)

```
100      IF Y = 8 THEN 110 ELSE 150
110         PRINT "Y IS EIGHT"
150 '    IFEND
```

Example (With NOT but lacking ELSE)

```
100      IF NOT(Y = 8 ) THEN 150
110         PRINT "Y IS EIGHT"
150 '    IFEND
```

Example (ANSI Minimal)

```
100      IF Y < > 8 THEN 150
110         PRINT "Y IS EIGHT"
150 '    IFEND
```

Another special version of the IF ... THEN ... ELSE structure is sometimes called the CASE structure. It is really a sequence of simple IF ... THEN ... ELSEs.

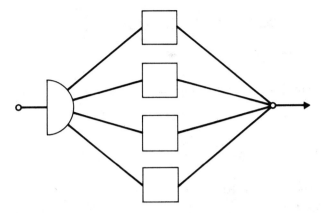

Fig. A-4   Flow Diagram for Expanded Decision

Example (TRS-80 Level II BASIC)

```
100      IF B = 1 THEN 110 ELSE 130
110        PRINT "GEORGE"
120        GOTO 230         'IFEND
130      IF B = 2 THEN 140 ELSE 160
140        PRINT "PAUL"
150        GOTO 230         'IFEND
160      IF B = 3 THEN 170 ELSE 190
170        PRINT "JOHN"
180        GOTO 230         'IFEND
190      IF B = 4 THEN 200 ELSE 220
200        PRINT "RINGO"
210        GOTO 230         'IFEND
220      PRINT "BEATLE OUT OF BOUNDS"
230 '    IFEND
```

Notice how in all the examples two apostrophe (') statements masquerade as other BASIC statements. These statements mimic the new structured BASIC developed at Dartmouth College (where the original BASIC was developed). You should use both the apostrophe ELSE and the apostrophe IFEND in your programs and indent all lines of code five spaces, so the apostrophe ELSE and the apostrophe IFEND can be aligned with the IF . . . THEN statement.

Also notice how indentation is used to show off the structure of all decisions. For further details on these ideas see *The Little Book of BASIC Style* by John M. Nevison (Addison-Wesley, 1978).

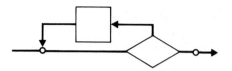

Fig. A-5   Flow Diagram for Repetition

Repetition

By far the trickiest structure in a computer program is the loop. The loop sends the program back to an earlier line and makes the program repeat statements.

Example

```
100      FOR X = 1 TO 10
110          PRINT X
120      NEXT X
130 '
```

```
100      IF C > 600 THEN 150
110          LET C = C + 33
120          PRINT C
130      GOTO 100
150 '
```

Both of these loops continue repeating until a certain condition is met. The FOR-NEXT pair repeats ten times (until X exceeds 10). The second loop continues until the value of C exceeds 600. Technically the FOR-NEXT construction could be rewritten with an IF . . . THEN and a GOTO. In practice, however, it is better to convert all possible loops to the FOR-NEXT construction. The second example could be rewritten as follows.

Example

```
100      FOR I = 1 TO 100000
110          IF C > 600 THEN 150
120          LET C = C + 33
130          PRINT C
140      NEXT I
150 '
```

While other logical flows are possible in BASIC, the above three flows—sequence, decision, and repetition—are all that are necessary to write a sound program. In fact, your program will be better if you ruthlessly confine yourself to these three structures. Good structure distinguishes the the clear program from the confused program, the correct from the incorrect.

Some Rules of Thumb on Style and Structure in BASIC

1. Always point IF . . . THEN . . . ELSE statements down the page. The line numbers after the THEN and ELSE should never refer up the page to an earlier number.
2. Use a FOR-NEXT pair whenever possible. They are a safe way to make loops in BASIC and your program will be safer if you use them to make loops.
3. Never use the GOTO statement anywhere but in your IF . . . THEN . . . ELSE structures.
4. Indent consistently.

PROGRAM PARAGRAPHS

Some ideas occur frequently in business computer programs. Among the most common is the simple loop for reading a subscripted variable.

```
100      FOR I = 1 TO 4
110          READ X(I)
120      NEXT I
130      DATA 10, 11, 9, 7
```

This loop does the same thing as the following two lines.

```
100      READ X(1), X(2), X(3), X(4)
110      DATA 10, 11, 9, 7
```

Once a program has values for a subscripted variable, it will often sum up the values.

```
100      LET S = 0
110      FOR I = 1 TO 4
120          LET S = S + X(I)
130      NEXT I
140      PRINT "SUM IS "; S
```

To increase a number by 12 percent use the following.

```
100      LET X =  1.12 * X
```

To decrease a number by 20 percent use this.

```
100      LET X = .80 * X
```

To round off a number use this.

```
100      LET X = INT(X + .5)
```

To round off dollars to the nearest penny use this.

```
100      LET X = (INT(X*100 + .5))/100
```

To print nine numbers across a 72-character line use this.

```
100      FOR C = 1 TO 9
110          PRINT TAB((C−1)*8); X(C);
120      NEXT C
```

To insert a blank line after every five lines of print use this.

```
100      FOR R = 1 TO 11
110          PRINT "THIS IS LINE "; R
120          IF (R/5) = INT(R/5) THEN 130 ELSE 140
130              PRINT
140 '            IFEND
150      NEXT R
```

A doubly subscripted variable can hold a table of data. In the examples that follow the variable T is doubly subscripted as T(R,C). R is the row subscript and C is the column subscript.

To read the first row in the table use this.

```
100      LET R = 1
110      READ T(R,1), T(R,2), T(R,3), T(R,4)
120      DATA    10,    22,    13,    24
```

To read a long row try this. (Reads 15 items.)

```
100     LET R = 1
110     FOR C = 1 TO 15
120         READ T(R,C)
130     NEXT C
140     DATA 10,9,8,14,−77,3,8,999,12,−2,88,.34,3.25,6.90,3
```

To read in several rows in a table. (Reads 12 variables.)

```
100     FOR R = 1 TO 4
110         FOR C = 1 TO 3
120             READ T(R,C)
130         NEXT C
140     NEXT R
150     DATA 14, 13, 12
152     DATA 3, 2, 1
154     DATA 33, 44, 55
156     DATA −100, −200, −333
```

To make a new column from two old ones (for every row).

```
100     FOR R = 1 TO 4
110         LET T(R,7) = T(R,1) + T(R,3)
120     NEXT R
```

To make a new row from two old ones (for every column).

```
100     FOR C = 1 TO 3
110         LET T(5,C) = (T(1,C) + T(3,C)) * 1.15
120     NEXT C
```

To sum across the fifth row.

```
100     LET R = 5
110     LET S = 0
120     FOR C = 1 TO 3
130         LET S = S + T(R,C)
140     NEXT C
150     PRINT "THE SUM FOR ROW "; R; "IS "; S
```

To sum down every column.

```
100      FOR C = 1 TO 3
110          FOR R = 1 TO 5
120              LET S(C) = S(C) + T(R,C)
130          NEXT R
140          PRINT "THE SUM FOR COLUMN "; C; "IS "; S(C)
150      NEXT C
```

THE LARGER PROGRAM

No piece of a finished program should exceed one page in length. Code that performs a common function should be collected in one place. Repeatedly used code should be written once. All of these concerns require that a program be broken into subroutines. A medium-sized program might have the following structure (Fig. A.6).

The main program calls four major subroutines, SUB-A, SUB-B, SUB-C, and SUB-D. These subroutines in turn call additional subroutines. In the example, the bottom subroutines are two utilities called UTIL-1 and UTIL-2.

In order to call a subroutine you should use a GOSUB statement. By itself, the GOSUB appears to be no different from the GOTO. However, the GOSUB has a partner, the RETURN statement. At the end of

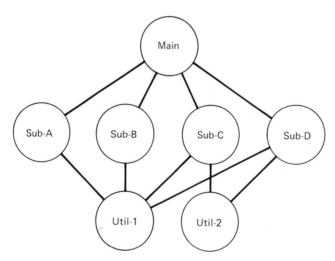

Fig. A-6   Structure Chart of a Medium-Sized Program

the subroutine, the RETURN statement returns to the line following the GOSUB that most recently called the subroutine. The RETURN remembers which GOSUB to return to.

If the subroutine gets data passed into it, the names of the variables should be noted on a REM IN: line. Any variables that carry out information—that is, any that can possibly have been altered—should be noted in a REM OUT: line. Here is what the program behind the structure chart looks like.

```
100 REM    FORM    14 SEPTEMBER 1980    J.M.NEVISON
110 '
120 REM    A PROGRAM TO DEMONSTRATE THE USE OF
130 REM    SUBROUTINES.
140 '
150 REM    VARIABLES:
160 REM        N . . . . . . . . . . . THE NUMBER
170 '
250 REM    MAIN PROGRAM
255 '
260        PRINT "MAIN PROGRAM"
270        GOSUB 500          'SUB-A
280        IF (N/2) = INT(N/2) THEN 290 ELSE 310
290          GOSUB 600        'SUB-B
300          GOTO 330         'IFEND
310 '      ELSE
320          GOSUB 700        'SUB-C
330 '      IFEND
340        GOSUB 800          'SUB-D
350        STOP
360 '
370 '
500 REM    SUBROUTINE: SUB-A
510 REM      IN: --
520 REM      OUT: N
530 '
535 REM    INPUT A NUMBER, N.
537 '
540        PRINT TAB(3); "SUB-A"
545        PRINT TAB(25); "YOUR NUMBER, PLEASE";
550        INPUT N
560        GOSUB 900          'UTIL-1
570 RETURN
580 '
590 '
```

```
600 REM    SUBROUTINE: SUB-B
610 REM      IN: N
620 REM    OUT: --
630 '
635 REM    LABEL AN EVEN NUMBER.
637 '
640        PRINT TAB(3); "SUB-B"
645        PRINT TAB(25); "N IS AN EVEN NUMBER"
650        GOSUB 900          'UTIL-1
680 RETURN
682 '
684 '
700 REM    SUBROUTINE: SUB-C
710 REM      IN: N
720 REM    OUT: N
730 '
732 REM    LABEL AND DOUBLE AN ODD NUMBER.
733 '
740        PRINT TAB(3); "SUB-C"
745        PRINT TAB(25); "N IS AN ODD NUMBER"
750        GOSUB 900          'UTIL-1
760        GOSUB 950          'UTIL-2
770        GOSUB 900          'UTIL-1
780 RETURN
782 '
784 '
800 REM    SUBROUTINE: SUB-D
810 REM      IN: N
820 REM    OUT: --
830 '
832 REM    QUADRUPLE THE FINAL NUMBER.
834 '
840        PRINT TAB(3); "SUB-D"
850        GOSUB 900          'UTIL-1
860        GOSUB 950          'UTIL-2
870        GOSUB 950          'UTIL-2
880        GOSUB 900          'UTIL-1
882 RETURN
884 '
886 '
900 REM    SUBROUTINE: UTIL-1
910 REM      IN: N
920 REM    OUT: --
930 '
932 REM    PRINT THE NUMBER, N.
934 '
940        PRINT TAB(6); "UTIL-1"
942        PRINT TAB(25); "N IS NOW "; N
944 RETURN
946 '
948 '
```

```
950 REM    SUBROUTINE: UTIL-2
960 REM      IN: N
970 REM    OUT: N
980 '
982 REM    DOUBLE THE NUMBER, N.
984 '
990        PRINT TAB(6); "UTIL-2"
992        LET N = 2 * N
994 RETURN
996 '
997 '
998        END
```

RUN

FORM   15 SEP 80 20:45

MAIN PROGRAM
  SUB-A
           YOUR NUMBER, PLEASE? 4

    UTIL-1
         N IS NOW 4
  SUB-B
         N IS AN EVEN NUMBER
    UTIL-1
         N IS NOW 4
  SUB-D
    UTIL-1
         N IS NOW 4

    UTIL-2
    UTIL-2
    UTIL-1
         N IS NOW 16

```
RUN

FORM     15 SEP 80  20:45

MAIN PROGRAM
  SUB-A
              YOUR NUMBER, PLEASE? 5

    UTIL-1
              N IS NOW  5
  SUB-C
              N IS AN ODD NUMBER
    UTIL-1
              N IS NOW  5
    UTIL-2
    UTIL-1
              N IS NOW  10
  SUB-D
    UTIL-1
              N IS NOW  10

      UTIL-2
      UTIL-2
      UTIL-1
              N IS NOW  40
```

As you work on your own program, first sketch out its major parts, then go back and sketch out the details of each part. Keep refining the detail until you can write a piece of code less than a page long. Continue in this fashion until you have completed the program. By working down from the main idea to the small details you will maintain control of your idea and of your computer program.

References

1. Dwyer, T., and Critchfield, M., *BASIC and the Personal Computer*, Reading MA: Addison-Wesley, 1978.
2. Linger, R.C., Mills, H.D., and Witt, B.I., *Structured Programming*, Reading MA: Addison-Wesley, 1979.
3. Kemeny, J.G., and Kurtz, T.E., *BASIC Programming*, 3rd edition, New York: Wiley, 1980.
4. Nevison, J.M., *The Little Book of BASIC Style*, Reading, MA: Addison-Wesley, 1978.
5. Orr, Kenneth T., *Structured Systems Development*, New York: Yourdon Press, 1977.
6. Yourdon, E., *Techniques of Program Structure and Design*, New York: Prentice-Hall, 1976.

B

Utility Programs

*A man is rich in proportion to the number of things which he
can afford to let alone.*

Henry David Thoreau

To make it easier for the reader to assemble a large program, each
utility program in this appendix has been written so it will convert easily
to a subroutine. If you want to use one as a subroutine in one of your
programs, you should make the following changes:

1. Remove the READ and DATA statements for variables that
   will be passed down to the subroutine.
2. Remove the PRINT statements for variables that will be passed
   back to the main routine.
3. Be sure to integrate the subroutine's variables into the list at
   the top of the main program.
4. Change the program title line to a subroutine title line and
   immediately follow it with the IN and OUT lines.
5. Change the END statement to a RETURN statement.

The last two programs in the appendix, BAR and SEVEN, illustrate how to apply these rules in practice.

```
READ      19 OCT 80  16:11

2000 REM    READ      27 SEPTEMBER 1980  J.M. NEVISON
2002 '
2004 REM    © COPYRIGHT 1980 BY JOHN M. NEVISON ASSOCIATES
2010 '
2020 REM    ASSIGN UP TO 100 NUMBERS TO THE SUBSCRIPTED
2030 REM    VARIABLE, X(), AND COUNT THE NUMBERS BY
2040 REM    USING −.999999 TO INDICATE THE END OF THE LIST.
2050 '
2060 REM    VARIABLES:
2070 REM        I............LOOP INDEX VARIABLE
2080 REM        N...........NUMBER OF ITEMS OF DATA
2090 REM        X() .........LIST OF DATA
2100 '
2110 REM    DIMENSIONS:
2120        DIM X(100)
2130 '
2140 REM     IN: --
2150 REM    OUT:  N, X()
2160 '
2170        FOR I = 1 TO 100
2180            READ X(I)
2190            IF X(I) = −.999999 THEN 2210
2200        NEXT I
2210 '
2220        LET N = I − 1
2230 '
2240        DATA 12, 92, 27, 45, 36
2250 '
2260 REM    ALL DATA MUST BE ENTERED ABOVE THIS LINE
2270        DATA −.999999
2280 '
2282        FOR I = 1 TO N
2284            PRINT X(I);
2286        NEXT I
2288        PRINT
2289        PRINT "N IS "; N
2290 '
2300        END


READ      19 OCT 80  16:11

 12  92  27  45  36
N IS  5
```

PERCENT   19 OCT 80   16:12

```
2400 REM    PERCENT     26 SEPTEMBER 1980    J.M. NEVISON
2410 '
2420 REM    © COPYRIGHT 1980 JOHN M. NEVISON ASSOCIATES
2430 '
2440 REM    PRINT A TABLE OF NUMBERS, X(), AND
2450 REM    THEIR PERCENTAGES.
2460 '
2470 REM    VARIABLES:
2480 REM        I . . . . . . . . . . . THE INDEX OF THE LOOP
2490 REM        N . . . . . . . . . THE NUMBER OF ITEMS IN THE LIST
2500 REM        P . . . . . . . . . PERCENTAGE
2510 REM        S() . . . . . . . . THE SUMS
2520 REM        X() . . . . . . . . EACH NUMBER
2530 '
2540 REM    DIMENSIONS:
2550        DIM X(100)
2560 '
2570 REM     IN: N, X()
2580 REM    OUT: --
2590 '
2591        LET N = 5
2592        FOR I = 1 TO N
2593            READ X(I)
2594        NEXT I
2595        DATA 17, 2, 9, 6, 21
2597 '
2600        LET S(1) = 0
2610        FOR I = 1  TO N
2620            LET S(1) = S(1) + X(I)
2630        NEXT I
2640 '
2650        PRINT "NUMBER", "% OF TOTAL"
2660        PRINT
2670 '
2680        LET S(2) = 0
2690        FOR I = 1  TO N
2700            LET P = INT(X(I)/S(1) * 100 + .5)
2710            PRINT X(I), P
2720            LET S(2) = S(2) + P
2730        NEXT I
2740 '
2750        PRINT "————", "————"
2760        PRINT S(1), S(2); " *"
2770        PRINT
2780        PRINT
2790        PRINT "* PERCENTAGES MAY NOT ADD TO 100 DUE TO ";
2800        PRINT "ROUNDING ERRORS."
2810 '
2820        END
```

PERCENT   19 OCT 80 16:12

NUMBER	% OF TOTAL
17	31
2	4
9	16
6	11
21	38
——	——
55	100 *

* PERCENTAGES MAY NOT ADD TO 100 DUE TO ROUNDING ERRORS.

MAX   19 OCT 80 16:13

```
2900 REM    MAX    27 SEPTEMBER 1980   J.M. NEVISON
2910 '
2920 REM    © COPYRIGHT 1980 BY JOHN M. NEVISON ASSOCIATES
2930 '
2940 '
2950 REM    FIND THE MAXIMUM IN A LIST OF NUMBERS.
2960 '
2970 REM    VARIABLES:
2980 REM        I............THE INDEX OF THE LOOP
2990 REM        M..........THE MAXIMUM NUMBER
3000 REM        N..........THE NUMBER OF ITEMS
3010 REM        X() ........EACH NUMBER
3020 '
3030 REM    DIMENSIONS:
3040        DIM X(100)
3050 '
3060 REM        IN:  N, X()
3070 REM    OUT:  M
3080 '
3081        LET N = 5
3082        FOR I = 1 TO N
3083            READ X(I)
3084        NEXT I
3085        DATA 17, 9, 2, 6, 21
3086 '
3090        LET M = X(1)
3100 '
```

```
3110      FOR I = 2  TO N
3120         IF X(I) > M THEN 3130 ELSE 3140
3130            LET M = X(I)
3140 '        IFEND
3150      NEXT I
3160 '
3162      PRINT "MAXIMUM IS "; M
3164 '
3170      END
```

MAX   19 OCT 80 16:15

MAXIMUM IS 21

SORT   19 OCT 80 16:16

```
3200 REM    SORT    27 SEPTEMBER 1980      J.M. NEVISON
3210 '
3220 REM      © COPYRIGHT 1980 BY JOHN M. NEVISON ASSOCIATES
3230 '
3240 REM    SORTS A MIXED BATCH OF NUMBERS, X(),
3250 REM    INTO ASCENDING ORDER.  GOOD FOR BATCHS
3260 REM    OF LESS THAN 50.
3270 '
3280 REM    VARIABLES:
3290 REM       I . . . . . . . . . . . THE INDEX VARIABLE
3300 REM       L . . . . . . . . . . THE LEAD ITEM OF THE CURRENT LIST
3310 REM       N . . . . . . . . . . THE NUMBER OF ITEMS IN THE BATCH
3320 REM       X() . . . . . . . . THE BATCH OF NUMBERS
3330 REM       X . . . . . . . . . . THE EXCHANGE VARIABLE
3340 '
3350 REM    DIMENSIONS:
3360       DIM X(100)
3370 '
3380 REM     IN: N, X()
3390 REM    OUT: X() <SORTED>
3400 '
3401      LET N = 5
3402      FOR I = 1 TO N
3403         READ X(I)
3404         PRINT X(I);
3405      NEXT I
3406      PRINT
3407      DATA 17, 2, 6, 9, 21
3408 '
```

```
3420        FOR L = 1 TO N-1
3430          FOR I = L+1 TO N
3440            IF X(I) < X(L) THEN 3450 ELSE 3480
3450              LET X = X(I)
3460              LET X(I) = X(L)
3470              LET X(L) = X
3480 '          IFEND
3490          NEXT I
3500        NEXT L
3510 '
3511        FOR I = 1 TO N
3512          PRINT X(I);
3513        NEXT I
3514        PRINT
3515 '
3520        END
```

RUN

SORT   19 OCT 80 16:18

```
17   2   6   9   21
 2   6   9  17   2'
```


SORTII   19 OCT 80 16:19

```
3600 REM    SORTII    27 SEPTEMBER 1980    J.M. NEVISON
3610 '
3620 REM    © COPYRIGHT 1980 BY JOHN M. NEVISON ASSOCIATES
3630 '
3650 REM    SORTS A BATCH OF NUMBERS, X(), INTO
3660 REM    ASCENDING ORDER.  GOOD FOR BATCHES FROM 50-100.
3670 '
3680 REM    REFERENCE:  D.L. SHELL, "A HIGH-SPEED SORTING
3690 REM                PROCEDURE," COMMUNICATIONS OF THE
3700 REM                ACM, (JULY, 1959), PP. 30-32.
3710 '
3720 REM    VARIABLES:
3730 REM       E$..........EXCHANGE MARKER
3740 REM       G...........THE GAP
3750 REM       I...........INDEX VARIABLE
3760 REM       N...........THE NUMBER OF ITEMS IN THE LIST
3770 REM       S...........THE STEP ACROSS THE GAP
3780 REM       T...........THE TOP OF THE PASS THROUGH THE
3785 REM                   NUMBERS
3790 REM       X() .........THE BATCH OF NUMBERS
3800 REM       X...........EXCHANGE VARIABLE
3810 '
```

```
3820 REM    DIMENSIONS:
3830        DIM X(100)
3840 '
3850 REM      IN:  N, X()
3860 REM     OUT:  X() <SORTED>
3870 '
3871        LET N = 5
3872        FOR I = 1 TO N
3873            READ X(I)
3874            PRINT X(I);
3875        NEXT I
3876        PRINT
3877        DATA 17, 2, 6, 9, 21
3878 '
3890 REM    COMPARES ITEMS ACROSS A GAP N/2 WIDE
3892 REM    UNTIL THERE ARE NO MORE EXCHANGES, THEN
3900 REM    CUTS THE GAP IN HALF AND REPEATS.
3910 '
3920        LET G = N
3930 '
3940        IF G <= 1 THEN 4110
3950            LET G = INT(G/2)
3960            LET T = N - G
3970            LET E$ = "NO EXCHANGE"
3980              FOR I = 1 TO T
3990                  LET S = I + G
4000                  IF X(I) > X(S) THEN 4010 ELSE 4050
4010                      LET X = X(I)
4020                      LET X(I) = X(S)
4030                      LET X(S) = X
4040                      LET E$ = "EXCHANGE"
4050 '                IFEND
4060              NEXT I
4070              IF E$ = "NO EXCHANGE" THEN 4090
4080            GO TO 3970
4090 '
4100        GO TO 3940
4110 '
4111        FOR I = 1 TO N
4112            PRINT X(I);
4113        NEXT I
4114        PRINT
4115 '
4120        END
```

SORTII   19 OCT 80 16:20

```
 17   2   6   9   21
  2   6   9   17   21
```

PLOT   19 OCT 80 16:21

```
4200 REM    PLOT    27 SEPTEMBER 1980    J.M. NEVISON
4210 '
4220 REM    © COPYRIGHT 1980 JOHN M. NEVISON ASSOCIATES
4230 '
4240 REM    PLOTS ALL POINTS IN THE REGION X1–X2, Y1–Y2.
4250 REM    THE REGION ON PAPER IS W9 CHARACTERS WIDE (Y'S)
4260 REM    AND L9 LINES LONG (X'S).
4270 '
4280 REM    VARIABLES:
4290 REM        G() . . . . . . . . . THE GRAPH ON WHICH POINTS
4295 REM                              ARE MARKED
4300 REM        I,J . . . . . . . . . . INDEX VARIABLES
4310 REM        N . . . . . . . . . . . THE NUMBER OF POINTS
4320 REM        O . . . . . . . . . . . OUTSIDE POINT COUNTER
4330 REM        X(),Y() . . . . . . THE COORDINATES OF THE POINTS
4340 REM        X1 . . . . . . . . . LEFT BOUNDARY OF THE PLOT
4350 REM        X2 . . . . . . . . . RIGHT BOUNDARY OF THE PLOT
4360 REM        Y1 . . . . . . . . . BOTTOM BOUNDARY OF THE PLOT
4370 REM        Y2 . . . . . . . . . TO BOUNDARY OF THE PLOT
4380 '
4390 REM    CONSTANTS:
4400        LET L9 = 20      'LENGTH OF THE PLOT IN LINES
4410        LET W9 = 36      'WIDTH OF THE PLOT IN CHARS
4420 '
4430 REM    DIMENSIONS:
4440        DIM G(20,36), X(100), Y(100)
4450 '
4460 REM        IN:  N, X(), Y(), X1, X2, Y1, Y2
4470 REM    OUT:  --
4480 '
4481        LET X1 = 0
4482        LET X2 = 50
4483        LET Y1 = 0
4484        LET Y2 = 50
4485        LET N = 20
4486        FOR I = 1 TO N
4487            READ X(I),Y(I)
4488        NEXT I
4489        DATA 1,1, 5,5, 15,15, 30,30, 50,50
4490        DATA 1.4,3.8, 8,10, 44,10, 37,11, 38.6,3.9
4491        DATA 23,−7, −12,−55, 16,0, 0, 48, 45,45
4492        DATA 2,4, 3,9, 4,16, 5,25, 6,36
4493 '
```

```
4500      LET O = 0
4510      FOR I = 1 TO L9
4520         FOR J = 1 TO W9
4530            LET G(I,J) = 0
4540         NEXT J
4550      NEXT I
4560 '
4570      FOR I = 1 TO N
4580         IF (X(I) > = X1) AND (X(I) < = X2) THEN 4590 ELSE 4680
4590            IF (Y(I) > = Y1) AND (Y(I) < = Y2) THEN 4620 ELSE 4680
4620            LET X(I) = X(I) / (X2 − X1)
4630            LET Y(I) = Y(I) / (Y2 − Y1)
4640            LET X(I) = INT(X(I)*(L9−1) + 1.5)
4650            LET Y(I) = INT(Y(I)*(W9−1) + 1.5)
4660            LET G(X(I),Y(I)) = G(X(I),Y(I)) + 1
4670            GOTO 4695
4680 '       ELSE
4690            LET O = O + 1
4695 '       IFEND
4700      NEXT I
4710 '
4720      PRINT "POINTS:"; N; "    ON:"; N−O; "   OFF:"; O
4730      PRINT "X FROM "; X1; "TO "; X2; "DOWN THE PAGE"
4740      PRINT "Y FROM "; Y1; "TO "; Y2; "ACROSS THE PAGE"
4750      PRINT "* INDICATES ONE (OR MORE) POINTS"
4760      PRINT
4770      PRINT "I";
4780      FOR J = 1 TO W9+1
4790         PRINT "−";
4800      NEXT J
4810      PRINT "Y"
4820      FOR I = 1 TO L9
4830         PRINT "I";
4840         FOR J = 1 TO W9
4850            IF G(I,J) = 0 THEN 4860 ELSE 4880
4860               PRINT " ";
4870               GOTO 4895
4880 '            ELSE
4890               PRINT "*";
4895 '            IFEND
4900         NEXT J
4910         PRINT
4920      NEXT I
4930      PRINT "X"
4940 '
4950      END
```

PLOT   19 OCT 80 16:25

POINTS: 20   ON: 18   OFF: 2
X FROM 0 TO 50 DOWN THE PAGE
Y FROM 0 TO 50 ACROSS THE PAGE
* INDICATES ONE (OR MORE) POINTS

```
| --------------------------------------Y
|   *                                  *
|      *    *
|      *       *       *        *
|         *
|
|
| *            *
|
|
|
|
|              *
|
|
|        *
|     *
|        *                      *
|
|                                 *
|
X
```

HIST   19 OCT 80 16:26

```
5000 REM    HIST    28 SEPTEMBER    J.M. NEVISON
5010 '
5020 REM    © COPYRIGHT 1980 BY JOHN M. NEVISON ASSOCIATES
5030 '
5040 REM    PRINT A HISTOGRAM OF THE DISTRIBUTION OF A
5050 REM    LIST OF NUMBERS, X().
5060 '
5070 REM    VARIABLES:
5080 REM        H() . . . . . . . . THE LENGTH OF EACH HISTOGRAM BAR
5090 REM        I . . . . . . . . . . . THE HISTOGRAM INTERVAL
5100 REM        J,K . . . . . . . . . INDEX VARIABLES
5110 REM        M . . . . . . . . . . THE MAXIMUM H()
5120 REM        N . . . . . . . . . . THE NUMBER OF ITEMS IN THE LIST
5130 REM        X() . . . . . . . . THE NUMBERS IN THE LIST
5140 REM        X1 . . . . . . . . . THE LOW END OF THE HISTOGRAM
5150 REM        X2 . . . . . . . . . THE HIGH END OF THE HISTOGRAM
5160 '
```

```
5170 REM    CONSTANTS:
5180        LET H9 = 20       'NUMBER OF HISTOGRAM BARS
5190        LET L9 = 35       'LENGTH OF THE LARGEST BAR
5200 REM                      CHARS ACROSS THE PAGE
5210 '
5220 REM    DIMENSIONS:
5230        DIM H(20), X(100)
5240 '
5250 REM      IN:  N, X(), X1, X2
5260 REM    OUT:  --
5270 '
5271        LET X1 = 0
5272        LET X2 = 100
5273        LET N = 40
5274        FOR J = 1 TO N
5275            READ X(J)
5276        NEXT J
5277        DATA 77, 26, 88, 86, 75, 76, 83, 86, 90, 68
5278        DATA 71, 55, 83, 77, 71, 66, 74, 76, 86, 60
5279        DATA 85, 70, 93, 91, 80, 83, 88, 94, 96, 74
5280        DATA 66, 78, 79, 88, 86, 84, 90, 78, 75, 79
5281 '
5290 REM    PLACE X()'S IN THE RIGHT HISTOGRAM BAR, H(K),
5300 REM    AND CHECK FOR A NEW MAXIMUM.
5310 '
5320        LET I = (X2 − X1)/H9
5330        LET M = L9
5340 '
5350        FOR J = 1 TO N
5360            LET K = INT(H9*X(J)/(X2−X1) + 1.5)
5370            LET H(K) = H(K) +1
5380            IF H(K) > M THEN 5390 ELSE 5400
5390              LET M = H(K)
5400 '          IFEND
5410        NEXT J
5420 '
5430 REM    PRINT OUT HISTOGRAM
5440 '
5450        PRINT "FROM"; X1; " TO "; X2; "IN INTERVALS OF "; I
5460        PRINT "MAXIMUM POSSIBLE HEIGHT IS "; M; "POINTS"
5470        PRINT "EACH POINT IS "; M/L9; "UNITS"
5480        FOR J = 1 TO H9
5490            PRINT "I";
5500            FOR K = 1 TO INT(H(J)/M*(L9−1) + .5)
5510              PRINT "*";
5520            NEXT K
5530            PRINT
5540        NEXT J
5550 '
5560        END
```

```
HIST     19 OCT 80  16:27

FROM 0  TO  100 IN INTERVALS OF  5
MAXIMUM POSSIBLE HEIGHT IS  35 POINTS
EACH POINT IS  1 UNITS
|
|
|
|
|
| *
|
|
|
|
|
| *
| *
| * *
| * * * *
| * * * * * * * *
| * * * * *
| * * * * * * * * * *
| * * * * * *
| * * *
```

```
PIE      19 OCT 80  16:28

5600 REM   PIE     29 SEPTEMBER 1980    J.M. NEVISON
5610 '
5620 REM   © COPYRIGHT 1980 BY JOHN M. NEVISON ASSOCIATES
5630 '
5640 REM   DRAW A PIE CHART FOR A LIST OF NUMBERS, X().
5650 REM   TO ADJUST TO YOUR SCREEN OR PRINTER, YOU
5660 REM   MAY MOVE THE CENTER OF THE CIRCLE, (R1,C1),
5670 REM   AND CHANGE THE RADIUS OF THE CIRCLE, R2.
5680 REM   TO GET RID OF THE 'FOOTBALL EFFECT,'
5690 REM   CHANGE F7.
5700 '
```

```
5710 REM    VARIABLES:
5720 REM        C . . . . . . . . . . COLUMN INDEX
5730 REM        C1 . . . . . . . . . COLUMN OF CENTER
5740 REM        C9 . . . . . . . . . LARGEST COLUMN
5750 REM        F7 . . . . . . . . . THE 'FOOTBALL' FACTOR
5760 REM        G$() . . . . . . . THE GRAPH ON WHICH THE CHART
5765 REM                    IS DRAWN
5770 REM        I . . . . . . . . . . . INDEX VARIABLE
5780 REM        N . . . . . . . . . . NUMBER OF ITEMS IN THE LIST
5790 REM        P1 . . . . . . . . . PI
5800 REM        P() . . . . . . . . PERCENTAGES OF X()'S
5810 REM        R . . . . . . . . . . ROW INDEX
5820 REM        R1 . . . . . . . . . ROW OF CENTER
5830 REM        R9 . . . . . . . . LARGEST ROW
5840 REM        R2 . . . . . . . . RADIUS OF CIRCLE
5850 REM        R3 . . . . . . . . PARTIAL RADIUS
5860 REM        T . . . . . . . . . . TOTAL VARIABLE
5870 REM        X() . . . . . . . . THE LIST OF NUMBERS
5880 '
5890 REM    IN: N, X()
5900 REM    OUT: --
5910 '
5911        LET N = 4
5912        FOR I = 1 TO N
5913            READ X(I)
5914        NEXT I
5915        DATA 1, 3, 5, 7
5916 '
5920        LET C1 = 30
5930        LET R1 = 20
5940        LET R2 = 20
5950        LET P1 = 3.1415926
5960        LET F7 = .75
5970        LET C9 = INT((C1+(1/F7)*R2) +1)
5980        LET R9 = INT((R1+F7*R2) + 1)
5990 '
6000 '
6010        PRINT "PIE GOES FROM COLUMN ";C1−(1/F7)*R2; "TO "; C9
6020        PRINT "PIE GOES FROM ROW "; R1−F7*R2; "TO ";R9
6030        PRINT
6040 '
6050 REM    DIMENSIONS: BE SURE G$() IS (R9,C9)
6060        DIM G$(40,60)
6070 '
6080 REM    BLANK THE GRAPH PAPER
6090 '
6100        FOR R = 1 TO R9
6110            FOR C = 1 TO C9
6120                LET G$(R,C) = " "
6130            NEXT C
6140        NEXT R
6150 '
```

```
6160 REM    FIND SUM AND PERCENTAGES
6170 '
6180      LET T = 0
6190      FOR I = 1 TO N
6200          LET T = T + X(I)
6210      NEXT I
6220      FOR I = 1 TO N
6230          LET P(I) = X(I)/T
6240      NEXT I
6250 '
6260 REM    SET CENTER OF PIE
6270 '
6280      LET G$(R1,C1) = "*"
6290 '
6300 REM    SET RIM OF PIE
6310 '
6320      FOR I = 0 TO 2 * P1 STEP P1/10
6330          LET R = F7 * R2 * SIN(I)
6340          LET C = (1/F7) * R2 * COS(I)
6350          LET C = C + C1
6360          LET R = R + R1
6370          LET G$(INT(R+.5),INT(C+.5)) = "*"
6380      NEXT I
6390 '
6400 REM    DRAW PIE SLICES
6410 '
6420      LET T = 0
6430      FOR I = 1 TO N
6440          LET T = (P(I)*2*P1) + T
6450          FOR J = 1 TO 5
6460              LET R3 = J/5 * R2
6470              LET R = R1 + F7 * R3 * SIN(T)
6480              LET C = C1 + (1/F7) * R3 * COS(T)
6490              LET G$(INT(R+.5),INT(C+.5)) = "*"
6500          NEXT J
6510      NEXT I
6520 '
6530 REM    PRINT THE PICTURE
6540 '
6550      FOR R = R9 TO 1 STEP -1
6560          FOR C = 1 TO C9
6570              PRINT G$(R,C);
6580          NEXT C
6590          PRINT
6600      NEXT R
6610      END
```

PIE   19 OCT 80 16:28

PIE GOES FROM COLUMN 3.33333 TO 57
PIE GOES FROM ROW 5 TO 36

AMORT   19 OCT 80 16:29

```
6700 REM    AMORT    21 OCTOBER 1980    J.M. NEVISON
6710 '
6720 REM    © COPYRIGHT 1980 BY JOHN M. NEVISON ASSOCIATES
6730 '
6740 REM    GIVEN THE AMOUNT OF A LOAN, X, THE
6750 REM    NUMBER OF YEARS OVER WHICH IT WILL BE REPAID, Y,
6760 REM    AT THE ANNUAL INTEREST RATE, I, PRINT OUT A
6770 REM    SCHEDULE OF THE INTEREST AND PRINCIPLE IN EACH
6780 REM    MONTHLY PAYMENT.
6790 '
6800 REM    VARIABLES:
6810 REM        I............THE ANNUAL INTEREST RATE
6820 REM        I1 ..........THE MONTHLY INTEREST
6830 REM        M...........MONTHLY INDEX VARIABLE
6840 REM        P...........THE MONTHLY PAYMENT
6850 REM        X...........THE LOAN AMOUNT
6860 REM        Y...........THE NUMBER OF YEARS OF THE LOAN
6870 '
6880 REM    IN: I, X, Y
6890 REM    OUT: --
6900 '
6901        LET I = .105
6902        LET X = 1000
6903        LET Y = 2
6904 '
6910 REM    THE PAYMENT FOR EACH MONTH
6920        LET P = X*((I/12)/(1−(1/(1+(I/12))^(Y*12))))
6930 '
6940        PRINT "LOAN AMOUNT: "; X
6950        PRINT "ANNUAL INTEREST RATE: "; I
6960        PRINT "NUMBER OF MONTHLY PAYMENTS: "; Y*12
6970        PRINT "MONTHLY PAYMENT AMOUNT: "; P
6980        PRINT
6990 '
7000        PRINT "MNTH INTEREST", "PRINCIPAL", "BALANCE DUE"
7010        FOR M = 1 TO (Y*12)
7020            LET I1 = (I/12)*X
7030            LET X = X − (P-I1)
7040            PRINT M; I1, (P−I1), X
7050        NEXT M
7060        END
```

AMORT   19 OCT 80 16:29

LOAN AMOUNT: 1000
ANNUAL INTEREST RATE: 0.105
NUMBER OF MONTHLY PAYMENTS: 24
MONTHLY PAYMENT AMOUNT: 46.376

MNTH	INTEREST	PRINCIPAL	BALANCE DUE
1	8.75	37.626	962.374
2	8.42077	37.9553	924.419
3	8.08866	38.2874	886.131
4	7.75365	38.6224	847.509
5	7.4157	38.9603	808.549
6	7.0748	39.3012	769.247
7	6.73091	39.6451	729.602
8	6.38402	39.992	689.61
9	6.03409	40.342	649.268
10	5.6811	40.6949	608.573
11	5.32502	41.051	567.522
12	4.96582	41.4102	526.112
13	4.60348	41.7726	484.34
14	4.23797	42.1381	442.201
15	3.86926	42.5068	399.695
16	3.49733	42.8787	356.816
17	3.12214	43.2539	313.562
18	2.74367	43.6324	269.93
19	2.36188	44.0142	225.916
20	1.97676	44.3993	181.516
21	1.58827	44.7878	136.728
22	1.19637	45.1797	91.5488
23	0.801052	45.575	45.9738
24	0.402271	45.9738	3.76925E−5

DEPA   19 OCT 80 16:31

```
7100 REM    DEPA    19 OCTOBER 1980    J.M. NEVISON
7110 REM    DEPRECIATION-A
7120 '
7130 REM    © COPYRIGHT 1980 BY JOHN M. NEVISON ASSOCIATES
7140 '
7150 REM    COMPUTE THE STRAIGHT LINE DEPRECIATION ON
7160 REM    AMOUNT, X, DEPRECIATED OVER Y YEARS.
7170 '
```

```
7180 REM    VARIABLES:
7190 REM        D() ........ DEPRECIATION EACH YEAR
7200 REM        I ........... INDEX VARIABLE FOR YEAR LOOP
7210 REM        X .......... INITIAL AMOUNT
7220 REM        Y .......... YEARS DEPRECIATED (LIFE OF
7225 REM                          INVESTMENT)
7230 '
7240 REM     IN:  X, Y
7250 REM    OUT:  D()
7260 '
7261        LET X = 1000
7262        LET Y = 8
7263 '
7270        PRINT "STRAIGHT LINE DEPRECIATION OF $"; X; "OVER ";
7280        PRINT Y; "YEARS."
7290        PRINT
7300        PRINT "YEAR", "DEPRECIATION"
7310        FOR I = 1 TO Y
7320            LET D(I) = X/Y
7330            PRINT I, D(I)
7340        NEXT I
7350        END
```

DEPA   19 OCT 80 16:32

STRAIGHT LINE DEPRECIATION OF $ 1000 OVER 8 YEARS.

YEAR	DEPRECIATION
1	125
2	125
3	125
4	125
5	125
6	125
7	125
8	125

DEPB   19 OCT 80 16:32

```
7400 REM    DEPB     19 OCTOBER 1980     J. M. NEVISON
7410 REM    DEPRECIATION-B
7420 '
7430 REM    © COPYRIGHT 1980 BY JOHN M. NEVISON ASSOCIATES
7440 '
7450 REM    COMPUTE THE DOUBLE DECLINING BALANCE
7460 REM    DEPRECIATION WITH CONVERSION TO STRAIGHT LINE
7470 REM    FOR AN AMOUNT X WITH A LIFE OF Y YEARS.
7480 '
7490 REM    VARIABLES:
7500 REM       B . . . . . . . . . . BALANCE REMAINING
7510 REM       D1 . . . . . . . . . DOUBLE DECLINING DEPRECIATION
7520 REM       D2 . . . . . . . . . STRAIGHT LINE DEPRECIATION
7530 REM       D() . . . . . . . . THE CHOSEN DEPRECIATION
7540 REM       I . . . . . . . . . . . INDEX VARIABLE FOR YEAR LOOP
7550 REM       X . . . . . . . . . . INITIAL AMOUNT
7560 REM       Y . . . . . . . . . . YEARS DEPRECIATED (LIFE OF
7265 REM                     INVESTMENT)
7570 '
7580 REM    IN: X, Y
7590 REM    OUT: D()
7600 '
7601      LET X = 1000
7602      LET Y = 8
7603 '
7610      PRINT "DOUBLE DECLINING BALANCE DEPRECIATION";
7620      PRINT " OF $"; X; "OVER "; Y; "YEARS."
7630      PRINT
7640      PRINT "YEAR", "DOUBLE DCLN", "STRAIGHT LINE",
7645      PRINT "BALANCE"
7650      LET  B = X
7660      FOR I = 1 TO Y
7670          LET D1 = B * 2/Y
7680          LET D2 = B/(Y − I + 1)
7690          IF D1 > D2 THEN 7700 ELSE 7740
7700              LET D(I) = D1
7710              LET B = B − D(I)
7720              PRINT I, D(I), , B
7730              GOTO 7780
7740 '        ELSE
7750              LET D(I) = D2
7760              LET B = B − D(I)
7770              PRINT I, , D(I), B
7780 '        IFEND
7790      NEXT I
7800      END
```

DEPB   19 OCT 80 16:34

DOUBLE DECLINING BALANCE DEPRECIATION OF $ 1000 OVER 8 YEARS.

YEAR	DOUBLE DCLN	STRAIGHT LINE	BALANCE
1	250		750
2	187.5		562.5
3	140.625		421.875
4	105.469		316.406
5		79.1016	237.305
6		79.1016	158.203
7		79.1016	79.1016
8		79.1016	0

DEPC   19 OCT 80 16:35

```
7900 REM    DEPC    19 OCTOBER 1980    J.M. NEVISON
7910 REM    DEPRECIATION-C
7920 '
7930 REM    © COPYRIGHT 1980 BY JOHN M. NEVISON ASSOCIATES
7940 '
7950 REM    COMPUTE THE SUM-OF-YEARS'-DIGITS DEPRECIATION ON
7960 REM    AMOUNT, X, DEPRECIATED OVER Y YEARS.
7970 '
7980 REM    VARIABLES:
7990 REM       D() ........ DEPRECIATION EACH YEAR
8000 REM       I............ INDEX VARIABLE FOR YEAR LOOP
8010 REM       X........... INITIAL AMOUNT
8020 REM       Y........... YEARS DEPRECIATED (LIFE OF
8025 REM                       INVESTMENT)
8030 '
8040 REM    IN:  X, Y
8050 REM    OUT:  D()
8060 '
8061        LET X = 1000
8062        LET Y = 8
8063 '
8070        PRINT "SUM-OF-YEARS'-DIGITS DEPRECIATION";
8080        PRINT " OF $"; X; "OVER "; Y; "YEARS."
8090        PRINT
8100 '
8110 REM    FORMULA FOR SUM OF 1 TO Y
8120        LET S = Y * (Y+1)/2
8130 '
8140        PRINT "YEAR", "DEPRECIATION"
8150        FOR I = 1 TO Y
8160           LET D(I) = X * ((Y-I+1)/S)
8170           PRINT I, D(I)
8180        NEXT I
8190        END
```

DEPC   19 OCT 80 16:35

SUM-OF-YEARS'-DIGITS DEPRECIATION OF $ 1000 OVER 8 YEARS.

YEAR	DEPRECIATION
1	222.222
2	194.444
3	166.667
4	138.889
5	111.111
6	83.3333
7	55.5556
8	27.7778

SMOOTH   19 OCT 80 16:37

```
8200 REM    SMOOTH    19 OCTOBER 1980    J.M. NEVISON
8210 '
8220 REM    © COPYRIGHT 1980 BY JOHN M. NEVISON ASSOCIATES
8230 '
8240 REM    APPLY 'THREE ON THREE' SMOOTHING TO A
8250 REM    SERIES OF NUMBERS, X(). THE RESULTANT X(I) IS
8260 REM    (1/9)*X(I−2) + (2/9)*X(I−1) + (3/9)*X(I)
8270 REM        + (2/9)*X(I+1) + (1/9) X(I+2)
8280 REM    FOR VALUES OF I FROM 3 TO (N−2).
8290 '
8300 REM    VARIABLES:
8310 REM        I...........INDEX VARIABLE FOR LOOP
8320 REM        N...........NUMBER OF ITEMS IN SERIES
8330 REM        X().........THE SERIES OF NUMBERS
8340 REM        Y().........THE TEMPORARY SERIES
8350 '
8360 REM    DIMENSIONS:
8370        DIM X(100), Y(100)
8380 '
8390 REM     IN:  N, X()
8400 REM    OUT:  X(0) <SMOOTHED>
8410 '
8411        LET N = 25
8412        FOR I = 1 TO N
8413           READ X(I)
8414           PRINT I; X(I),
8415        NEXT I
8416        PRINT
8417        PRINT
8418        DATA 1,2,3,4,5,5,4,3,2,1,1,2,3,4,5,5,4,3,2,1,1,2,3,4,5
8419 '
```

```
8420        FOR I = 2 TO N−1
8430            LET Y(I) = (X(I−1) + X(I) + X(I+1))/3
8440        NEXT I
8450        LET Y(1) =X(1)
8460        LET Y(N) = X(N)
8470 '
8480        FOR I = 2 TO N−1
8490            LET X(I) = (Y(I−1) + Y(I) + Y(I+1))/3
8500        NEXT I
8510 '
8511        FOR I = 1 TO N
8512            PRINT I; X(I),
8513        NEXT I
8514        PRINT
8515 '
8520        END
```

SMOOTH   19 OCT 80 16:37

1	1	2	2	3	3	4	4	5	5
6	5	7	4	8	3	9	2	10	1
11	1	12	2	13	3	14	4	15	5
16	5	17	4	18	3	19	2	20	1
21	1	22	2	23	3	24	4	25	5

1	1	2	2	3	3	4	3.88889	5	4.44444
6	4.44444	7	3.88889	8	3	9	2.11111	10	1.55556
11	1.55556	12	2.11111	13	3	14	3.88889	15	4.44444
16	4.44444	17	3.88889	18	3	19	2.11111	20	1.55556
21	1.55556	22	2.11111	23	3	24	4	25	5

BETA   19 OCT 80 16:38

```
8600 REM   BETA    19 OCTOBER 1980    J.M. NEVISON
8610 '
8620 REM   © COPYRIGHT 1980 BY JOHN M. NEVISON ASSOCIATES
8630 '
8640 REM   FIND THE SYSTEMATIC RISK (BETA) OF STOCK X() IN
8650 REM   MARKET M().  LOW RISK = 0; HIGH RISK = 2.
8660 '
8670 REM   REFERENCE:  COPELAND, THOMAS E., AND J. FRED
8680 REM                          WESTON, "FINANCIAL THEORY AND
8690 REM                          CORPORATE POLICY,"  READING, MA:
8700 REM                          ADDISON-WESLEY PUBLISHING COMPANY,
8710 REM                          1979, P. 164.
8720 '
8730 REM   VARIABLES:
8740 REM        B.......... BETA--THE SYSTEMATIC RISK
8750 REM        I........... INDEX OF LOOP
8760 REM        N.......... NUMBER OF PERIODS
8770 REM        M.......... MARKET AVERAGE VALUE
8780 REM        M() ........ MARKET VALUES
8790 REM        S1.......... SUM OF MARKET-STOCK COVARIANCE
8800 REM        S2.......... SUM OF MARKET VARIANCE
8810 REM        X........... STOCK AVERAGE VALUE
8820 REM        X() ........ STOCK VALUES
8830 '
8840 REM   DIMENSIONS:
8850       DIM M(100), X(100)
8860 '
8870 REM      IN: N, M(), X()
8880 REM   OUT: B
8890 '
8891       LET N = 23
8892       FOR I = 1 TO N
8893          READ X(I)
8894       NEXT I
8895       DATA 63, 92, 66, 56, 102, 96, 73, 89, 61, 85
8896       DATA 56, 52, 36, 78, 57, 26, 27, 22, 44, 9
8897       DATA -22, -15, 10
8898 '
8899       FOR I = 1 TO N
8900          READ M(I)
8901       NEXT I
8902       DATA 171, 162, 205, 161, 263, 257, 185, 201, 138, 202
8903       DATA 136, 103, 72, 143, 88, 54, 59, 43, 87, 30
8904       DATA -19, -2, 34
8905 '
```

```
8910        LET X = 0
8920        LET M = 0
8930        FOR I = 1 TO N
8940            LET X = X + X(I)
8950            LET M = M + M(I)
8960        NEXT I
8970        LET X = X/N
8980        LET M = M/N
8990 '
8994        LET S1 = 0
8998        LET S2 = 0
9000        FOR I = 1 TO N
9010            LET S1 = S1 + ((M(I)−M) * (X(I)−X))
9020            LET S2 = S2 + ((M(I)−M) * (M(I)−M))
9030        NEXT I
9040 '
9050        LET B = S1/S2
9060 '
9061        PRINT "BETA IS "; B
9062 '
9070        END
```

BETA   19 OCT 80 16:38

BETA IS 0.408911

BAR   19 OCT 80 16:49

```
100 REM    BAR     28 SEPTEMBER 1980    J.M. NEVISON
110 '
120 REM    © COPYRIGHT 1980 BY JOHN M. NEVISON ASSOCIATES
130 '
140 REM    PRINT A BARCHART FROM A LIST OF UP TO 100 NUMBERS.
150 '
160 REM    VARIABLES:
170 REM        I............INDEX VARIABLE
180 REM        L............LENGTH OF BAR
190 REM        M............MAXIMUM NUMBER FROM THE LIST
200 REM        N............THE NUMBER OF ITEMS OF DATA
210 REM        P............PERCENT OF TOTAL FOR EACH NUMBER
220 REM        S............SUM OF NUMBERS
230 REM        X()..........THE NUMBERS AS DATA
240 '
250 REM    DIMENSIONS:
260        DIM X(100)
270 '
```

```
280 REM    MAIN PROGRAM
290 '
300       GOSUB 370         'READ THE DATA
310       GOSUB 530         'FIND THE MAXIMUM
320       GOSUB 680         'PRINT THE CHART
330 '
340       STOP
350 '
360 '
370 REM    SUBROUTINE: READ THE DATA
380 REM       IN: --
390 REM      OUT:  X(), N
400 '
410       FOR I = 1 TO 100
420           READ X(I)
430           IF X(I) = −.999999 THEN 450
440       NEXT I
450 '
460       LET N = I − 1
470 '
480       DATA 12, 92, 27, 45, 36
490       DATA −.999999
500 RETURN
510 '
520 '
530 REM    SUBROUTINE: FIND THE MAXIMUM
540 REM       IN:  X(), N
550 REM      OUT:  M
560 '
570       LET M = X(1)
580 '
590       FOR I = 2 TO N
600           IF X(I) > M THEN 610 ELSE 620
610             LET M = X(I)
620 '         IFEND
630       NEXT I
640 '
650 RETURN
660 '
670 '
```

```
680 REM    SUBROUTINE: PRINT THE CHART
690 REM       IN:  X(), M, N
700 REM    OUT: --
710 '
720 REM    COMPUTE THE PERCENT OF TOTAL, THE LENGTH OF THE
730 REM    BAR, AND THEN PRINT OUT THE BAR AND THE PERCENT.
740 '
750        FOR I = 1 TO N
760            LET L = INT(X(I)/M * 50 + .5)
770 '
780            PRINT TAB(8); "."
790            PRINT X(I); TAB(8); "+";
800 '
810            FOR J = 1 TO L
820                PRINT "*";
830            NEXT J
840            PRINT
850 '
860        NEXT I
870 '
880 RETURN
890 '
900 '
910        END
```

BAR   19 OCT 80 16:50


```
      .
 12  +*******
      .
 92  +**************************************************
      .
 27  +***************
      .
 45  +**********************
      .
 36  +*******************
```

```
SEVEN    19 OCT 80  16:54

100 REM  SEVEN    28 SEPTEMBER 1980    J.M. NEVISON
101 '
102 REM  © COPYRIGHT 1980 JOHN M. NEVISON ASSOCIATES
105 '
110 REM  FIND THE 7-NUMBER SUMMARY OF A BATCH OF NUMBERS.
115 REM  (BY VARYING THE TRANSFORMATION OF X() ON SUCCESSIVE
120 REM  RUNS, ONE CAN FIND THE TRANSFORMATION THAT
122 REM  LINES UP MID-SPREADS.)
125 REM  FUNCTIONS TO TRY INCLUDE:
130 REM  X^2, X, X^(1/2), LOG(X), −X^(−1/2), −X^(−1), −X^(−2)
135 '
140 REM  REF:  JOHN W. TUKEY, "EXPLORATORY DATA ANALYSIS,"
145 REM        READING, MASS.:  ADDISON-WESLEY PUBLISHING
150 REM        COMPANY, 1977.
155 '
160 REM  VARIABLES:
170 REM     D() .......... THE DEPTH OF THE LETTER VALUES
171 REM     E$ ........... EXCHANGE MARKER
173 REM     G ............ THE SORT GAP
175 REM     I ............ INDEX VARIABLE
177 REM     N ............ THE NUMBER OF ITEMS
178 REM     S ............ STEP OVER SORT GAP
180 REM     S() .......... SUMMARY VALUES
181 REM     T ............ TOP OF PASS THROUGH NUMBERS
182 REM     X ............ EXCHANGE VARIABLE
183 REM     X() .......... THE LIST OF NUMBERS (SORTED)
185 '
190 REM  CONSTANTS:
200      LET S9 = 3         'NUMBER OF SUMMARY VALUES =
205 REM                       2*S9 + 1
220 '
225 REM  DIMENSIONS:
230      DIM X(100)
235 '
260 REM  MAIN PROGRAM
265 '
270      GOSUB 2000         'READ
275      GOSUB 3600         'SORTII
277 '
278 REM  THIS IS THE PLACE WHERE X() CAN BE TRANSFORMED
280      FOR I = 1 TO N
282          LET X(I) = LOG(X(I))
284      NEXT I
286      LET T$ = "LOG"
310 '
```

```
315        GOSUB 340          'DEPTHS AND SUMMARY VALUES
320        GOSUB 515          'PRINT OUT
325  '
330        STOP
335  '
337  '
340 REM     SUBROUTINE: DEPTHS AND SUMMARY VALUES
345 REM        IN: X()
350 REM     OUT: D(),S()
355  '
360 REM     DEPTHS ARE THE DISTANCE TO THE NEAREST END OF THE
365 REM     ORDERED DATA. THEY ARE EITHER A WHOLE NUMBER  OR A
370 REM     NUMBER AND A HALF. QUARTERS AND EIGHTHS, LIKE
375 REM     THE MEDIAN, ARE EITHER NUMBERS IN THE ROW (WHEN
380 REM     DEPTH IS A WHOLE NUMBER), OR THE AVERAGE OF
382 REM     TWO ADJACENT VALUES.
385  '
390        FOR I = 1 TO 2*S9 + 1
395            LET D(I) = 0
400            LET S(I) = 0
405        NEXT I
410  '
415        LET D(0) = N
420        FOR I = 1 TO S9
425            LET D(I) = (INT(D(I−1)) + 1) / 2
430        NEXT I
435  '
440        FOR I = 1 TO S9
445            IF D(I) = INT(D(I)) THEN 450 ELSE 465
450                LET S(I) = X(D(I))
455                LET S(I+S9) = X((N+1) − D(I))
460                GOTO 485
465  '            ELSE
470                LET D = INT(D(I))
475                LET S(I) = (X(D) + X(D+1)) / 2
480                LET S(I+S9) = (X(N+1−D) + X(N−D)) / 2
485  '            IFEND
487        NEXT I
490  '
495 RETURN
500  '
```

```
505 REM    SUBROUTINE:  PRINT OUT
510 REM      IN:  X(), D(), L()
515 REM    OUT: --
520 '
525       PRINT "HEIGHTS OF THE HIGHEST POINT IN 50 STATES"
530       PRINT "UNIT--(100 FEET)"
535       PRINT
540       PRINT "NUMBER OF DATA:"; N
545       PRINT
550       PRINT TAB(11); "DEPTH"; TAB(18); "MID";
555       PRINT TAB(29); T$; " SUMMARY"; TAB(51); "SPREAD"
560       PRINT TAB(18); " ------------------------------"
565       PRINT "MEDIAN    "; D(1); TAB(17); S(1);
570       PRINT TAB(26); "I"; TAB(32); S(1); TAB(48); "I"
575 '
580       PRINT "HINGE(QTR)"; D(2); TAB(17); (S(2+S9) + S(2))/2;
585       PRINT TAB(26); "I"; TAB(28); S(2); TAB(38);S(2+S9);
590       PRINT TAB(48); "I"; TAB(50); S(2+S9)-S(2)
595 '
600       PRINT "EIGHTH    "; D(3); TAB(17); (S(3+S9) + S(3))/2;
605       PRINT TAB(26); "I"; TAB(28); S(3); TAB(38); S(3+S9);
610       PRINT TAB(48); "I"; TAB(50); S(3+S9)-S(3)
615 '
620       PRINT "EXTREMES "; 1; TAB(17); (X(N) + X(1)) / 2;
625       PRINT TAB(26); "I"; TAB(28); X(1); TAB(38); X(N);
630       PRINT TAB(48); "I"; TAB(50); X(N)-X(1)
635 '
640 RETURN
645 '
650 '
```

```
2000 REM    SUBROUTINE: READ
2001 REM      IN: --
2002 REM    OUT:  N, X()
2003 '
2020 REM    ASSIGN UP TO 100 NUMBERS TO THE SUBSCRIPTED
2030 REM    VARIABLE, X(), AND COUNT THE NUMBERS BY
2040 REM    USING −.999999 TO INDICATE THE END OF THE LIST.
2050 '
2060 REM    VARIABLES:
2070 REM        I . . . . . . . . . . . LOOP INDEX VARIABLE
2080 REM        N . . . . . . . . . . NUMBER OF ITEMS OF DATA
2090 REM        X() . . . . . . . . . LIST OF DATA
2100 '
2130 '
2160 '
2170        FOR I = 1 TO 100
2180            READ X(I)
2190            IF X(I) = −.999999 THEN 2210
2200        NEXT I
2210 '
2220        LET N = I − 1
2230 '
2232        DATA 3, 32, 63, 144, 4, 34, 66, 144, 8, 35, 67, 145
2234        DATA 5, 8, 35, 72, 203, 12, 36, 88, 13, 40, 112, 16
2236        DATA 126, 17, 44, 127, 18, 48, 128, 18, 49, 131
2238        DATA 20, 50, 20, 53, 132, 23, 53, 24, 54, 135
2240        DATA 24, 57, 138, 28, 138, 41
2250 '
2260 REM    ALL DATA MUST BE ENTERED ABOVE THIS LINE
2270        DATA −.999999
2280 '
2300 RETURN
2301 '
2302 '
```

```
3600 REM    SUBROUTINE: SORTII
3601 REM      IN:  N, X()
3602 REM    OUT:  X() <SORTED>
3603 '
3650 REM    SORTS A BATCH OF NUMBERS, X(), INTO
3660 REM    ASCENDING ORDER.  GOOD FOR BATCHES FROM 50-100.
3670 '
3680 REM    REFERENCE:  D.L. SHELL, "A HIGH-SPEED SORTING
3690 REM                        PROCEDURE," COMMUNICATIONS OF THE
3700 REM                        ACM, VOL 2, (JULY, 1959), PP. 30-32.
3710 '
3720 REM    VARIABLES:
3730 REM       E$..........EXCHANGE MARKER
3740 REM       G...........THE GAP
3750 REM       I............INDEX VARIABLE
3760 REM       N...........THE NUMBER OF ITEMS IN THE LIST
3770 REM       S...........THE STEP ACROSS THE GAP
3780 REM       T...........THE TOP OF THE PASS THROUGH THE
3785 REM                        NUMBERS
3790 REM       X() .........THE BATCH OF NUMBERS
3800 REM       X...........EXCHANGE VARIABLE
3810 '
3840 '
3890 REM    COMPARES ITEMS ACROSS A GAP N/2 WIDE
3892 REM    UNTIL THERE ARE NO MORE EXCHANGES, THEN
3900 REM    CUTS THE GAP IN HALF AND REPEATS.
3910 '
3920       LET G = N
3930 '
3940       IF G <= 1 THEN 4110
3950          LET G = INT(G/2)
3960          LET T = N - G
3970          LET E$ = "NO EXCHANGE"
3980             FOR I = 1 TO T
3990                LET S = I + G
4000                IF X(I) > X(S) THEN 4010 ELSE 4050
4010                   LET X = X(I)
4020                   LET X(I) = X(S)
4030                   LET X(S) = X
4040                   LET E$ = "EXCHANGE"
4050 '                IFEND
4060             NEXT I
4070             IF E$ = "NO EXCHANGE" THEN 4090
4080          GO TO 3970
4090 '
4100       GO TO 3940
4110 '
4120 RETURN
4121 '
4122 '
4123       END
```

SEVEN   19 OCT 80 16:56

HEIGHTS OF THE HIGHEST POINT IN 50 STATES
UNIT--(100 FEET)

NUMBER OF DATA: 50

	DEPTH	MID	LOG SUMMARY			SPREAD
MEDIAN	25.5	3.8277 I	3.8277		I	
HINGE(QTR)	13	3.85712 I	2.99573	4.7185	I	1.72277
EIGHTH	7	3.73511 I	2.56495	4.90527	I	2.34033
EXTREMES	1	3.20591 I	1.09861	5.31321	I	4.21459

C

Current Equipment

Men have become the tools of their tools.

Henry David Thoreau

When you bought your first car, you had some idea what you wanted because you knew how you were going to use it. Buying your first computer will be much like buying your first car: the more you know about how you are going to use it, the wiser your purchase will be.

KNOW YOUR NEEDS

One way to learn about computers is to learn to program on a friend's computer before you buy your own. If you don't feel you have the time to learn to program before you buy, at least remember the old car buyer's axiom, "Ask the man who owns one," and be sure to talk to a couple of people who are doing the kind of thing you would like to be doing with your computer. They may have some ideas that you haven't thought of. They will surely give you advice on most aspects of the particular equipment they own and on how well it is serviced in your area.

You are now in a position to think through what you will want to do with your computer. If the equipment is for fun, you may want color graphics. If it is for financial modeling, you may want a printer to give you results on paper. If it is for inventory control, you may need a lot of disc memory.

So just as when buying a car, you will have to shop for the computer with the combination of features you will need to do what you want to do. A wise shopper doesn't buy extras that he or she doesn't need.

Unfortunately, a computer is like a car in another way. There are so many different combinations of features and tricks that the only way to really understand what's going on is to test drive the thing. At the store, insist that you be allowed to play on exactly the configuration that you intend to buy. Remember, it's your last chance to find major problems before you part with your money.

GET GOOD SERVICE

Sometime after you purchase your computer, it will break down. When this happens, you will again be struck by the similarity between your computer and your car. Both get taken for granted as long as they are working. But when either your computer or your car malfunctions, everything grinds to a halt until it is repaired. So just as with buying a car, good service is an important part of your purchase.

Depending on your needs, "good" can mean fast, or reliable, or cheap. If you will use the computer for business "good" means fast and reliable. Be sure the service is good before you buy.

BUY A BRAND NAME

Computers are where automobiles were in 1910. Lots of companies are in the market and it is not clear who will survive the next five years' competition. Right now (1980), two manufacturers stand out: Radio Shack and Apple. Other large firms that sell personal computers include Heathkit (one of which is a Digital Equipment Corporation computer), Hewlett-Packard, and Texas Instruments. Other possibilities include Atari, Commodore Pet, Compucolor, Cromenco, Exidy, and Ohio Scientific.

The programs in this book will all run on the largest-selling personal computer: the Radio Shack TRS-80. The version of BASIC is called Level II. The amount of main memory needed is 16,000 characters (16K), and the mass storage device can be a tape cassette. The price of the whole system is presently $849 (for Model I) or $999 (for Model III).

Radio Shack's BASIC has a wonderful feature: it preserves indentation in the program. Most BASICs on personal computers destroy indentation. For the person who is serious about adopting a good programming style and writing well-structured programs (see Appendix A), indentation is essential.

Apple is Radio Shack's major competition. Their color and high resolution graphics are quite interesting. If you buy an Apple, you will need to employ a trick if you wish to preserve indentation. The trick turns a bad feature into a good one. APPLESOFT BASIC allows you to type:

```
100 LET A = 2 : LET B = 4
```

The colon (:) separates two statements on a single line. Putting more than one statement on a line is a terrible programming practice, but you can put the colon to a good use as a pseudo-indentation. For example:

```
100 FOR I = 1 TO 5
110 :  PRINT I
120 :  PRINT I*3.1415926
130 :  LET B = I * 3
140 NEXT I
```

For most BASICs that destroy indentation, the same trick will work. Use the character that separates statements to generate pseudo-indentation.

Both Hewlett-Packard and Texas Instruments are sound business enterprises that can be expected to stand behind their products with considerable expertise.

Heathkit offers Digital Equipment Corporation's computers to the hobbyist at a reasonable price. Both Heath and DEC enjoy excellent reputations for quality products and good service.

Many of the other computers mentioned earlier are fine products. One of them may become the General Motors of the industry. Several will probably not survive the decade's competition. There is no way of knowing which is which.

So you can see, buying a computer really is like buying a car. It should be no surprise that the more work you put into making a wise selection, the greater the chances are that you will be happy with what you finally buy.

D

About VisiCalc

Man's capacities have never been measured; nor are we to judge of what he can do by any precedents, so little has been tried.

Henry David Thoreau

Imagine having a large ledger sheet in front of you with rows numbered 1, 2, 3, ... and columns lettered A, B, C, ... Imagine being able to write a number or a title anywhere on the sheet. Imagine directing the sheet to let column C be the sum of column A plus column B and having column C magically appear. Imagine correcting a mistake in column A and having everything that used that number automatically readjusted to the corrected value.

Imagine needing to insert three more new rows and the ledger sheet giving you three blank lines right where you needed them. Imagine wanting to compare column A to column Z and the ledger sheet automatically folding itself so the two columns were side by side. You fill this ledger with your projected income statement, cash flow, and balance sheet. Imagine changing a single value to ask "what if?" and seeing the ledger sheet automatically readjust all the calculations to reflect the new value.

Imagine VisiCalc.

VisiCalc does all these things (and more) on the screen of your computer. If you have a printer, you can get a paper copy of your work. If you have a disc memory, you may store your work for later revision. Tables that were made with VisiCalc can be read by BASIC programs and vice versa.

Not every small computer has VisiCalc available. Currently it is available on Apple, Atari, Hewlett-Packard, IBM, Pet, and Radio Shack computers. Soon it will be available on others. A similar program called

Supercalc runs on the Heathkit H-8 and H-89 and on the Xerox 820 computers. Because VisiCalc is so handy, every program in this book that can be easily written in VisiCalc is marked with an asterisk (*) in the Program Index. Conversion from BASIC to VisiCalc will be straightforward. For example, the first program in the book might look like this in VisiCalc:

```
A1 = YEAR
B1 = AMOUNT
C1 = RATE
A2 = 0
B2 = 100
C2 = 1.15
A3 = A2 + 1
A4 = A3 + 1
A5 = A4 + 1
A6 = A5 + 1
B3 = C2 * B2
B4 = C2 * B3
B5 = C2 * B4
B6 = C2 * B5
```

The actual VisiCalc table would look like this:

	A	B	C
1	YEAR	AMOUNT	RATE
2	0	100.00	1.15
3	1	115.00	
4	2	132.25	
5	3	152.09	
6	4	174.90	

Changing the initial amount, B2, or the interest rate, C2, will change the entire table.

The second program in the book, INFLATE, might look like the photograph on the next page in VisiCalc.

If you have VisiCalc, you might want to try converting a few of the programs marked with an asterisk in the Index of Programs.

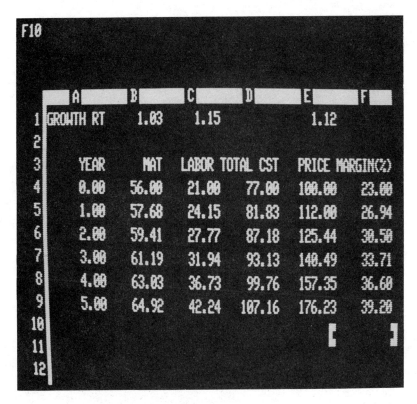

Fig. D-1   A Handy VisiCalc Program

Program Index

CHAPTER 1

INFLATE(*) Projects profit margin in product with inflationary costs.
SALES Plots past years' and current year's monthly sales.

CHAPTER 2

PLAN(*) Projects an income statement five years.
CASHPLAN Projects an income statement and cash flow and reconciles debt with available cash.
TABLE(*) Adds rows and columns in a table of numbers.

CHAPTER 3

X-RAY(*) Allocates fixed costs among products and computes each product's contribution to profits.
SHARE(*) Computes and prints relative market share for each product.
GROWTH Models experience-curve competition among three companies in a market.

CHAPTER 4

PRESENT(*) Gives the net present value of a future stream of cash flow at a given discount rate. (Can also be used to find the internal rate of return.)
RISKY Provides a framework for building monte-carlo models to assess risk in business situations. Models a company's future stock price as an example.

Indicates program can be easily translated into VisiCalc.

CHAPTER 5

QUERY Selects, manipulates, and prints information extracted from a "data base".

CHAPTER 6

GANTT Prints a simple Gantt chart for a series of jobs.
CPM-I Computes the critical path for a series of jobs, and prints an enhanced Gantt chart and a table of values.
CPM-II Computes the critical path for a series of jobs, prints an enhanced Gantt chart, a table of values, and a resource density histogram.
CPM-III Performs the work of CPM-II on the actual project as it unfolds and prints an enhanced Gantt chart that compares the actual job to the planned job.
TIMELY(*) Estimates how long a project composed of several small jobs will take to complete.

CHAPTER 7

INVENTRY Models the material in an inventory.
INV Models the costs of managing an inventory.
INVENT Models the costs of managing an inventory with historical, or random, patterns of demand.

CHAPTER 8

DIET Solves a resource allocation problem by brute force.
SIMPLEX Solves linear programming problems by the Simplex Method.

CHAPTER 9

DECIDE Evaluates decision trees.

CHAPTER 10

LINEFIT Calculates the "least-squares" best-fitting line through a set of points (also known as the regression line) and plots the results.
NEXTMNTH Projects next month's value from a best-fitting line to values of the last 12 months, a line of the last 11 months, 10 months, ... , and 2 months.
FINDTIME Finds a possible meeting time among several individuals' schedules, and plots the schedules.

APPENDIX A

PROG1 – PROG20 Illustrate elementary BASIC statements.
FORM Illustrates the use of subroutines.

APPENDIX B

READ Reads and counts initial data.
PERCENT(*) Prints a table of numbers and their percentages of total.

MAX(*) Finds the maximum in a list of numbers.
SORT Sorts a small list of numbers. (Can be modified to alphabetize a list of names.)
SORTII Sorts a large list of numbers.
PLOT Plots all points in a region.
HIST Plots a histogram of a list of numbers.
PIE Plots a pie chart of a set of numbers.
AMORT Prints a mortgage-repayment (loan-amortization) schedule.
DEPA Calculates straight-line depreciation.
DEPB Calculates depreciation by doubly-declining-balance converting to straight-line.
DEPC Calculates sum-of-years'-digits depreciation.
SMOOTH Smooths the values in a time series.
BETA Finds the systematic risk (Beta) of a stock, X, in a market, M.
BAR Plots a bar chart of a list of numbers.
SEVEN Prints a seven-number summary of a list of numbers.

Index

ABS function, 25
Absolute value, 25
Accounting rate of return, 68, 71
Actual finish, 127, 139
Actual start, 127, 139
Actual work history, 127
Administrative costs, 36
After-tax profits, 68
Alternative futures, 55
Alternative scenarios. *See* What if
AMORT subroutine listing, 289
Analyses, 37–39
  of payback period, 68
Annual inventory extremes, 156
Apostrophes, 4, 13
Apple computers, 306, 307, 309
Assignment, 33. *See also* LET statement
  problem in, 205
Atari computers, 306, 309

Back orders, 154, 170
Bar charts, 7, 8
BAR subroutine listing, 296–298
BASIC functions
  ABS, 25
  TAB, 95, 148, 250–251
BASIC statements
  DATA, 38, 54, 215, 245, 257–258
  FOR, 4, 162, 178, 200, 227, 256
  GOSUB, 65, 156, 200, 268–272
  GOTO, 200
  IF ... THEN ... ELSE, 25, 43, 83, 92,
    151, 155, 175, 200, 215, 245, 259,
    261–265
  INPUT, 245, 258
  LET, 6, 253–255. *See also* Assignment
  NEXT, 4, 256
  PRINT, 14, 33, 151, 250–256
  READ, 54, 83, 257
  REM, 13, 256
  RETURN, 65, 200, 268–272
  RUN, 38
Bell-shaped distributions, 141, 145
Best fit, 221, 222, 226
Beta distributions, 141
BETA subroutine listing, 295–296

Blank lines, 4, 253
Border variables, 179, 180, 188
Brute-force approach, 178
Budgets, 31
  capital, 13, 67, 72
  capital-equipment, 13
  help with, 29–31
  review of, 15

Capital, 149, 157
  budgeting of, 13, 67, 72
  cost of, 68, 69, 70, 71, 72, 73
  planning of, 67
  spending of, 73
Capital-equipment budgets, 13
Carrying inventories, 156–160
  cost of, 156, 157, 160, 170, 171
Cash flow, 22–25, 69, 73, 227
Cash surplus, 22
CASHPLAN program, 14
  listing of, 26–28
Change factors, 37, 42
Changes in supply, 170–171
Colons, 307
Commas, 251, 252
Comments, 10, 13, 211
Commodore Pet computers, 306, 309
Competitive effects, 77
Competitive growth, 49–55
Compound growth 3–4
Compound interest, 4
Compucolor computers, 306
Computational accuracy, 180
Computed zeros, 200
Computers. *See* Microcomputers
Constants, 64
Control
  of costs, 66
  of inventory, 150
  of project, 125–127
Corporate data base, 88–89
Cost curves, 44, 50, 52, 55
Cost-experience curves, 52
Cost per unit, 44, 51
Costs
  administrative, 36

capital, 68, 69, 70, 71, 72, 73
carrying, 156, 157, 160, 170, 171
control of, 66
direct, 36, 37
fixed, 35, 36, 37, 42
handling, 36
information-gathering system, 150
inventory-control system, 150
inventory replenishment, 156, 157, 160, 170
labor, 4
least, 180, 185, 205
material, 4, 170
product, 36
real, 35
reduced, 185
set-up, 36
of shortages, 170
total, 160
CPM programs, 205
CPM-I program, 125
  listing of, 109–114
CPM-II program, 115, 125, 127
  listing of, 117–124
CPM-III program listing, 128–139
Critical path, 105, 106, 124, 139, 145, 205
Cromemco computers, 306
Curve fitting, 221
Curves
  bell-shaped, 141, 145
  cost, 44, 50, 52, 55
  cost-experience, 52
  experience, 43, 44, 45, 50, 52, 53
  fitting of, 221
  industry price, 54
  learning, 43
  price, 44, 50, 52, 54
  price-experience, 52
  slope of, 50, 221

Data base, 89, 90, 93
  administrator of, 90, 91
  management system for, 88, 89, 92
  users of, 89–93
Data dictionary, 89
Data integrity, 90
Data security, 90
DATA statements 38, 54, 215 245, 257–258
Debt, 15, 22, 24, 25, 51, 71, 72
DECIDE program listing, 212–214
Decision trees, 209, 210, 211, 216, 217
Demand, 150, 158, 160, 161–166, 169
  distribution of, 169
  for finished goods, 149
  history of, 165
  random, 164
Density functions, 141
DEPA subroutine listing, 289–290
DEPB subroutine listing, 291–292
DEPC subroutine listing, 292–293
Depreciation, 22
Deterioration of inventory, 156

Diet problem, 173–176
DIET program listing, 176–178
Digital Equipment Corporation, 306, 307
DIM statements, 14
Direct costs, 36, 37
Discounted cash flow, 69
Discount factors, 70
Distribution, 78, 79, 82, 83, 164, 165
  bell-shaped, 141, 145
  beta, 141
  demand, 169
  Gaussian, 141
  project, 143
  random, 169
  task, 142
Dollar value of inventory, 157
Duality principle, 188

Early start, 104, 106, 108
Econometric models, 226, 227
Economic conditions, 77
Economic order quantity (EOQ), 160
Edge values, 205, 206
Enlarged tableau, 204
EOQ. See Economic order quantity
Equalities, 189–192
Equity, 71
Error traps, 215
Excess inventory, 149
Exidy computers, 306
Expected value, 141, 145, 207, 208
Experience
  curves of, 43, 44, 45, 50, 52, 53
  value of, 43–46

Final tableau, 180
Financial models, 227
FINDTIME program, 233, 238
  listing of, 239–244
Finished goods, 149, 150
Finish node, 205
Fixed costs, 35, 36, 37, 42
Forecasts, 226, 227, 232
FORM subroutine listing, 269–272
FOR statements, 4, 162, 178, 200, 227, 256. See also Loops

Gantt chart, 100, 106–107, 108, 109, 114, 124, 139
Gantt, Henry, 100
GANTT program, 103
  listing of, 101–102
Gaussian distributions, 141
GOSUB statements, 65, 156, 200, 268–272
GOTO statements, 200
Government legislation, 77, 78
Graphs, 13, 46
  of sales, 7–12
Growth equation, 18, 19
GROWTH program, 55, 65
  listing of, 56–59
Growth rates, 18–19
Guest-cook problem, 99, 109

Handling costs, 36
Heathkit computers, 306, 307, 310
Hewlett-Packard computers, 306, 307, 309
HIST subroutine listing, 282–284
Histograms, 115, 124, 125, 139
    of random demand, 164

IBM computers, 309
IF ... THEN ... ELSE. 25. 43, 83, 92,
    151, 155, 175, 200, 215, 245, 259,
    261–265
Income statements, 16, 17, 22, 23
Independent variables, 227
Indicators, 181
Industry price, 52
    curve for, 54
Inequalities, 190
INFLATE program, 5
    listing of, 6
Inflation, 22, 71
    pricing in, 4–6
    rate of, 5
Information-gathering systems, 150
Initial inventory, 158
Initial tableau, 179, 180, 185
INPUT statements, 245, 258
Insurance, 156
Integrity of data, 90
Intercept, 221
Interest, 22, 51, 156
    compound, 4
    rate of, 51, 52
Intermediate parts, 149
Intermediate products, 150
Internal rate of return (IRR), 68, 70, 71
Inventory, 149, 150, 151–154
    annual extremes in, 156
    carrying, 156–160, 170, 171
    control of, 150
    dollar value of, 157
    initial, 158
    policies of, 170
    replenishment of. See Replenishment of
        inventory
INV program, 161
    listing of, 159
INVENT program listing, 167–169
INVENTRY program, 161
    listing of, 154–155
IRR. See Internal rate of return

Labor, 6
    cost of, 4
Late start, 106, 108
Learning curve, 43
Least cost, 180, 185, 205
Least-squares linear regression, 226
Legislation, 77, 78
LET statements, 6, 253–255. See also As-
    signment
Linear programming, 173
Linear regression, 226

LINEFIT program, 226, 227, 232
    listing of, 222–225
Line graphs, 7, 8
Line numbers, 65
Logarithmic scales, 44
Long-range planning, 13
Loops, 4, 5, 17, 21, 24, 25, 70, 79, 82,
    161, 175, 200, 211, 215, 257–258
Lowest possible cost. See Least cost

Main routine, 87
Margin of profit, 4, 5, 24, 45, 149
Market growth, 46, 59–64
Market risk, 71
Market share, 45, 46, 49, 51, 52, 53, 66
Market volume, 45
Marketing decisions, 216–218
Materials, 6, 149, 156
    cost of, 4, 170
    model of, 150–154
Material requirements plan (MRP), 227
Maximization, 186
MAX subroutine listing, 276–277
Mean, 145
Meeting scheduling, 233–238
Microcomputers, 13, 15, 29, 70, 85, 88,
    149, 239
    selecting for use, 305–307
Minimization, 180
Minimum cost. See Least cost
Minimum price, 178
Models, 22, 29, 44, 49, 50, 54, 77, 82, 170
    econometric, 226, 227
    financial, 227
    material, 150–154
    pricing, 5
Modified tableau, 180
MRP. See Materials requirements plan

Nature's game, 208, 211
Net income, 22
Net present value (NPV), 54, 67, 68, 70,
    71, 72, 73
Networks, 104, 105, 106, 109, 204, 205
NEXT statements, 4, 256. See also Loops
NEXTMNTH program listing, 229–232
Nodes, 205, 209, 210, 211, 215
NPV. See Net present value
N-simplex, 179
Numerical accuracy, 200
Numeric variables, 215

Obsolescence, 157
Office computer training, 13
Ohio Scientific computers, 306

Payback period, 68, 69, 71
PERCENT subroutine listing, 275–276
PIE subroutine listing, 284–287
Pivot column, 181, 182, 183
Pivot element, 182, 183, 191
Pivot row, 182, 183
Pivot selection, 182

Pivoting, 182
PLAN program, 28
  listing of, 19–21
Plane, 227
Planning
  long-range, 13
  of projects, 125
PLOT subroutine listing, 280–282
Predecessors, 104, 107, 108, 109
  table of, 107–109
PRESENT program listing, 73–74
Present value, 54, 67, 68, 70, 74
Price, 6, 185
  curve of, 44, 50
  growth of, 5
  slack in, 179
  total, 180
Price-experience curve, 52
Pricing, 178
  in inflation, 4–6
  model of, 5
PRINT statements, 14, 33, 151, 250–256
Probability-density function, 140
Product costs, 36
Production, 149
Production line, 173
Production managers, 173
Profit, 24, 36, 37, 38, 42, 51, 52, 54, 66,
  170
  after-tax, 68
  margin of, 4, 5, 24, 45, 149
Programs
  AMORT, 289
  BAR, 296–298
  BETA, 295–296
  CASHPLAN, 14, 26–28
  CPM, 205
  CPM-I, 109–114, 125
  CPM-II, 115, 117–124, 125, 127
  CPM-III, 128–139
  DECIDE, 212–214
  DEPA, 289–290
  DEPB, 291–292
  DEPC, 292–293
  DIET, 176–178
  FINDTIME, 239–244
  FORM, 269–272
  GANTT, 101–102, 103
  GROWTH, 55, 56–59, 65
  HIST, 282–284
  INFLATE, 5, 6–7
  INV, 159, 161
  INVENT, 167–169
  INVENTRY, 61, 154–155
  LINEFIT, 222–225, 226, 232
  MAX, 276–277
  NEXTMNTH, 229–232
  PERCENT, 275–276
  PIE, 284–287
  PLAN, 19–21, 28
  PLOT, 280–282

PRESENT, 73–74
QUERY, 93–94
READ, 274
RISKY, 79–81, 82–84
SALES, 10–11, 13–14
SEVEN, 299–304
SHARE, 47–48
SIMPLEX, 192, 200
SMOOTH, 293–294
SORT, 277–278
SORTII, 278–279
TABLE, 30, 31–33, 48
TIMELY, 146–148
X-RAY, 39–42
Projects
  control of, 125–127
  distribution of, 143
  mean of, 145
  planning of, 125
  scheduling of, 114–117
Quantified problems, 29
Quantity discounts, 170–171
Query language, 90, 92
QUERY program listing, 93–94
Radio Shack TRS-80 computer, 21, 306, 309
Random demand, 164
Random distributions, 169
Random numbers, 83, 165
Random-number generator, 75
Rate of return. *See* Return on investment
Raw materials. *See* Materials
READ statements, 54, 83, 257
READ subroutine listing, 274
Real costs, 35
Reduced costs, 185
Relative market share, 46, 49
REM statements, 13, 256
Remarks. *See* Comments
Reordering, 151, 156, 157, 158, 160, 163
  cost of, 160
  trial-and-error approach to, 161
Reorder period, 161, 169
Replenishment of inventory, 156–160
  cost of, 156, 157, 160, 170
  delay in, 161
  period for, 158
  policy on, 162, 163
Resources, 124, 125
  density chart for, 124
  histogram of, 124, 125, 139
  limits of, 117
  requirements for, 116
  scarce, 114, 116
Return on investment (ROI), 68, 70, 157
RETURN statements, 65, 200, 268–272
Risks, 75–79, 219
  market, 71
  systematic, 72
RISKY program 82–84
  listing of, 79–81

ROI. *See* Return on investment
RUN command, 38

Sales, 15, 16, 17, 22, 37, 51
    graphing of, 7–12
    growth of, 18
SALES program, 13–14
    listing of, 10–11
Scarce resources, 114, 116
Scheduling
    of meetings, 233–238
    of projects, 114–117
Security of data, 90
Semicolons, 250
Set-up costs, 36
SEVEN subroutine listing, 299–304
SHARE program listing, 47–48
Shortages, 170
Simplex method, 179, 180, 181–185
SIMPLEX program, 192, 200
    listing of, 193–199
Simulations, 82, 84
Slack, 105, 106, 108, 179, 185, 188, 189
Slope of curves, 50, 221
SMOOTH subroutine listing, 293–294
Smoothing, 141
Solution, 180, 181, 185, 189, 192, 203,
    204, 205
SORT subroutine listing, 277–278
SORTII subroutine listing, 278–279
Staff training, 13
Standard deviation, 83, 141, 143, 144, 145
Starting times, 124, 125
Start node, 205
Start-up, 50
Stepping-stone method, 206
Stock prices, 77
Storage, 156
String variables, 13, 14, 215
Structure, 86–88
Structured programming, 86
Subroutines, 65, 87, 124, 139, 199, 244,
    245, 269–272
    AMORT, 289
    BAR, 296–298
    BETA, 295–296
    DEPA, 289–290
    DEPB, 291–292
    DEPC, 292–293
    FORM, 269–272
    HIST, 282–284
    MAX, 276–277
    PERCENT, 275–276
    PIE, 284–287
    PLOT, 280–282
    READ, 274
    SEVEN, 299–304
    SMOOTH, 293–294
    SORT, 277–278
    SORTII, 278–279
Subscripted variables, 14, 21, 265–268

Successor, 104
Supercalc, 309–310
Supply, changes in, 170–171
Surplus of cash, 22
Systematic risk, 72

TAB function, 95, 148, 250–251
TABLE program, 30, 48
    listing of, 31–33
Tables, 13, 18, 21, 29, 30, 33, 36, 37, 45,
    46, 68, 69, 70, 92, 106, 139, 143, 206.
    See also Tucker Tableau
    predecessor, 107–109
    transportation, 205
Takeover bids, 77
Tasks, 140
    distribution of, 142
Tax rates, 72
Terminals, 13, 39
Texas Instrument computers, 306, 307
Thoreau, Henry David, 3, 15, 35, 67, 85,
    99, 149, 173, 207, 221
Time estimation, 139–140, 145
TIMELY program listing, 146–148
Time value of money, 71, 73
Total cost, 160
Total price, 180
Transportation problems, 202–206
Transportation table, 205
Trapping errors, 215
Trial-and-error approach to reordering, 161
TRS-80 computer, 21, 306, 309
Tucker Tableau, 179–180, 181, 186, 188,
    190, 203, 204

Uncertain future, 207
Utility value, 219

Values
    absolute, 25
    edge, 205, 206
    expected, 141, 145, 207, 208
    of experience, 43–46
    of inventory, 157
    of money, 71, 73
    net present, 67, 68, 70, 71, 72
    present, 54, 67, 68, 70, 74
    utility, 219
Variables, 13, 14, 17, 21, 29, 64, 82, 87,
    92, 162, 182, 226
    border, 179, 180, 188
    independent, 227
    in INFLATE program, 6
    numeric, 215
    string, 13, 14, 215
    subscripted, 14, 21, 265–268
VisiCalc, 309–311

Well-behaved systems, 189
Working capital, 22

Xerox computers, 310
X-RAY program listing, 39–42

This book was designed by Nancy Ross McJennett and set in London Times and Helios. It was composed on a Wang/GSI CAT 8 typesetter from text supplied in computer-readable form by the author to an Ibycus computing system at Logoi Systems, Hanover, New Hampshire.

A complete set of the programs in this book may be purchased on cassette or disc from:

John M. Nevison Associates
26 Main Street
Concord, MA 01742
(617) 369–4214